# Conversations with Philip Roth

Literary Conversations Series
*Peggy Whitman Prenshaw*
*General Editor*

# Conversations with Philip Roth

*Edited by George J. Searles*

University Press of Mississippi
Jackson and London

Copyright © 1992 by the University Press of Mississippi
All rights reserved
Manufactured in the United States of America

95   94   93   92      4   3   2   1

The paper in this book meets the guidelines for permanence and durability of the
Committee on Production Guidelines for Book Longevity of the Council on Library
Resources.

**Library of Congress Cataloging-in-Publication Data**

Roth, Philip.
    Conversations with Philip Roth / edited by George J. Searles.
       p.   cm. — (Literary conversations series)
    Includes index.
    ISBN 0-87805-557-6 (alk. paper). — ISBN 0-87805-558-4 (pbk. :
alk. paper)
       1. Roth, Philip—Interviews. 2. Novelists, American—20th
    century—Interviews. I. Searles, George J. (George John), 1944–       .
    II. Title. III. Series.
    PS3568.0855Z465   1992
    813'.54—dc20                                                91-48004
                                                                    CIP

British Library Cataloging-in-Publication data available

## Books by Philip Roth

*Goodbye, Columbus and Five Short Stories.* Boston: Houghton Mifflin, 1959.
*Letting Go.* New York: Random House, 1962.
*When She Was Good.* New York: Random House, 1967.
*Portnoy's Complaint.* New York: Random House, 1969.
*Our Gang (Starring Tricky and His Friends).* New York: Random House, 1971.
*The Breast.* New York: Holt, Rinehart and Winston, 1972.
*The Great American Novel.* New York: Holt, Rinehart and Winston, 1973.
*My Life as a Man.* New York: Holt, Rinehart and Winston, 1974.
*Reading Myself and Others.* New York: Farrar, Straus and Giroux, 1975.
*The Professor of Desire.* New York: Farrar, Straus and Giroux, 1977.
*The Ghost Writer.* New York: Farrar, Straus and Giroux, 1979.
*A Philip Roth Reader.* New York: Farrar, Straus and Giroux, 1980.
*Zuckerman Unbound.* New York: Farrar, Straus and Giroux, 1981.
*The Anatomy Lesson.* New York: Farrar, Straus and Giroux, 1983.
*Zuckerman Bound: A Trilogy and Epilogue.* New York: Farrar, Straus and Giroux, 1985.
*The Counterlife.* New York: Farrar, Straus and Giroux, 1987.
*The Facts: A Novelist's Autobiography.* New York: Farrar, Straus and Giroux, 1988.
*Deception.* New York: Simon and Schuster, 1990.
*Patrimony: A True Story.* New York: Simon and Schuster, 1991.

# Contents

# Introduction

Philip Roth is surely among the most gifted of contemporary American writers. A keen-eyed observer of social nuances, a probing analyst of human motivations, and a masterly prose stylist, he has been called the literary heir of Henry James. This is high praise, but well earned. In novels such as *Letting Go* (1962), *The Professor of Desire* (1977), and *The Counterlife* (1987), he has played inventive variations upon his fundamental theme: the difficulty of reconciling the opposed demands of the self and the social contract, particularly in the arena of close interpersonal relationships. Parents and children, husbands and wives, friends and lovers in Roth's fiction encounter problems because they are unable to strike a balance between involvement and detachment, between indulgence and restraint. Usually this failure is linked to sexual avidity, and the resulting dramas are enacted within the thorny context of conflicting ethnic and cultural mores. As Roth said in his first public interview, "My fiction is about people in trouble."

But Roth has sometimes been in trouble himself, at least according to his detractors. For there is another, decidedly *un*-Jamesian Philip Roth: an irreverent, taboo-flouting *tummler* whose boisterous hi-jinks have offended the sensibilities of some readers while incurring the outright wrath of others. This is the Roth of *Goodbye, Columbus* (1959) and—especially—the notorious *Portnoy's Complaint* (1969), books that were accused of fostering distorted perceptions of American Jewish life. And many critics also rejected Roth's several experimental works—*Our Gang* (1971), *The Breast* (1972), and *The Great American Novel* (1973)—dismissing them as little more than glib digressions. Indeed, during the 1970s Roth became the Peck's Bad Boy of the American literary scene, burdened, as he explained to Joyce Carol Oates, with a rather salacious public image "spawned by *Portnoy's Complaint* and compounded largely out of the fantasies that book gave rise to because of its 'confessional' strategy."

From the vantage point of the post-Rushdie 1990s, however, the furor that greeted Roth's early work seems perhaps naive. Surely the satire of *Goodbye, Columbus* is quite mild in retrospect, and even *Portnoy's Complaint* is for the most part no more shocking than much of what passes for popular entertainment by today's permissive standards. Moreover, Roth's experimental books were really very typical of their moment—a time when writers like Donald Barthelme, John Hawkes, and Robert Coover (to cite just a few obvious examples) were testing the limits of fiction in works far more unconventional. *Portnoy's Complaint* and the experimental fictions that followed it were part of a whole spate of confessional narratives including Frederick Exley's *A Fan's Notes* (1968), Erica Jong's *Fear of Flying* (1973), and many others. As Roth told *The Paris Review,* "I didn't ever feel so free as . . . in the 60s, to indulge myself in comic performance. . . . the dynamic, stagey atmosphere . . . inspired me to try out a new voice . . . a less page-bound voice. . . . So did . . . the rage and rebelliousness that were in the air, the vivid examples I saw around me of angry defiance and hysterical opposition. This gave me a few ideas for my act."

Certainly the most amusing comments that Roth has ventured concerning *Portnoy's Complaint* appear in his *American Poetry Review* interview with the Italian critic Walter Mauro:

> the massive, late-sixties assault upon sexual customs came nearly twenty years after I myself hit the beach and began fighting for a foothold on the erotic homeland held in subjugation by the enemy. I sometimes think of my generation of men as the first wave of determined D-day invaders, over whose bloody, wounded carcasses the flower children subsequently stepped ashore to advance triumphantly toward the libidinous Paris we had dreamed of liberating as we inched inland on our bellies, firing into the dark. "Daddy," the youngsters ask, "what did you do in the war?" I humbly submit they could do worse than read *Portnoy's Complaint* to find out.

Clearly, Roth places great value upon the cathartic function of humor, and is deeply aware of the relationship between the serious and the comic, the rational and the irrational. An underlying sense of fundamental duality fuels Roth's literary imagination, and drives these interviews as well. He told George Plimpton, for example, that what he most admired about the Second City Company was their "joining of precise social observation with extravagant and dreamlike fantasy," and although Roth is himself essentially a social realist, the word "fantasy" occurs again and again throughout the interviews. Even Roth's much-applauded style reflects this quality of dynamic opposition, as the high culture and the low, the belletristic and the vernacular, vie for supremacy—sometimes with a single paragraph. Roth has said, "Sheer Playfulness and Deadly Seriousness are my closest friends," and this balancing of inimical tendencies is a feature of his very demeanor. Interviewers repeatedly describe him as "courteous," "gentlemanly," and "professorial," and he is. But they also tell us that he is "stretched taut," and "capable of the ascerbic touché," that "just underneath this benign appearance there is a ferocious concentration and mental rapacity." James Atlas describes Roth's "raucous banter" as "discordant, manic, ebullient," asserting that he "has the verve of a Borscht circuit comedian."

Although it has been said that Roth dislikes interviews, he has granted well over fifty during the course of his career. Some of these, of course, have been essay-interviews, in which a writer from *Time, Newsweek, Maclean's,* or some other popular magazine or newspaper has built a feature article upon the novelist's remarks, often on the occasion of book publication. And Roth has been quite forthcoming about his work, never hesitating to correct a popular misconception or clarify the intended focus of a particular volume. Hence we have many capsule assessments that leave little doubt as to Roth's intentions in a given work:

> *My Life As a Man* is about the surprises that manhood brings; *The Professor of Desire* is about the surprises that desire brings; and *The Ghost Writer* is about the surprises that the vocation of writing brings.

> *When She Was Good* is about a young woman's brutal disappointment in the weaknesses and failing of her father and her husband, and the rage in her to make them better men. It's about extreme moral ambitiousness and its pitfalls—so, in its own way, is *Letting Go.*

> *The Counterlife* is a rather fullish exploration of the alternatives to one's existence. Its obsession is with the transformation of lives.

Elsewhere, in more formal "Question & Answer" exchanges such as the *Paris Review* interview, the self-conducted interview in *Partisan*

*Review,* and the *Ontario Review* conversation with Oates, Roth expounds at greater length upon a broad range of topics. He is particularly concerned with ensuring that his attitude toward his own Jewishness be correctly understood, and it is interesting to contrast his early, almost testy, remarks on this subject with his more recent observations, which tend to approach the topic in less personal terms. Particularly cogent in this regard are his comments in the interview reprinted from Asher Z. Milbauer and Donald G. Watson's *Reading Philip Roth* (1988). In this piece Roth places the issue in the broad context of recent social history, pointing out that Jewish readers today are less likely to take issue with his books, not only because of his now more affirmative treatment of Jewish subject matter, but also because "Jewish readers aren't quite so responsive to other people's ideas (real or imaginary) of what constitutes socially acceptable Jewish behaviour. . . . American Jews are less intimidated by Gentiles than they were when I began publishing in the 1950s, they are more sophisticated about anti-Semitism and its causes. . . ."

His comments on other writers are also instructive, as he alludes not only to long-revered canonical figures like Tolstoy, Rilke, and Gogol, but also to contemporaries such as Updike, Styron, and Mailer. Among current writers, though, it is Saul Bellow whom Roth mentions most often. This is not surprising, in view of Roth's having dedicated *Reading Myself and Others* (1975) to Bellow, calling him "the 'other' I have read from the beginning with the deepest pleasure and admiration." Earlier, in the National Educational Television interview with Jerre Mangione (1966), Roth had explained that Bellow was important to him because he had "laid claim upon certain areas of experience that no Jewish writer had before, and also took a certain attitude toward this experience. That is, he really knocked off the reverence and the piety, and that was a great relief, that you could really examine this material and treat it like a novelist, rather than as a public relations man." Elsewhere, however, Roth has repudiated the idea of an "American-Jewish" mode of writing, pointing out that he, Bellow, and Bernard Malamud (the three writers said to constitute the vanguard of such a school) differ with respect to "age, upbringing, regional origin, class, temperament, education, intellectual interests, moral ideologies, literary antecedents, and artistic aims and ambitions."

As that lengthy catalog suggests, Roth can wax emphatic, even insistent. But throughout these interviews the reader is also struck by a very different quality: Roth's essential humility in the face of the creative process. As he told George Plimpton, "the subway is jammed with people . . . full of ideas for novels they cannot begin to *write*. I am often one of them." And he has no illusions about the role of literature in an essentially materialistic society. In the excellent *Paris Review* interview he said that he has influenced the culture "Not at all," and in that same piece he observed that "I work in a society where as a writer everything goes and nothing matters, while for the Czech writers I met in Prague, nothing goes and everything matters." The overall impression conveyed by this collection of interviews is that of a self-confident, highly intelligent man impatient with foolish questions and pat answers, and totally devoted to his art. At the same time Roth emerges as still the jokester, quick with the witty or off-beat remark. And in the two pieces that conclude the volume, we see a decidedly mellowed, nostalgic Roth, looking back with almost wistful fondness upon his childhood and his graduate-school days. This is consistent, of course, with the tone of Roth's recent autobiographical books, *The Facts* (1988) and *Patrimony* (1991).

By its very nature, any anthology of this sort will inevitably exhibit at least some degree of overlap from selection to selection, as interviewers often lend to ask similar questions, to which the subject provides predictably comparable answers. And this is exaggerated somewhat by the chronological ordering of the pieces (the standard approach in the Literary Conversations series). In general, however, Roth tends not to repeat himself excessively. Hence the interviews included here are reprinted verbatim—with no deletions—to preserve the shape and rhythm of each. There has been no editorial intrusion, except to correct obvious typographical miscues in the originals, to regularize punctuation in a few instances, and to remove subheads and italicize book titles in the newspaper reprints.

*Conversations With Philip Roth* would not have been possible at all, however, without the support of a number of helpful people for whom acknowledgement is certainly in order. I am indebted first, of course, to the many interviewers whose exchanges with the novelist are included here, and to the various magazines, newspapers, journals, *et al.* in which they originally appeared. Thanks also to my

typist, Barbara Granato of the Mohawk Valley Community College
Life Sciences Department, and to JoAnne Werner and Sherry Day of
the college library, who helped me locate some of the more elusive
sources. I wish also to express my gratitude to Seetha A-Srinivasan,
of the University Press of Mississippi, who provided astute guidance
at every stage of the project. A special thank-you goes to Philip Roth
himself, for his accessibility and invaluable assistance. And I thank my
wife, Ellis, for her encouragement, her excellent editorial advice, and
her love.

GJS
October 1991

# Chronology

1933      Born 19 March in Newark, New Jersey, second son of Herman and Bess (Finkel) Roth

1950      Graduates from Weequahic High School (Newark); enrolls at Newark Colleges of Rutgers University.

1951      Transfers to Bucknell University; serves as founding editor of the campus literary magazine *Et Cetera,* contributing fiction and satire.

1954      B.A. in English, *magna cum laude,* Phi Beta Kappa; publishes first story, "The Day It Snowed," in *Chicago Review.*

1955      M.A. in English, University of Chicago; enlists in Army, August 1955 (is discharged with back injury, August 1956); "The Contest for Aaron Gold" in *Epoch.*

1956      Ph.D. candidate for one academic quarter, University of Chicago; Instructor, University of Chicago (1956–58); "The Contest for Aaron Gold" included in *Best Short Stories of 1956.*

1957–58    Reviewer for *New Republic,* publishing thirteen pieces on film and television.

1958–59    Moves from Chicago to Manhattan's Lower East Side; "The Conversion of the Jews," "Epstein," and "Goodbye, Columbus" in *Paris Review.*

1959        Marries Margaret Martinson Williams; "Conversion of the
            Jews" included in *Best Short Stories of 1959*; "Epstein"
            receives *Paris Review's* Aga Khan Award; "Defender of
            the Faith" in *New Yorker*, "Eli, the Fanatic" in *Commen-
            tary*; first book, *Goodbye, Columbus* and *Five Short
            Stories*; receives Houghton Mifflin Literary Fellowship and
            National Institute of Arts and Letters Grant.

1959–60     Lives in Rome on Guggenheim Fellowship; in September
            joins faculty of University of Iowa Writers Workshop;
            National Book Award and Daroff Award of Jewish Book
            Council of America for *Goodbye, Columbus*; "Defender
            of the Faith" included in *Best Short Stories of 1960* and
            *O. Henry Prize Stories of 1960*.

1962        Writer-in-Residence, Princeton University (1962–64);
            receives Ford Foundation Grant; "Novotny's Pain"
            in *New Yorker*; *Letting Go*.

1963        Legally separates from wife, sublets apartment on West
            Side of Manhattan, begins five years of psychoanalysis;
            first visit to Yaddo in Saratoga Springs—to spend four to
            eight weeks there annually until 1972; "The Psychoana-
            lytic Special" in *Esquire*.

1964        Moves to East 10th Street, Manhattan; "Novotny's Pain"
            included in *O. Henry Prize Stories of 1964*.

1965        Begins teaching one semester a year at the University of
            Pennsylvania (1965–77).

1967        Visiting lecturer, SUNY Stony Brook; suffers near-fatal
            attack of appendicitis and peritonitis; *When She Was
            Good*.

1968        Estranged wife dies in automobile accident.

1969      Moves to East Eighties apartment in Manhattan; *Portnoy's Complaint;* Paramount film version of *Goodbye, Columbus.*

1970      Rents house in Woodstock, New York, and lives there virtually full-time; elected to National Institute of Arts and Letters; "On the Air" in *New American Review.*

1971      Visits Prague for first time (returns annually until denied entry visa in 1976); *Our Gang; Unlikely Heroes* (stage adaptation of "Defender of the Faith," "Epstein," and "Eli, the Fanatic") opens on Broadway.

1972      Buys eighteenth-century farmhouse in northwestern Connecticut and moves there as full-time resident; elected to American Academy of Arts and Sciences; *The Breast;* Warner Brothers film version of *Portnoy's Complaint.*

1973      *The Great American Novel;* ". . . Looking at Kafka" in *American Review*

1974      Becomes founder and General Editor of Penguin's new "Writers From the Other Europe" series; *My Life As A Man.*

1975      *Reading Myself and Others*

1976      Enters into long-term relationship with the British actress Claire Bloom (the couple will spend half of each year in London, half in Connecticut).

1977      *The Professor of Desire*

1979      Receives honorary doctorate from Bucknell University; *The Ghost Writer.*

1980      *A Philip Roth Reader*

1981        Mother dies; *Zuckerman Unbound.*

1983        *The Anatomy Lesson*

1984        BBC/PBS "American Playhouse" television version of
            *The Ghost Writer,* featuring Claire Bloom.

1985        Receives honorary doctorate from Bard College; *Zucker-
            man Bound.*

1987        Receives honorary doctorates from Columbia University
            and Rutgers University; National Book Critics Circle
            Award in Fiction; returns from London to live year-round
            in the United States; *The Counterlife.*

1988        Distinguished Visiting Professor, Hunter College; National
            Jewish Book Award for Fiction from J. W. B. Jewish Book
            Council, for *The Counterlife; The Facts.*

1989        Receives honorary doctorate from University of Hartford;
            undergoes quintuple bypass surgery; father dies.

1990        Marries Claire Bloom; *Deception.*

1991        Receives honorary doctorate from Brandeis University;
            National Arts Club Medal of Honor for Literature; *Patri-
            mony.*

1992        Receives honorary doctorate from Dartmouth College.

# Conversations with Philip Roth

# The NBA Winner Talks Back
## Martha McGregor/1960

From *The New York Post Magazine*, 3 April 1960, 11. © 1960
by *The New York Post*. Reprinted by permission.

Twenty-seven-year-old Philip Roth, winner of the National Book
Award for his *Goodbye, Columbus* (Houghton Mifflin) was interviewed at the Astor before he flew back to Rome where he is working
on a novel.

"What is the new book about? At the risk of being rude, I'd rather
not go into that," Roth said.

But he had fewer inhibitions when it came to discussing the controversy over certain of the stories in *Goodbye, Columbus*.

"When 'Defender of the Faith' was published in *The New Yorker* I
got letters from, oh, rabbis and just plain citizens who were out-
raged." Their indignation was directed at the characterization of an
Army private who used his religion, which was Jewish, to obtain
special favors.

"I tried to answer everybody and tell them where they had misunderstood. I don't think 'Defender of the Faith' is an anti-Semitic story.

"I think there's a lot of anxiety among Jews and a real foundation
for it—being Jewish has never been easy. The whole people has had
a terrible experience. The last war was such a ghastly thing and we
have all had private experiences that have left us terribly unhappy.

"This anxiety led some readers to overlook the fact that there are
*two* Jewish characters in 'Defender of the Faith' and that they are
absolute opposites. Grossbart is a rat, but Marx is a man of great
decency and loyalty.

"However, the story is by no means about the Jews. It's about
individuals who happen to be Jewish. There is a kind of reverse
prejudice that says all Jews are good, all Catholics are good, all
Negroes are good, all of any minority are good.

"It's just a damn lie and it does a great deal of harm to our sense
of reality. Any criticism of any individual is regarded as critical of the
whole group."

1

Roth's work has been most consistently attacked by Charles Angoff. "He doesn't do it once, he does it a dozen times, printing the same article different places—lots of Jewish community papers.

"I just read one today in which he says my book and *Marjorie Morningstar* and *Exodus* would all make Spinoza and Aristotle unhappy.

"The point is he is writing about the past and I'm not. He's spokesman for a certain kind of Jewish writing, a sentimentalized immigrant fiction.

"My advice to him is to write a book about why he hates me—it might give insights into me and him, too."

Another point of controversy is Roth's satirical handling of Jewish suburban life. "I can't deny I have feelings of anger and censure as a human being and a Jew, although I would say this is not particularly a Jewish problem, but an American problem.

"How to act when you've made it—the whole problem of affluence and success are highlighted here. Jews who came 40 or 50 years ago in poverty and alienation now find themselves affluent. It's not easy to be affluent. They're living two lives. The same questions come up: 'Who am I? How do I act? What do I do?'

"My work does not offer answers. I am trying to represent the experience, the confusion and toughness of certain moral problems. People always ask what's the message. I think the worst books are the ones with messages. My fiction is about people in trouble."

# Philip Roth

## Jerre Mangione/1966

Transcription of National Educational Television interview (16 mm B/W, 30 min.) produced by Jerome Tookin. © 1966 by National Educational Television. Printed by permission.

Philip Roth's first major work, *Goodbye, Columbus*, appeared in 1959. The critic [Irving] Howe has said of Roth, "what many writers spend a lifetime searching for—a unique voice, a secure rhythm, a distinctive subject—seems to have come to Philip Roth totally and immediately." *Goodbye, Columbus* won the National Book Award in 1959, and his novel *Letting Go*, published in 1961, received both great adulation and great abuse from literary critics. He is now completing another major work of fiction.

**Mangione:** How much Yiddish was spoken at home by your parents?

**Roth:** Oh, very little Yiddish was spoken. When Yiddish was spoken, it was not spoken so that I would understand, but so that I *wouldn't* understand. That is, it was the language of secrecy, the language of surprises and chagrin. So I learned very little; I didn't pay much attention to it. What I heard, however, wasn't always English, at the other extreme. I heard a *kind* of English that I think was spoken by second-generation people in what was essentially a very tightly enclosed Jewish neighborhood in Newark. My knowledge of Yiddish is *very* slight. People say things and I don't know what they're talking about. Apparently I don't spell it right, either, when I do it in my books. I've been told that.

**Mangione:** But some of the critics give the impression that you know a great deal of Yiddish. For example, I remember one critic who attributed great meaning to the fact that you had called the main character in *Goodbye, Columbus* Neil "Klugman."

**Roth:** Yeah. That was Irving Howe. But *he* knows a lot of Yiddish . . . much more than I do. I wanted a kind of name that wasn't

3

recognizably Jewish (like Cohen or Ginsberg or whatever), that wasn't ordinary, wasn't conventionally Jewish, but one that had a Jewish sound to it. Now, in the deepest reaches of my unconscious, I might have been aware of its Yiddish meaning; I don't believe I was.

**Mangione:** Did you read a fellow named Joseph Landis on the subject? He's written an article called "The Sadness of Philip Roth." He said that "Klugman" has two meanings: If you say "KLUGman" it means "clever fellow," but if you say "KLOOGman" it means "mourner" or "sad fellow." And he talks about the fact that you are struck with sadness when you see what is happening.

**Roth:** Landis is a Klugman, in the first sense. No, I don't know; that kind of speculation about the meanings of names or the derivations of names doesn't really concern me very much. When I wrote those stories I wasn't trying to be clever, particularly, and in many ways they weren't terribly "literary," as I think of them. They were kind of responses to my background, responses to my origins, and they were also written independently, one of the other. I had no sense they'd be brought together in a book, or that the book would have a kind of Yiddish or Jewish theme. In fact, when the book came out and received the kind of criticism it did and the kind of attention it did, I was very surprised. I was perhaps being too innocent. But nevertheless I was very surprised by the way it was received, as a kind of regional book, a book about a particular group. Now maybe I shouldn't have been so surprised. To me the stories weren't so much about the breakdown of the American Jewish community, as some of the critics said.

**Mangione:** Yes. They kept talking about the fact that you were portraying a people whose values were breaking down because they were joining the mainstream of middle-class America, which was in this "swampland of prosperity." I think that was one of the expressions that [Saul] Bellow used.

**Roth:** Yeah, Bellow had a nice expression—I remember it well—in his review, which appeared in *Commentary.* He talked about the Patimkins (the leading characters in *Goodbye, Columbus*) as living in "pig heaven." That was more the spirit in which the book had been written. I'm not a sociologist, and my categories weren't sociological. The *comedy* of the thing got me—the comedy of this particular kind of Jewish affluence, the comedy of certain Jewish predicaments. I think of the book, really, taken altogether, even though it has a kind of sad or melancholy edge to it, as a *comic* book, and the situation as funny, very often.

**Mangione:** When you say "the book," do you also include the short stories that go with *Goodbye, Columbus,* or are you talking about specifically the novella *Goodbye, Columbus?*

**Roth:** No, I mean the whole thing taken together. For instance, "The Conversion of the Jews" is a story about a kid who goes up on a roof and threatens to jump. It's not a grim story, it's comic— sometimes at the expense of this kid himself, sometimes at the expense of the other people. But the comedy really doesn't derive from any satire directed at the characters, but out of the bizarre nature of the experience. Also, I think a certain kind of comedy comes out of the fact that there's a bizarre experience in a kind of recognizable setting. There's something recognizable about what the people *say* in that story.

**Mangione:** I suppose it's hard to be comic without being serious at the same time. You can't help but base your comedy on serious things. I was thinking, for example, of the story "Eli, the Fanatic," which says some pretty serious things. One of the things it says, it seems to me, is something that you more or less keep saying in various ways throughout all your writing. And it's expressed by dialogue between Eli's wife and Eli. She says, "You won't do any- thing in moderation. That's how people destroy themselves." And he says, "I do *everything* in moderation. That's my trouble."

**Roth:** Yeah, that's a good bit of dialogue to point to . . . I didn't remember it. But that problem of how far to go—how far to go, especially when you have large personal ambitions, large moral aspirations . . . how far do you go with them? In a way, that's not so much the subject of the novella *Goodbye, Columbus* as it is, say, of "Eli, the Fanatic," about a man who's driven to sort of create right out of a situation, to create a kind of "good order," and of a story like "Defender of the Faith," where you get Sargeant Marx, who's appalled by the behavior of this soldier, and doesn't know how far to go to stop him. He's very hesitant to be savage, very hesitant to be openly cruel. He really can't deal with his cruelty. He doesn't know how necessary it is. And also, of course, what happens in that story is that it conflicts with his sense of being a civilized man. It may be that his sense of civilization is narrow, or mistaken. It's this theme that I picked up in *Letting Go,* the novel that followed *Goodbye, Columbus.* And in a way I see *Letting Go* coming out of—not directly, but in a hazy kind of way—"Defender of the Faith" and "Eli, the Fanatic." The central problem is, really, "How far do you go? How far do you penetrate into the suffering and the error and the mistakes," say, "in other lives?" And so both the hero, Gabe Wallach, and even the other hero, Paul Herz, are battling between maintaining some kind of authentic self, and some sense of detachment. Because, after all, there's only so much one can do. But the problem for them is to determine *how* much one can do, how much one ought to do, how much is necessary—to feel yourself not just fully human or fully civilized, but manly, to feel yourself altogether a man. And I think that's the kind of problem those two heroes face in *Letting Go,* and I think that if you look back you'll see it in those two stories we mentioned in *Goodbye, Columbus.* As for the novella, you don't see it, but you do get someone dealing with the question "What kind of man am I going to be?" More broadly, "What kind of *person* am I going to be? What kind of life am I going to live?"

**Mangione:** The novella, of course, is very impressive to me, and the excited reviews that it received were, I think, pretty much deserved. I found a great deal more compassion there than a writer of comedy usually has, and I found sort of a tough-minded philosophy and a kind of tough-minded prose. It was very direct. There were many things about it that struck me as having their roots in Russian literature. This is why I was interested in your background. That is, I kept thinking of Dostoevsky, believe it or not, and Gogol, of course.

**Roth:** Well, as for literary antecedents for *Goodbye, Columbus,* there really weren't any to speak of. Again, I'd go back to speaking of it just as a way of instantly and immediately dealing with my experience. There were writers I had read, writers who had begun to interest me in literature, first as a reader and then as a writer. The first one, when I was fourteen or fifteen, was Howard Fast. His moral passion got to me. Then, later on, Thomas Wolfe. These are writers I haven't read since, but who opened me up. And then at the time I was writing *Goodbye, Columbus,* I was teaching English at the University of Chicago, so I was just reading all kinds of people, none of whom really attached to me particularly.

**Mangione:** The book was published when you were twenty-six years old, but you probably started to write it, I suppose, when you were twenty-two or twenty-three.

**Roth:** Yeah, the first stories.

**Mangione:** What struck me was your complete understanding of the swimming pool set, and at the same time of these people who seem to come from Sholom Aleichem, in a certain sense. The two hardly ever go together. In other words, the same writer usually doesn't understand those two different kinds of people.

**Roth:** Well, "the swimming pool set," even as you said it, seemed to me a comic way of describing these people, because the comedy really derives from the fact that they're *not* the swimming pool set, that in fact behind them are people who are not the swimming pool set, that the whole country club culture is something that was foreign to the Jewish experience in Europe, even foreign to the Jewish experience here. And in fact, the country club set is the very thing that made certain Jews very nervous when they got here. And I think that, in a way, what you've touched upon is the *center* of the joke in *Goodbye, Columbus,* what creates the comedy.

**Mangione:** When I first read *Goodbye, Columbus,* reading the whole book, I couldn't help wondering, of course, what had come first, which story you wrote first, which were the early stories. When in your progression did the novella come along?

**Roth:** Well, there were other stories that I wrote. I was very Southern for a while. You know, when you begin to write you just sort of lash out, or else you copy something, and I remember writing a very southern story that had nothing to do with me or my voice or my concerns, but had to do with the literature I was reading at the time. But the first story of that [*Goodbye, Columbus*] group I wrote when I was in the Army, when I was twenty-one or twenty-two, and that was "The Conversion of the Jews." It's not a story that I'm terribly fond of now. In fact, next fall the Modern Library, much to my delight, is going to bring out *Goodbye, Columbus* as a Modern Library book. And I had occasion to read the book over again about four months ago. And I was given the opportunity to revise some of the stories—to change them—because they were written so long ago. At first I had pretty much decided I would change some of the stories, so I sat down with a pencil and went through them, and it was hopeless. Because I was making great changes—in "The Conversion of the Jews," particularly—but I was not at one with the ideas and feelings that had caused it to be written, so I thought the best thing would be to just let it be.

**Mangione:** When *Letting Go* was published, it got kind of mixed reviews. It got very enthusiastic reviews. But even the writers who said that this more or less established your position as a major American novelist found fault with it. They found it too long. One of them said it sprawled and sagged. And they found a great deal to criticize about the ending. Did you get anything constructive from these people? You certainly received more criticism—that is, more articles, very thoughtful articles—written about your work than most writers ever do, and I wonder whether you found that you were benefitting from some of the observations made by these critics.

**Roth:** No, I didn't benefit too much. Some of them made me very sick.

**Mangione:** Many of them, I know, are very superficial; reviewers can be very superficial.

**Roth:** The most intelligent review I read of the book was by Stanley Edgar Hyman, who reviewed the book in *The New Leader*. He didn't like the book particularly (he liked aspects of it), but he directed his attention to matters that were crucial to me, that were at the center of the book for me. For instance, the criticism of the ending: Only a few people have mentioned that to me. Other people have criticized the hero. In fact, people have been very pious and moralistic about him. For instance, another critic (or rather, a novelist serving his time as a critic) was Saul Bellow, who counter-criticized *Letting Go.* He said that the hero had no love for any man or any place or any thing. And to be sure, neither Paul Herz nor Gabe Wallach has as much love for any man as Moses Herzog has for himself. But that's hard to do when you're dealing with others. I felt there was a lot of moralizing about the hero—moralizing like that. And rather than understanding that the problems of pursuing life, of pushing one's way into it, of being drawn by the mystery of pain and suffering and mistakes and error—that that was treated problematically. I was interested in finding out the size of the problem, really . . . what it means to enter life and what it means to be detached. My own feelings about the hero—which are still unsettled—are these:

that in many ways Gabe Wallach would've been wise to be *more*
detached. In a way, neither of the men in the book has understanding of what might be called the courage of detachment. They're
not familiar with suffering. And that's in part what the book is about,
their discovering that there are some things that are unresolvable.
That's what the ending of the book is about. You'll remember that at
the end of the book Gabe Wallach, the hero (wealthy, attractive,
man-about-town. . . . wealthy, attractive, and energetic young man),
is driven by the frustrations he's endured in a year of his life to take a
baby on a wild chase down to Gary, Indiana. And there he comes
across a man who doesn't understand him at all, or want to: Harry
Bigoness. And what Gabe comes up against at the end is someone
who can't be moved by his intelligence, by his money, by his
persuasiveness, by his moral code. He can't even be moved by the
fact of the baby. And that's what Gabe wanted to present him with,
the human fact. The ending seems very necessary to me. I wouldn't
defend it aesthetically; the book is full of errors, but it derives from
my sense of what the problem was. I wanted him to come up against,
at the end of the book, something that was indeed larger than him,
but something that had nothing to do with being more intelligent or
even more charitable than he was.

**Mangione:** Well, perhaps you were presenting him in a charitable
light by having him engage in an act of fanaticism, sort of an
assertion, which is something I find in your other stories. For example, "Eli, the Fanatic": he is a man who feels he has to do something
that seems mad to everyone else, but he does it with a sense of
performing a moral right.

**Roth:** Right, exactly. The word "fanatic" is a fine word to describe
a concern of mine . . . that is, a moral fanaticism. It seems to be a
concern. . . . I didn't know it was until I wrote. It happens in the book
I'm working on now [*When She Was Good*]. I didn't see the similarity
of theme in this book—a similarity to *Letting Go,* a similarity that
goes back to "The Defender of the Faith" and "Eli, the Fanatic." But
there it is again: a kind of investigation of moral force, moral ambition. In this book you get a character—it's a woman (a girl, really)—
who in a way resembles Gabe Wallach and Paul Herz, because for all
the moral passion, and all the sense that one is finally created as a
person by way of one's moral interests, nevertheless there's a kind of

moral ignorance. There's a deep innocence in these people, a deep innocence about the nature of evil. They don't expect it should really *be* there. That's what makes them think that if they hurl themselves against the wall they'll finally break it down. What happens, however, in, say, *Letting Go,* the image that comes to mind, is of two kids fighting in a playground. They get held back by their friends, and then somebody decides to let go of them, and they come together, and they don't really like it so much, once they're in there. The same thing happens to Gabe Wallach. He's working like hell to intensify his life. And so he gets it, and it's a surprise to him. Now the character in the book I'm writing now—the young girl—never really backs away, keeps going and going and going until she destroys herself. There's a story of Kleist's called "Michael Kohlhaas," in which you again get a character who's driven by a moral passion, a moral aspiration, which the world cannot contain. The world has to destroy him.

**Mangione:** What about the *mood* of this new book? Will it be like the other books—that is, more or less social realism (I hate that term, but it's fairly descriptive)—or will it be more fantastic?

**Roth:** Well, in a way it's both. That is, it doesn't take place in a Jewish milieu; it takes place in the middle west, the middle of America. The locale is not definitely stated because I didn't want to write a book about Iowa or Minnesota or Wisconsin. I wanted to write about an area, a region—a region where certain ideas control the people who live there.

**Mangione:** Fairly recent ideas, perhaps . . . not ideas that have come over from Europe?

**Roth:** No. Native home-grown, *American* ideas. Very much a book about America! Right now I'm playing around with section titles—just to inform myself, really—and I've called one section "O Beautiful for Spacious Skies." It's about ambition in the middle of America. To speak of fantasy, there's a kind of nightmarish, driven quality about the narrative. It's really a kind of horror story. It's a very grim story, and I'll be glad when I'm finished writing it, really. Yet it somehow is embedded in a realistic setting, and there's even a satiric edge to the book. There's a real kind of mingling or mixing of modes, and the success of the book will depend upon this kind of mixing. The problem for me has been in determining what my attitude toward the experience really is—whether I do think it's ridiculous or whether I think it's horrible.

**Mangione:** I gather it'll be more satirical than your other work.

**Roth:** No, no. Except for that title—"O Beautiful for Spacious Skies" (which isn't the title of the *book*)—I don't think it's *as* satiric, actually. It's just that it has a strange, nightmarish quality. I don't know what more I can say about it.

**Mangione:** I know that you're interested in the theater. I've read a number of reviews written by you about Broadway plays and off-Broadway plays. Do you envision writing for the theater? You have a great sense of dialogue, a fine ear.

**Roth:** Well, I wrote a play. Last year I took some time away from the novel and wrote a play—a long play and two short plays—just trying to get away from the book for a time. And it takes more than a sense of dialogue and it takes more than an ear. In fact, I found my ear sort of bottled up when I got to work on the play, because the formal problems became so great. That is, the problems of letting the reader know what attitude to take toward what's going on—all the things you do *stylistically* in a novel, or you do by all kinds of narrative manipulations. I didn't know quite how to do that in the play. But I really want to get back to that. There are scenes in the play that I'm terribly fond of, that I think are very funny. And as soon as I finish this novel—someday—I want to try to finish the long play and the two one-act plays, which, by the way, are totally fantastic. And there I did find I did have a different kind of writing experience. That is, the form absorbed the fantastic material in a pleasing way. The form and the fantasy seemed to come together.

**Mangione:** Were you able to work with an actors' company, as you set out to do?

**Roth:** Yeah, I was lucky. At the time, I had some Ford Foundation money to indulge this playwriting interest, and at the American Place Theatre here in New York, the place that did Robert Lowell's play, they did a reading just for me. So I got a chance to hear it, and that of course thoroughly confused me. And what's happening now is that I'm forgetting the reading, which was awfully good, but I'm forgetting it, because you get the sound of the actors' voices in your ear, and you get a sense of what the director thinks the play is about, and somehow it confuses you.

**Mangione:** I would think that it would confuse anyone. I wish we had more time, because there are so many questions I want to ask you. For example, I'm constantly surprised that you are grouped with Malamud and Bellow, who are so much older than you are. I think there's an eighteen or nineteen year difference there.

**Roth:** Age has nothing to do with it. [laughter]

**Mangione:** I know, but somehow I gather here a kind of literary father/son relationship. I don't mean by that that you send Bellow on Father's Day a gift—I don't mean that at all.

**Roth:** No, I don't.

**Mangione:** But there is a certain similarity. For example, *Herzog* itself: The title *Herzog* immediately reminded me of Paul Herz. I thought it was kind of an extension of it, and as I read *Herzog* I couldn't help feeling that I was reading a sequel to *Letting Go.*

**Roth:** No, I don't think so. I feel very strongly about Saul Bellow's work. I'm a great admirer of his.

**Mangione:** I know. You've said you consider him the most important writer in America today.

**Roth:** Sure, I think so. And I also strongly admire Malamud's work. I think Bellow is important, and important to me personally, and important to a lot of other writers, for several reasons. One is that he laid claim upon certain areas of experience that no Jewish writer had before, and also took a certain attitude toward this experience. That is, he really knocked off the reverence and the piety, and that was a great relief, that you could really examine this material and treat it like a novelist, rather than as a public relations man. Not that other writers hadn't done that before him.

**Mangione:** Daniel Fuchs had done it in his novels, to a certain extent, but not to the same extent.

**Roth:** And not with the same kind of accomplishment that you get in Bellow's novels. Also there's a kind of linguistic freedom. Needless to say, there's very little comparison between the style in my books and the style in Bellow's. It isn't that you are directly influenced by, or directly take from, another writer, but he enlightens you about possibilities in your own experience. He enlightens you about possibilities in literature, and I think that many Jewish writers took heart from—this is expressing it too piously, really—that freedom, that spirit, that wit . . . the fact that you could be funny in certain ways, and funny about certain things.

**Mangione:** That departure from Marjorie Morningstar, or, as a friend of mine calls it, "Marjorie Morningsickness."

**Roth:** I can't top it.

From Philip Roth's apartment in Greenwich Village in New York, National Educational Television has been privileged to bring you a conversation between Mr. Roth and Jerre Mangione.

# Will This Finally Be Philip Roth's Year?

## Howard Junker/1969

From *New York*, 13 January 1969, 44–47. © 1969 by *New York*. Reprinted by permission.

"Why don't you speak to some of my real close friends," suggests Philip Roth to help the reporter start his piece on one of America's best, most serious novelists. "Tiny Tim. Tim. Ti, we call him. Of course, we knew Tim before Susan discovered him. Sue. Suzy Q. Suzy Q. Sontag."

And Roth *spritzes* into his latest theory:

"Now there are all these Jew Freaks, you see. This is the Age of the Jew Freak. Barbra Streisand. And the Becks, Paul Krassner, Abbie Hoffman.

"The Age of the Jewish moralist is over. It's the Age of the Jew Freak. Abe Fortas as Lenny Bruce, right? They made him into Lenny Bruce. Abe Fortas gets up and Strom Thurmond says: 'Dirty Jew, showing them dirty movies!'

"They don't want Jew moralists anymore, they want the Jew Freak. The Jew Freak who will try anything."

"Well," says the reporter. "You just turned the corner in time."

"Yeah. Red Rover, Red Rover, Red Roth come over. I just made it."

Roth has, at last, made it. At last is not quite the term, however, for ten years ago, at 26, Roth won the National Book Award for *Goodbye, Columbus*. Still, that collection of stories, hailed as a breakthrough in describing the New Jew, the suburban, emancipated Jew, the Jew caught between Brownsville (not the *shtetl*) and Bronxville, between vulgarity, cynicism and moral earnestness—the achievement, said the heavy critics, would truly come when Roth eased off the surface brilliance, the caricature he did so well, and wrote serious prose fiction. Which he did, producing *Letting Go* (1962), a sprawl-

14

ing, closely observed, conscience-wracked saga of two young academics on the road toward manliness, and *When She Was Good*
(1967), a study of an emasculating bitch and her *shmuck* of a
husband, told in a Midwestern twang.

But the trouble was that if these two books were not glib, know-it-
all, insouciant, they were dreary. At least they would have been
dreary, went the pious, circumspect opinion, if they were not so
good, so obviously the ambitious failures of a genuine talent.

And then something happened. Roth kicked the nice Jewish boy
bit, the stance of the Jamesian moral intelligence, and unleashed his
comic, foul-mouthed, sex-obsessed demon. His true self.

The result, *Portnoy's Complaint,* does for masturbation what
*Jurgen* did for coitus. Ostensibly the guilt-edged *kvetching* of one
Alex Portnoy on Dr. Spielvogel's couch, the book is hilarious, vicious,
explicit. The ultimate in true confessions, the ultimate in wailing the
woes of the Jewish family, the ultimate in exploiting the possibilities
of pop porno, the ultimate in stream-of-consciousness. . . .

Roth began writing about analysis on or about the time he himself
began seeing a psychiatrist some five years ago. At one point, he
even considered a cycle of Spielvogel stories: "Like the York cycle of
mystery plays, a lot of people would have this doctor, but you'd
never see him." Only two of these stories, still in the deeply realistic,
highly polished conscience-wracked style of early Roth, were published. "The Psychoanalytic Special" (in *Esquire*) describes a woman
beginning her analysis, taking the one-oh-five into the city and Dr.
Spielvogel: "At the start of her analysis she was involved mostly
in complaining anyways." Then she learns to resist her impulses to
promiscuity, shunning a dark gentleman who rides the same train.
And while this self-restraint bolsters her ego, finally it's frustrating.
"Truly," she concludes, having lost track of the dark stranger, "it was
awful if this was what it was going to be like, being better."

Both the material and the process of *Portnoy's Complaint* are
analytic. "The book is *about* talking about yourself," says Roth. "The
method is the subject. One of the reasons for using complaint in the
title (rather than "The Jewish Blues," "Whacking Off" or "Civilization and Its Discontents"—the titles of the sections) is to say to the
reader I KNOW (it's about complaint)."

Portnoy has plenty to complain about: his seductive, oblivious,

C-a-n-c-e-r-and-polio-obsessed, dietary-rules-and-regulations-obsessed mother and his constipated, insurance-selling father. And then all those *goys* everywhere, all around. And those other kids, like Ba-ba-lu Mandel, so marvelously sophisticated about matters sexual, while young Portnoy, in the tentative sanctuary of his family's bathroom, among other even more public places, solaces himself by masturbating.

Grown up, common decency is no less a heavy burden for Portnoy. Even when blessed with the ultimate, a West Virginia, lowdown, Jet Set sexpot, The Monkey, Portnoy suffers. She wants the decency he wants to abandon. "With a life like mine, Doctor, who needs dreams?"

But wait! *Portnoy's Complaint* will not officially be published until February 21. And pub date is sacred. Like opening night on Broadway, it is the pseudo-event after which reviews may appear. Should they appear too soon 1) the product might not have reached the stores (not the case on B'way) and 2) the impact, that is, the free publicity, would be dissipated. So reviewers, usually in advance of pub date, out of courtesy hang fire.

Yet, as with most big books in these days of multiple sales, much of *Portnoy's* has already appeared, as it was written, as short stories in the April '67 *Esquire,* the summer '67 *Partisan Review* and the *New American Review* 1 and 3. And partly because NAR was widely reviewed, so was *Portnoy.* By the middle of last May, *Time* was calling it, "the most brilliant piece of radical humor in years." By mid-July even the *New York Times* had admitted there was "no question it will be one of the most talked about books of the winter."

Candida Donadio, empress of the literary agents, is not talking about client Roth. She fears sibling rivalry amongst her other charges—Bellow, Friedman, Heller *et al*—and fears another bad experience with an interviewer. So she sticks to her job, which, for Roth, was getting a $250,000 advance from Random House; selling movie rights to independent producer Sidney Beckerman ("I don't think it's going to be any tougher to put on the screen than *What's New Pussycat.* . . .") for $250,000; paperback rights to Bantam for $350,000; book club rights to the Literary Guild for an estimated $60,000; as well as the sections to magazines.

When he first moved to New York, Roth lived in a basement flat in what was not yet called the East Village. Recently he has lived on the top floor of a midtown, concrete waffle. His view, which he occasionally surveys with mini-binoculars, extends from a gold-domed antique sky-scraper in the mid-20s to Chase Manhattan Plaza. His three-room apartment has the clean, spare taste of a sensible decorator.

The poster of Jack Kennedy restraining a virulent LBJ looks out from the kitchen. Daguerreotypes of the '47 and '51 Dodgers are taped near the refrigerator which, says Roth, paying tribute to Lenny Bruce's description of a hooker's fridge, "is filled with beer, an old corsage and a bowl of tuna fish gone green."

Books line the walls. On an end table, beneath a stark abstraction, there are titles such as *Hunger, Vibrations, The Divided Self, Ariel, The Origins of Totalitarianism.* All the magazines from *Newsweek* to *Ramparts.* A Norwegian blanket draped over a wicker rocker. A big, heavy slab of dark wood of a desk. An Olivetti portable, yellow legal pads. An ottoman beside the lounger. TV on a wire stand. "I'm addicted to the 7 o'clock news," says Roth, who switches to Huntley-Brinkley when Eric Sevareid comes on. "His shoulders are too big. They overlap my screen."

Tall, dark, handsome Philip Roth has the lean, flat body of a swimmer. Now that he has recovered from the appendix-peritonitis of late '67, he is especially trim. And he works out in the afternoons in his living room, in a blue tank suit, listening to rock 'n' roll, a subject he is being tutored in by Al Goldman (recent field trips: Albert King, Jimi Hendrix).

Friends used to tease Roth about looking like another lefty, Sandy Koufax, whom Roth once saw in a World Series striking out that great *goy,* Mickey Mantle, three times in a row—"What a day for literature!" But Roth now denies that resemblance, probably harboring a secret notion that with his five o'clock shadow and widow's peak set off by a receding hairline, he looks like a literary Dick Nixon. Or, as David Levine sketched him at Truman Capote's party, like a nice, bull-necked, Jewish John L. Lewis. In short, put John Updike's nose on Thomas P.F. Hoving, grow the hair to a frizz around the ears—and you have Philip Roth.

"If I were to do something with you," he says, excusing himself from being "followed" instead of merely being interviewed, "it would be, in a way, false. I don't do that much. I mean, I really save my energies. I don't like to stay up late, because then I don't get up early enough to work.

"It may not be apparent from my work, but I'm very obsessive about writing. It's the best thing to be obsessive about. Otherwise, you're obsessive about your health or whatever."

Roth has the moves and dialects of a stand-up comic. He is a great mimic, whose wit is laced with dirty words, whose eye notices every girl that passes on the street, whose ear picks up on every innuendo in a conversation.

The *New York Review* assigned Roth to cover one of Lenny Bruce's trials. But then Bruce got sick, the trial was postponed and Roth went off to Yaddo, the artist's colony in Saratoga, N.Y., of which he is now a director. So nothing came of Bruce by way of reportage.

On the other hand, the first few pages of Bruce's autobiography, *How To Talk Dirty and Influence People,* is like the archetype of *Portnoy's Complaint,* both in the manner in which the bits are strung together and in the kind of material used.

Unlike Bruce, Roth has little of the (paranoid) social crusader in him. Roth is intensely private, though he is deeply concerned about the war and the draft and has signed certain petitions (perhaps partly influenced by his girl friend, a Princess Casamassima who works in the anti-draft movement and, last fall, modeled for the *Times'* Sunday magazine fashion spread).

Roth can be Campy, especially at those times when his delivery demands squeals and shrieks and giggles. Those moments which require—or perhaps spring from—the spiteful fury of a mama's boy, those moments when Roth would like to be a Jew Freak. Of course, he is not one. He still wears Bass Weejuns, for crissakes.

Then again, Roth can be a clam, laying an open palm on his cheek as if afraid to touch. Or clenching his thumb—until noticed. Or enunciating professionally, dispassionately, all deep tones, deep, dark eyes.

The gift of the self-dramatic has always been there. It was there in graduate school when Roth would bounce around bits after class, bits about parents, sanctimonious rabbis, Uncle no-goodniks, with Ted Solataroff, now editor of the *New American Review* (and doing Roth for the *Atlantic*) and professor Arthur Geffin ("he makes me look like John Wayne").

But for a long time the gift was lost. Psychoanalysis obviously helped develop that sense of liberation, euphoria and exultant self-revelation so evident in *Portnoy's Complaint.* "That doctor salvaged his life," comments one friend.

Roth has also been freed, although in a way still largely hidden by the advent of money, and, in still another way, by the death of his estranged wife last May.

Thus, while there is still a lot of bitterness, uncertainty and *kvetching* left in Roth, he now surfaces as a *spritzer.* He bubbles, even when declining, over breakfast in the Palm Court of the Plaza (his turtle-neck having barred him from the Edwardian Room) to perform his most famous routine—"this would be a good place to do it"—a rabbi attacking Philip Roth, anti-Semite. "It's in bad taste," says Roth. "Not the routine—the rabbi!"

Stephen Crane, as well as the great Jewish gangster Abe "Longie" Zwillman, the Dodgers' Gene Hermanski, Sarah Vaughn, Jerry Lewis, Leslie Fiedler, LeRoi Jones and Philip Roth, came from Newark. Roth returned to his old neighborhood with the director of *Goodbye, Columbus,* Larry Peerce (*One Potato, Two Potato*). "I know there's a Jew around here somewhere," said Roth. But now the Jews have moved up and out to the suburbs. And the film was shot last summer in Westchester, starring Ali McGraw, a brunette of Irish descent.

Roth was raised to be a nice Jewish boy by parents who were both born in Newark. His paternal grandparents were married "somewhere in Austria-Hungary" before emigrating at the turn of the century, but his maternal grandparents met on the Lower East Side—"so I go way back on that side, been here since the 17th century."

In Newark, the Roths lived on the ground floor of a two-family house in a Jewish block, a block away from a mixed neighborhood and a block, in the other direction, from one-family-house Jews. Herman Roth sold insurance for Metropolitan Life and eventually became a manager. As the Portnoy stories appeared, he gave out

copies to friends, while Mrs. Roth, jokingly, declared that when the
book appears, she will leave the country.

Roth was bar mitzvahed, but early on stopped being religious. "He
once told an Israeli audience that, from the tradition, he had received
"a kind of psychology that can be translated into three words: 'Jews
are better.' " He also declared: "It seems to me that the largest
burden a Jew has is not having the courage to accept one's Jewishness, but having the courage to deny it."

He is now bored with all that talk about Jewishness, though most
of his best friends are Jewish and his current material is more Jewish
than ever. "My interest then," he says, "was in part determined by
the response to my book. You get thrust into situations in which you
play a role to a degree. And you try to convert it so it works for
you. You might as well; you have to do something."

Roth skipped a grade in grammar school and took English at
Newark's predominantly Jewish Weequahic High from Allen Ginsberg's aunt. Among other youthful memories, like going to see
the Newark Black Yankees with his father on Sunday afternoons, he
recalls having to wear the hand-me-downs of his older brother,
Sandy, now a big-time advertising art director.

After a year at Rutgers College in Newark, Roth transferred to
Bucknell: "I simply couldn't live at home anymore. And I had ideas,
little ideas, dreams of Coed, white bucks."

He did a lot of acting, edited the lit mag, got kicked out of a dorm
for having a girl in his room and graduated *magna* and Phi Beta
Kappa. In 1955 he took his master's at University of Chicago and
joined the army. As a clerk at Walter Reed, he shook Ike's hand—
"*President* Eisenhower. You were just a kid, then, boy." And in less
than a year he was discharged with a back injury suffered in basic (cf.
the *New Yorker* short story, "Novotny's Pain"), returning to New
York to look for a job in publishing and magazines, then returning to
Chicago as a PH.D. candidate and instructor.

"The '50s," Roth recalls, "were very much a time when the real
hero was Stevenson. To be a gentleman was a way of being manly. It
was a way of absorbing all your force and wit and aggression and
intelligence into one thing. And if you stuck with those qualities—
charm, elegance, intelligence—you'd be ok.

"For instance, the whole business of Henry James. I'd be in class

with all those Jew boys, and we'd have our hands up. Hey ya!
Heeyyaaaaa! I know the answer! *Whaddyamean, a Jew knows Henry
James?* We knew everything. We'd dominate the class."

Roth quickly began publishing in the *Chicago Review, Esquire* and
the *New Republic,* which picked up his piece on Ike's bedtime
prayer ("Good night, Lord, I want to thank you for helping me
today. You really stuck by me. I know, Lord, that I muffed a few and
I'm sorry about that. But . . . You take over from here. . . ."). For a
season, Roth was the *New Republic*'s regular film critic. At the same
time, William Styron's wife, Rose, was plucking a Roth story from the
*Paris Review* slush pile, and assistant associate editor Norman Pod-
horetz was pulling another from the *Commentary* slush pile.

Collected as *Goodbye, Columbus,* these stories were immediately
recognized—in reviews by Saul Bellow, Leslie Fiedler, Irving Howe
and Alfred Kazin—as the debut of a major talent. And in a year
without a major novel (*Confessions of a Spent Youth, Henderson the
Rain King, Malcolm, Naked Lunch, The Poorhouse Fair*), Roth won
the National Book Award, as well as the Jewish Book Council's
Daroff Award, the *Paris Review*'s Aga Khan award, a Guggenheim
and a National Institute of Arts and Letters award.

With *Goodbye, Columbus,* the late critic Benjamin Boroff once
explained to an Israeli audience, Roth became the gentile's "Baede-
ker, the guidebook to Jewish life." For the American Jews themselves, he became "a kind of shibboleth . . . they define themselves
and other people in terms of how they react to Roth. In the suburbs,
for example, there are always little cells, little revolutionary movements . . . set apart from the great mass of suburban people to whom
Mr. Roth is anathema."

It is hard to recapture that sense of revelation in *Goodbye, Columbus,* so familiar has the New—and the Old—Jew become. These are
days when the Golden Age of Jewish-American literature is a stale
joke. The Jew is no longer Everyman, the alienated, hypersensitive
Victim. That metaphor was twisted into parody by the black humor-
ists. Then it was turned on its head and kicked in the face by the
black revolutionaries (Jew as Victimizer). But things aren't all that
bad, not these days when the saga of the (German) Jewish robber
barons becomes a best seller and Leo Rosten compiles a dictionary
joke book called *The Joys of Yiddish.*

It is not easy for an author who wants to be called Novelist of the Year to wait for his book to be published. Roth has been looking at houses, at cars. He is moving to a new apartment. He is breaking up with his girl friend. Last spring he changed editors at Random House. Late summer in London he had some suits made, although as one friend observes, "one pair of trousers were cut so tight they look like an ad for the Mattachine Society."

"He's got his nose pressed against the sweet shop window," says another friend. "And those goodies, those marvelous goodies are almost too good for him. Yet I fear the mass-media adulation will get him nervous. The need to repeat the success. I hope America doesn't eat him."

But Roth is already back at work. "It's very terrifying," he says, "I hate this time, trying to find my way into something. I still can't write anything recognizable. But I know things I don't want to. I honest to Christ can't write anything again like 'he opened the door and went into the room and lit a cigarette. And ate the cigarette.'

"There's a lot of material I have—what's been going on, the war, friends of mine involved in anti-war stuff. And I wanna find out what else I know. I wanna kick a lot of the past.

"I feel kind of free. Like I've found my book. But I've always felt that way after each book, frankly."

Not long ago, Princeton sociologist-anthropologist Mel Tumin, who stores Roth's manuscripts in his basement, called Roth in the morning, when the phone is usually turned off.

"What are you doing?" Tumin asked. "Why're you answering the phone. That means you're not writing."

"No, I'm writing."

"What the hell you writing for. You're a rich man, for chrissakes. Get the hell out and go somewhere."

"Yeah. I gotta lotta money. I own a piece of a supermarket. I own a piece of a goldmine. But what the hell am I going to do? What's the difference if I gotta lotta money? What am I supposed to do? Not write?"

"Awwh, go enjoy."

"Wha? How the hell? Where?"

# Portnoy's Complaint by Philip Roth Looms as a Wild Blue Shocker and the American Novel of the Sixties
Albert Goldman/1969

From *Life*, 7 February 1969, 58, 61–64. © 1969 by the Time/ Life Company. Reprinted by permission.

The publication of a book is not often a major event in American culture. Most of our classics, when they first appeared, met with disappointing receptions, and even the much-ballyhooed best-sellers of recent years have rarely cut a great swath outside the lanes of publicity and journalism. But this year a real literary-cultural event portends and every shepherd of public opinion, every magus of criticism, is wending his way toward its site. Gathered at an old New York City inn called Random House, at the stroke of midnight on the 21st of February in this 5,729th year since the creation of the world, they will hail the birth of a new American hero, Alexander Portnoy. A savior and scapegoat of the '60s, Portnoy is destined at the Christological age of 33 to take upon himself all the sins of sexually obsessed modern man and expiate them in a tragicomic crucifixion. The gospel that records the passion of this mock messiah is a slender, psychotic novel by Philip Roth called *Portnoy's Complaint* (the title is a triple pun signifying that the hero is a whiner, a lover and a sick man). So great is the fame of the book even before its publication that it is being hailed as *the* book of the present decade and as an American masterwork in the tradition of *Huckleberry Finn*.

Heralded last year by several stunning excerpts in the serious literary magazines, *Portnoy* comes to us glowing not merely as a *succès d'estime* but as a *succès de scandale*—the scandal fuming up from the book's pungent language, a veritable attar of American obscenity; and from its preoccupations, foremost among which is the terrible sin of onanism. Presently the object of a cult, which passes selections from the sacred writing from hand to hand at sophisticated dinner parties so that all may have the opportunity to read aloud, *Portnoy* today is still an underground password. But the complete work is being readied for distribution by an international ring of literary agents who are cutting, packaging and peddling it like a deck of pure heroin. Soon it will be injected into every vein of contemporary culture: as hard-cover book, as soft-cover booklet, as book club offering, as foreign translation and as American movie. The TV rights remain as yet unsold, but even without them the book has already earned almost a million dollars prior to the first press run.

A million dollars in publicity is what the book will earn next. A chain reaction of cover stories and profiles and critiques and put-ons and put-downs and pictures and cartoons and slogans and quips has already begun to build toward a blast that may set a new record for publicity overkill.

The book that is being blown up by all of this puffing is not so much volatile as it is intense, probing, incisive. A diagnostic novel by a comic Freud, it focuses its lens of a beautifully cut and brightly stained slice of contemporary American life—all sick, black and blue. The hero, an Assistant Commissioner of Human Opportunity for the City of New York, is a man who exemplifies the cherished values of the Kennedy years. Brilliant and precocious as a student, successful as a lawyer, dedicated and sensitive as a public servant to the underprivileged, Alexander Portnoy has devoted his whole life to being good.

Yet when we discover this nicest of Nice Jewish Boys, he is lying on his back on a psychoanalyst's sofa, like an overturned cockroach, spewing out a frenzied stream of angry, resentful and self-defensive words. Honking through his beaky nose a heavy Jewish blues, he reels off an endless chronicle of suffering, degradation and terror, interspersed now and then with little grace notes of pleasure.

Though Alexander Portnoy's complaint is directed in the first instance against his smothering and seductive mother, and in the second against the succession of maddening females who have poisoned his life, the ultimate truth of his condition is that he has fallen victim to American history in the same way that Oedipus fell victim to fate. For struggle as he will, and analyze as best he can, Portnoy cannot escape the appalling fact that in the '60s Americans are seeking to live by two completely contradictory moral codes. Maintaining their allegiance to the traditional morality of monogamy, fidelity, self-sacrifice and the sublimation of sexual energies, Americans are almost equally sanctimonious about those "needs" and "rights" that include the license to experiment with every sort of sexual and sensuous behavior dictated by the most primitive instincts and passions. Walking about in a fallen world, with these two Edens warring in their heads, modern Americans are made borderline schizophrenics.

Something of this sense of the *Doppelgänger* that stalks us has been suggested in a great many works of contemporary literature and comedy. Indeed, the farcical gap between what all Americans are supposed to be and what they are has been the mainstay of our humor ever since this American dilemma found expression in the wit of the so-called "sick" comics of the mid-'50s. Lenny Bruce, Mort Sahl and Nichols & May were the first to exploit the awkward, spraddling moral stance of the new American; after them the comedy of the Yankee *schlemiel* was developed much further by a whole succession of Jewish novelists, including Saul Bellow, Joseph Heller, Wallace Markfield and Bruce Jay Friedman. For more than a decade these comic artists cultivated the themes and techniques brought to final fruition in *Portnoy*. For it has always been evident that, though this profound conflict between our better and worse selves might tear us apart, drive us to despair or make us crazy, it could never be treated with complete seriousness or with the literal-minded simplicity of the sexologists and the public moralists. Comedy alone could provide the lens through which this strangely contorted and grotesquely embarrassing American predicament could be examined.

Philip Roth's achievement in *Portnoy*, therefore, is not the discovery of a theme nor the invention of a mode, but the final perfection of an art, the comic art of this Jewish decade. His book combines in its irresistible funniness all the resources of the tradition: the relentless Marx Brothers energies of *Catch-22*, the self-pitying rhetoric of *Herzog*, the hovering Chagall figures of *Stern* and *A Mother's Kisses*, the pop art sprinkles of *To an Early Grave* and the self-lacerating ridicule of Lenny Bruce. Purging the Jewish joke and comic novel of their lingering parochialism, Roth has explored the Jewish family myth more profoundly than any of his predecessors, shining his light

into all its corners and realizing its ultimate potentiality as an archetype of contemporary life.

*Portnoy's Complaint* boldly transcends ethnic categories. Focusing
its image of man through the purest and craziest of stereotypes, the
book achieves a vision that, paradoxically, is sane, whole and profound. As intimate as the mirror on the bathroom wall, it affords its
readers glimpse after glimpse of themselves nakedly living the truths
and lies of their innermost lives. Looking into this mirror, the
reader—Jew or Gentile—will be caught between old shame and new
pride, between the instinct to cover up and the urge to bare all.
Torn, yet relieved by successive shocks of recognition, he will mur-
mur the healing formula of self-acceptance: "It is I."

So intense is the conflict between the two sides of Alexander Portnoy's fractured psyche, so classically clear is his syndrome, that he
has been accorded by his psychoanalyst the signal honor of having
his illness defined by his symptoms and labeled with his own name:
"Portnoy's Complaint—A disorder in which strongly felt ethical
and altruistic impulses are perpetually warring with extreme sexual
longings, often of a perverse nature. . . . Acts of exhibitionism,
voyeurism, fetishism, autoeroticism and oral coitus are plentiful; as a
consequence of the patient's 'morality,' however, neither fantasy nor
act issues in genuine sexual gratification, but rather in overriding
feelings of shame and the dread of retribution, particularly in the
form of castration."

Portnoy's personality derangement derives, of course, from his
childhood relationship with his Jewish mother. Alternately rocked in
the soothing seas of maternal solicitude and swamped by the terrifying tides of maternal domination, the boy grows up pathetically
seeking some one thing he can call his own. Not until puberty does
he discover what he is seeking. Masturbation offers him the thrill of a
secret, rebellious and wholly self-indulgent life. Behind a locked
bathroom door, his head thronging with erotic impulses, his ear alert
for the terrifying knock and the unanswerable challenge—"Alex,
what are you doing inside there?"—Portnoy comes to identify sex
with feelings of anxiety and remorse. But the power of his secret
pleasure propels him out into the world in search of the beautiful,
responsive creatures of his fantasies. Gentile girls with silky hair,

button noses and long slender legs are what he seeks: little beauties redolent of the perfume of America, the alien land that must be plowed to be possessed.

Questing like a nervous knight-errant in search of an erotic grail, he must pass through many encounters, many trying adventures, before he discovers the embodiment of his dreams standing at midnight on the corner of 52nd Street and Lexington Avenue. Springing off the highboard of life-as-fantasy with this girl, who is so appetitive and ignorant that he calls her "The Monkey," Portnoy tumbles head over heels in the most extravagant of all erotic, romantic, neurotic relationships.

Their dreamlike fall into the depths of sexual debauchery is at first thrilling—in this respect paralleling the stolen pleasures of his boyhood. But gradually they come to demand something more of each other than exchanges of erotic goodies, and the relationship splinters into angry words and exacerbated feelings. Finally, after having inveigled his mistress into a scene of climactic licentiousness, our hero abandons her as a crazy person who manaces his life and happiness.

Leaving the hysterical Monkey standing on the window sill of their hotel room in Athens, threatening to dash herself to death on the pavement below, Portnoy flees to Israel, where he meets a lady *kibbutznik,* a rugged, self-righteous amazon who reminds him of his mother. Attempting a crude physical seduction, he finds himself impotent. When he offers the lady an alternate form of gratification, she becomes enraged at his degeneracy and kicks him in the heart. Ending his sexual odyssey much where he began it, sprawling prostrate and helpless at the feet of a greatly desired but inaccessible woman, Portnoy concludes his long complaint with a protracted scream of pain.

*Portnoy* is not only a funny but an impassioned and angry book. Unlike every other Jewish writer since Heine, Philip Roth knows what's hurting him—and it isn't the *goyim.* He delivers his most soul-gratifying thrusts at those sentimentalized objects of mindless piety, the Jewish mama and papa, the emasculators of generations of Jewish men. Yet his anger is crossed by love for its targets, and is distinguished even further by an "Arise Ye Brothers of———" ardor, a rhapsodic sympathy for his fellow sufferers that bursts forth in passages of ironic eloquence. The crown of the book is his vision of a

Jewish *Ship of Fools,* a boatload of Nice Jewish Boys rolling on the
seas of guilt:

"I am on the biggest troop ship afloat . . . only look in through the
portholes and see us there, stacked to the bulkheads in our bunks,
moaning and groaning with such pity for ourselves, the sad and
watery-eyed sons of Jewish parents, sick to the gills from rolling
through these heavy seas of guilt—so I sometimes envision us, me
and my fellow wailers, melancholics and wise guys, still in steerage,
like our forebears—and oh sick, sick as dogs, we cry out intermittently, one of us or another, 'Poppa, how could you?' 'Momma, why
did you?' . . . the retching in the toilets after meals, the hysterical
deathbed laughter from the bunks, and the tears—here a puddle
wept in contrition, here a puddle from indignation—in the blinking of
an eye, the body of a man (with the brain of a boy) rises in impotent
rage to flail at the mattress above, only to fall instantly back, lashing
itself with reproaches. Oh, my Jewish men friends! My dirty-mouthed
guilt-ridden brethren! My sweethearts! My mates! Will this . . . ship
ever stop pitching? When? *When,* so that we can leave off complaining how sick we are—and go out into the air, and live!"

For many readers the strangest feature of *Portnoy* will be the fact
that its author is the same man who wrote *Letting Go* and *When She
Was Good,* books that reveal Roth's moral preoccupations and
literary skills but in no wise prepare one for the high jinks of this latest
work (though these high jinks do in fact mirror closely the style and
wit I and other friends of Roth have enjoyed for years in private
conversations and at parties). Indeed, since 1960, when at the
remarkably early age of 27 he won the National Book Award for
fiction with his first work, *Goodbye, Columbus,* Philip Roth has given
every indication of desiring to be counted among the handful of
recent authors more concerned with the values of traditional literature than they are with the currents of contemporary writing.

Educated at Bucknell and the University of Chicago, active for
many years as a teacher of English literature and creative writing at
Chicago, Princeton and Iowa, a familiar figure on the college lecture
platform and even behind the lectern of the synagogue, a contributor
to *Commentary* and *Partisan Review,* Roth has clung through his
whole career to the skirts of the university and has counted himself a

member of the intellectual and cultural elite. It was to this audience in
particular that this early work appealed.

With *Goodbye, Columbus,* a collection of canny, morally sophisticated stories written in a scrupulously impersonal style—the antithesis
of the verbal extravagance of *Portnoy*—Roth focused fiercely on the
life of middle-class America in the postwar years, particularly in the
American Jewish community where all the traditional values were
being submerged in the scuffle to obtain the good things of material
prosperity. This volume was followed in 1962 by *Letting Go,* a
long and thoughtful novel in which Roth articulated his moral obsession, the theme which underlies all his subsequent writing: the effort
of the self to break the bondage of narcissism by renouncing all
selfish gratification in favor of a self-sacrificing dedication to the
happiness of others. This Christian theme he treated, of course, with
a great deal of irony, steadily increasing the dosage, until in *Portnoy*
the theme is totally inverted and the hero struggles, with the reader's
covert approval, to cast off all traces of moralism and lead a life of
guiltless self-gratification.

It was while he was working on his third book, *When She Was Good,*
that I first met Philip Roth. Whether it was owing to some congenial-
ity of temperaments or simply to the fact that he knew that I had
spent a great many years running with a pack of Jewish comics that
included the late Lenny Bruce, our encounters soon assumed the
form of spontaneous staging sessions with Roth out in the spotlight
working the room like a stand-up comic. Typically we would meet by
chance at the Mayhews, a little breakfast shop in Manhattan's East
Sixties. I'd be sitting there enjoying the peace of the morning hour
and the soothing influence of an egg and butter, when my mood
would be shattered by a reproachful voice: "Albert, your father and I
have been worried sick about you!" Looking up I would see not my
Jewish mother magically transported from Santa Monica to New
York, but Philip Roth, glaring at me maniacally. Looking nothing like
the picture on the jackets of his books—that beautiful fem-man
face, with its cleft Cary Grant chin, bold intellectual nose and dis-
tantly gazing Mesmer-eyes—this was the comic-crazy Roth, the one
lost soul on the pilgrimage, a jarring presence sending out hysterical
waves in every direction.

Slipping into the chair next to mine, fixing me with a hooded maternal gaze, he would continue his exhortation in that guilt-inducing, this-is-not-your-mother-but-your-conscience voice: "Two weeks and not a word. How is it a writer, a person who sits all day behind a typewriter, can't put two words together to send to a mother who lives three thousand miles away?" Then a hyena laugh, fracturing that sorrowful maternal stare into the crazy lights and angles of a Cubist portrait. I'd be gagging, choking, caught between laughter at Philip and anger at my mother, wondering meanwhile (with an instinct as old as the race) what the *goyim* were thinking—particularly that thick-lensed cashier, who has stopped toting up his bills and is staring with astonishment at this strident newcomer.

By this time Philip would be too wound up to notice or to care what reaction he was getting. He'd be doing the Jewish Genet who has written this play called *The Terrace* in which there's a brothel for Nice Jewish Boys where you go every night and they dress you in Dr. Denton's kiddie pajamas and they bathe you and powder you and put mineral oil where it itches. Tucked into your bed, you fall asleep blissfully listening to a little radio with an orange dial. Next morning a voice calls softly, "Wake up, dear, it's time to get up." For that, Philip says, he'd gladly pay $50 a night.

Now the magic word "radio" triggers him into his "Blue Network" bit. "J-E-L-L-O!" He's doing all the voices from the Jack Benny show: smoothie Jack, fruity Dennis. Yes, yes, I remember them perfectly! But wait, he's reaching even further back for—wow!—*Mr. Kitzel!* Now he's sliding his voice way up in the air in an oral shrug, a vocal curlicue: "Mees-ter Benny!" Oh my pop epiphany, it's Schlep-perman! "Awesome, Philip, awesome."

After 15 or 20 minutes of this comic fuguing, the waiters would be throwing Philip looks, *Wall Street Journals* would be dropping and some old lady would be giving him the top lens. Everybody would be asking himself, "Who the hell is this guy? He must be some famous Jewish nightclub comedian who hasn't gotten to bed yet. Wow! He's really up there. Nine o'clock in the morning and still flying."

After all my years with the funny men, my response to Philip's antics was partly professional. I recognized in him a type not of the stage but of the Jewish living room, the candy store or luncheonette, where after school the kids take turns driving each other over the

edge into hysteria. He agreed that he had learned to be funny when
he was a child, probably on those daily walks from Chancellor Ave.
grade school in the Weequahic section of Newark to the little Hebrew
school 15 minutes away. In that precious quarter of an hour, those
highly regimented Jewish kids could blow off steam and subject the
pyramided pieties of their world to a healthy dose of desecratory
humor. For a few minutes they could afford to be bad.

Being bad and being funny were much the same thing in Roth's
mind, and I often had the feeling that when he wrote his fiction
he was intent upon being very good. Having as one of my own
obsessions the ideal of a Jewish comic who would be an artist and
not just a theatrical or literary entertainer, I often urged Roth to
exploit his comic gifts in fiction. I told him that his role was to be the
comic messiah, the redeemer of the Jewish joke. When I pressed my
arguments and exhorted him to write a novel that would match his
hidden talents, a book that would be black, sick, surreal, Kafkaesque,
unabashedly vulgar, obscene and Jewish, he would say with a sigh,
"Oh, Al."

In those days, *When She Was Good* was his primary obsession. He
had worked on it for years and rewritten it something like eight times.
In his apartment were four big cartons stuffed with manuscript. After
so many years of close-up work, he couldn't tell any longer what he
was doing; so one day he packed the latest draft into his briefcase
and left his rackety apartment for the calm of the 42nd Street
Library's reading room. There he read enough of what he had
written to realize that, despite the enormous pains he had lavished on
the book, it was still so defective that he could not think of publishing
it. Walking out into Bryant Park with its pigeons and hobos, he
contemplated the future. No longer was he a writer, he decided, nor
would he trade off his literary reputation by taking a succession of
teaching jobs. At 33 he was young enough to go into something else.
What would it be? Well, he could always go up to Harlem and be a
playground director and die.

Instead, he went off to Yaddo, a foundation-supported estate in
Saratoga Springs, which serves as a work retreat for writers, artists
and composers. (Roth's deep attachment to Yaddo owes something
to the beauty of the place—it is set among lakes and woods, with a

view of the distant Vermont mountains—but it is, really its character
as a sanctuary from city life, and more especially its comfort as a
surrogate home, a home without the annoyance of a family, that
explains his frequent and prolonged visits there.) Regulating his life
for as much as six months at a time by the soothing routine of the
place—they get you up early, feed you breakfast and pack you off to
work in a little cabin with a lunch box full of cold chicken and a
shiny apple—he was finally able to bring *When She Was Good* into
order and to publish it in 1967.

A stylistic *tour de force*, *When She Was Good* turns the tone of
*One Man's Family* back on itself to produce a highly ambiguous
literary texture whose irony is as subtle and deadly as the ripple in a
highly polished saw blade. The tension of the book is generated by
counterpointing the most gracious of all pop American tones against
the moral frenzy and insanity of the heroine, a Midwestern Medea
who embodies the horror of the Protestant ethic run amok.

Expecting high praise—at least from the more sophisticated critics—Roth was dismayed to find the reviewers yawning over his novel
and offering consoling phrases while they waited for his next book.
Perhaps *When She Was Good* was too subtle for those who sat down
to write about it. In any case, as soon as Roth had finished it his mind
righted itself and all the baffled energies that had blown this way and
that during five years of mental doldrums now became a steady
breeze which soon shaped itself into a voice—a voice rising and
falling with the complaining intonations of an angry and neurotic
Jewish boy.

For two years I had seen so little of Philip Roth that when I dialed his
number last summer I wasn't even sure whether he was still living in
New York. But having read the fourth installment of *Portnoy's Complaint* in *New American Review*, I had to toss in my penny's worth of
praise. Always glad to hear from an old playmate, Philip invited me
to his home in one of New York's tallest and baldest buildings. As I
walked into his apartment on the 21st floor, a flat lined with brown
metal bookcases like the stacks of a library, he greeted me with a
routine, singing in the strident voice of a Broadway musical comedy
star, "New York, New York, it's a wonderful town!" and gesticulating

toward the huge plate-glass windows of the room. Holding a high note, he drew the blind to reveal a stunning panorama of city skyline.

Stepping offstage, he slumped into an armchair and began to talk. Immediately, I caught a new note in his voice, a lilting note of optimism.

"Wow, what a year I've had!" He reels off an incredible yarn. It starts with his going to a publication party for William Styron's *Nat Turner*. Standing there in his new British tweeds, nibbling on an *hors d'oeuvre*, Philip begins to feel this pulsing pang in his right side. He'd had the same pain months before and figured he'd licked it, but now it grows worse and worse. The doctors can't tell what it is, so they put him in the hospital and his fever goes up and up, and finally, this crazy scene: A big, handsome surgeon dressed for a black-tie party is pressing down on his abdomen and Philip is going through the ceiling. Appendicitis is the diagnosis and immediate operation the plan, but when they cut him open they find that the cap blew off his gut days before and his belly is flooded with pus. They stick tubes into him from top to bottom and for days he wallows in delirium. Every time he comes out of it, he finds this exquisite woman, the woman he's been seeing almost every day for three years, standing at the foot of the bed wearing these strange sacklike dresses. "Get out of here!" he screams. "Go home and put a short skirt on. You look like you're dressed for my funeral." (And indeed, as he learned later, by the time they cut into him he was just two hours' walk from the grave—a shocking realization that flooded him with an awed feeling of pride and elation. He had wrestled the *Malekhamoves*—the angel of death—to a fall.)

Then there is his convalescence in Florida, an idyl of sun and water, and the finishing touches on *Portnoy,* and the growing feeling that he has his life back under control at last, when one morning, in this same living room—he's up on his feet now, showing me what happened—the phone rings and he hears his stepdaughter saying, "Mother has been killed." His estranged wife, Maggie, being driven across Central Park at five in the morning, had been instantly killed when the car smashed into a tree. Philip is stunned. He goes through the funeral arrangements in a trance. Then, just as he starts to pull himself together again—wham!—all the hullaballoo begins about *Portnoy.* Fame he's known before, but now, for the first time in his life, he has money—and everybody is shooting zingers into him. He passes the man next door, who says, "Oh, my neighbor, the million-aire!" But what can Philip say? Yesterday a messenger came to his door and gave him a royalty-advance check for a quarter of a million dollars. Philip gave him a tip. What's the tip on a quarter of a million? "I gave him a quarter, Al."

Now he's into his new book. He doesn't know where he's going: he has all these pieces of paper with one sentence on each page. He's just writing this stuff and throwing it away, groping for a new theme—some big semi-comic idea. And he's haunted by this phrase, a simple little phrase: "A terrible mistake has been made." Just that. Now he thinks he may write a book which will stand Kafka on his head. Sort of a marvelous idea:

"Instead of having a guy who is more and more pursued and trapped and finally destroyed by his tormentors, I want to start with a guy tormented and then the opposite happens. They come to the jail and they open the door and they say to you, 'A terrible mistake has been made.' And they give you your suit back, with your glasses and your wallet and your address book, and they apologize to you. And they say, 'Look, people from big magazines are going to come and write stories on you. And here's some money. And we're very sorry about this.' "

# Philip Roth's Exact Intent

## George Plimpton/1969

From *The New York Times Book Review,* 22 February 1969, 2
© 1969 by The New York Times Company. Reprinted by
permission.

*Would you say something about the genesis of* Portnoy's Complaint?
*How long has the idea of the book been in mind?*

Some of the ideas that went into the book have been in my mind
ever since I began writing. I mean particularly ideas about style and
narration. For instance, the book proceeds by means of what I began
to think of while writing as "blocks of consciousness," chunks of
material of varying shapes and sizes piled atop one another and held
together by association rather than chronology. I tried something
vaguely like this in *Letting Go,* and have wanted to come at a
narrative in this way again—or break down a narrative this way—
ever since.

Then there's the matter of language and tone. Beginning with
*Goodbye, Columbus,* I've been attracted to prose that has the turns,
vibrations, intonations, and cadences, the spontaneity and ease, of
spoken language, at the same time that it is solidly grounded on the
page, weighted with the irony, precision, and ambiguity associated
with a more traditional literary rhetoric. I'm not the only one who
wants to write like this, obviously, nor is it a particularly new aspiration on the planet; but that's the kind of literary idea, or ideal, I
was pursuing in this book.

*I was thinking more in terms of the character and his predicament
when I asked how long you had in mind the "idea of the book."*
I know you were. That's partly why I answered as I did.

*But surely you don't intend us to believe that this volatile novel of
sexual confession, among other things, had its conception in purely
literary motives?*
No, I don't. But the conception is really nothing, you know, beside
the delivery. My point is that until my "ideas"—about sex, guilt,

35

childhood, about Jewish men and their Gentile women—were
absorbed by an overall fictional strategy and goal, they were ideas
not unlike anybody else's. Everybody has "ideas" for novels; the
subway is jammed with people hanging from the straps, their heads
full of ideas for novels they cannot begin to *write*. I am often one
of them.

*Given the book's openness, however, about intimate sexual
matters, as well as its frank use of obscenity, do you think you would
have embarked upon such a book in a climate unlike today's? Or is
the book appropriate to these times?*
As long ago as 1958, in *The Paris Review,* I published a story
called "Epstein" that some people found very disgusting in its intimate sexual revelations; and my conversation, I have been told, has
never been as refined as it should be. I think that many people in the
arts have been living in a "climate like today's" for some time now;
the mass media have just caught up, that's all, and with them, the
general public. Obscenity as a usable and valuable vocabulary, and
sexuality as a subject, have been available to us since Joyce, Henry
Miller, and Lawrence, and I don't think there's a serious American
writer in his thirties who has felt restricted by the times particularly, or
suddenly feels liberated because these have been advertised as the
"swinging sixties." In my writing lifetime the use of obscenity has, by
and large, been governed by literary taste and tact and not by the
mores of the audience.

*What about the audience? Don't you write for an audience? Don't
you write to be read?*
To write to be read and to write for an "audience" are two
different matters. If you mean by an audience a particular readership
which can be described in terms of its education, politics, religion, or
even by its literary tone, the answer is no. When I'm at work I don't
really have any group of people in mind whom I want to communicate with; what I want is for the work to communicate itself as fully as
it can, in accordance with its own intentions. Precisely so that it can
be read, *but on its own terms.* If one can be said to have an audience
in mind, it is not any special-interest group whose beliefs and demands one either accedes to or challenges, but those ideal readers

whose *sensibilities* have been totally given, over to the writer, in exchange for his seriousness.

An example which will also get us back to the issue of obscenity. My new book, *Portnoy's Complaint,* is full of dirty words and dirty scenes; my last novel, *When She Was Good,* had none. Why is that? Because I've suddenly become a "swinger"? But then apparently I was "swinging" all the way back in the fifties, with "Epstein." And what about the dirty words in *Letting Go?* No, the reason there is no obscenity, or blatant sexuality either, in *When She Was Good* is that it would have been disastrously beside the point.

*When She Was Good* is, above all, a story about small-town Middle Westerners who more than willingly experience themselves as conventional and upright people; and it is their own conventional and upright style of speech that I chose as my means of narration—or, rather, a slightly heightened, somewhat more flexible version of their language, but one that drew freely upon their habitual clichés, locutions, and banalities. It was not, however, to satirize them, in the manner, say, of Ring Lardner's "Haircut," that I settled eventually on this modest style, but rather to communicate, by their way of saying things, their way of seeing things and judging them. As for obscenity, I was careful, even when I had Roy Bassart, the young ex-G.I. in the novel, *reflecting*—had him safely walled-up in his own head—to show that the furthest he could go in violating a taboo was to think "f. this and f. that." Roy's inability to utter more than the initial of that famous four-letter word, even to himself, was the point I was making.

Discussing the purposes of his art, Chekhov makes a distinction between "the solution of the problem and a correct presentation of the problem"—and adds, "only the latter is obligatory for the artist." Using "f. this and f. that," instead of The Word Itself, was part of the attempt to make a correct presentation of the problem.

*Are you suggesting, then, that in* Portnoy's Complaint *a "correct presentation of the problem" requires a frank revelation of intimate sexual matters, as well as an extensive use of obscenity?*

Yes, I am. Obscenity is not only a kind of language that is used in *Portnoy's Complaint,* it is very nearly the issue itself. The book isn't full of dirty words because "that's the way people talk"; that's one of the *least* persuasive reasons for using the obscene in fiction. Besides, few people actually talk the way Portnoy does in this book—this is a man speaking out of an overwhelming obsession: he is obscene because he wants to be saved. An odd, maybe even mad, way to go about seeking personal salvation; but, nonetheless, the investigation of this passion, and of the combat that it precipitates with his conscience, is what's at the center of the novel. Portnoy's pains arise out of his refusal to be bound any longer by taboos which, rightly or wrongly, he experiences as diminishing and unmanning. The joke on Portnoy is that for him breaking the taboo turns out to be as unmanning in the end as honoring it. Some joke.

So, I wasn't simply after verisimilitude here; I wanted to raise obscenity to the level of a subject. You may remember that, at the conclusion of the novel, the Israeli girl (whose body Portnoy has been wrestling her for on the floor of his Haifa hotel room) says to him, with loathing, "Tell me, please, *why* must you use that word all the time?" I gave her this question to ask him—and to ask at the end of this novel—altogether deliberately: Why he must is what the book is all about.

*Do you think there will be Jews who will be offended by this book?*
I think there will even be Gentiles who will be offended by this book.

*I was thinking of the charges that were made against you by certain rabbis after the appearance of* Goodbye, Columbus. *They said you were "anti-Semitic" and "self-hating," did they not?*
In "Writing About Jews," an essay I published in *Commentary,* in December 1963, I replied at length to those charges. Some critics who said that my work furnished "fuel" for anti-Semitism. I'm sure these charges will be made again—though the fact is (and I think there's even a clue to this in my fiction) that I have always been far more pleased by my good fortune in being born a Jew than my critics may begin to imagine. It's a complicated, interesting, morally demanding, and very singular experience, and I like that. I find myself in the historic predicament of being Jewish, with all its implications. Who could ask for more? But as for those charges you mention—yes, they probably will be leveled at me. Because of the U.N. condemnation of Israeli "aggression," and anti-Semitic rage flaring

up in the black community, many American Jews must surely be
feeling more alienated than they have in a long time; consequently, I
don't think it's a moment when I can expect a book as unrestrained
as this one to be indulged or even tolerated, especially in those
quarters where I was not exactly hailed as the Messiah to begin with.
I'm afraid that the temptation to quote single lines out of the entire
fictional context will be just about overwhelming on upcoming
Saturday mornings. The rabbis have got their indignation to stroke,
just as I do. And there are sentences in that book upon which a man
could construct a pretty indignant sermon.

*I have heard some people suggest that your book was influenced
by the nightclub act of Lenny Bruce. Would you consider Bruce, or
other stand-up comics such as Shelley Berman or Mort Sahl, or even
The Second City comics, as influence upon the comic methods you
employ in* Portnoy's Complaint?
   Not really. I would say I was more strongly influenced by a sit-
down comic named Franz Kafka and a very funny bit he does called
"The Metamorphosis." Interestingly, the only time Lenny Bruce and
I ever met and talked was in his lawyer's office, where it occurred to
me that he was just about ripe for the role of Joseph K. He looked
gaunt and driven, still determined but also on the wane, and he
wasn't interested in being funny—all he could talk about and think
about was his "case." I never saw Bruce perform, though I've heard
tapes and records, and since his death I've watched a movie of one
of his performances and read a collection of his routines. I recognize
and admire in him what I used to like about The Second City
company at its best, that joining of precise social observation with
extravagant and dreamlike fantasy.

*What about the influence of Kafka that you mention?*
   Well, of course, I don't mean I modeled my book after any work of
his, or tried to write a kafka-*like* novel. At the time I was beginning to
play with the ideas for what turned out to be *Portnoy's Complaint,* I
was teaching a lot of Kafka in a course I gave once a week at the
University of Pennsylvania. When I look back now on the reading I
assigned that year, I realize that the course might have been called
"Studies in Guilt and Persecution"—"The Metamorphosis," *The
Castle,* "In the Penal Colony," *Crime and Punishment,* "Notes from

Underground," *Death in Venice, Anna Karenina* . . . My own previous two novels, *Letting Go* and *When She Was Good,* were about as gloomy as the gloomiest of these blockbusters, and fascinated, obviously, as I still was by these dark books, I was actually looking for a way to get in touch with another side of my talent. Particularly after several arduous years spent on *When She Was Good,* with its unfiery prose, its puritanical, haunted heroine, its unrelenting concern with banality, I was aching to write something freewheeling and funny. It had been a long time between laughs. My students may have thought I was being strategically blasphemous or simply entertaining them when I began to describe the movie that could be made of *The Castle,* with Groucho Marx as K. and Chico and Harpo as the two "assistants." But I meant it. I thought of writing a story about Kafka writing a story. I had read somewhere that he used to giggle to himself while he worked. Of course! It was all *so funny,* this morbid preoccupation with punishment and guilt. Hideous, but funny. Hadn't I only recently sat smirking through a performance of *Othello*? And not just because it was badly done either, but because something in that bad performance revealed how *dumb* Othello is. Isn't there something ludicrous about Anna Karenina throwing herself under that train? For what? What after all had she done? I asked my students; I asked myself. I thought about Groucho walking into the village over which the Castle looms, announcing he was the Land Surveyor; of *course* no one would believe him. Of *course* they would drive him up the wall. They had to—because of that cigar.

Now the road from these random and even silly ideas to *Portnoy's Complaint* was more winding and eventful than I can describe here; there is certainly a personal element in the book, but not until I had got hold of guilt, you see, as a comic idea, did I begin to feel myself lifting free and clear of my last book and my old concerns.

# Joking in the Square

Walter Clemons/1971

From *Newsweek,* 8 November 1971, 110–111. © 1971 by
Newsweek, Inc. All rights reserved. Reprinted by permission.

Philip Roth was at work on a novel, his first since *Portnoy's Complaint,* when he saw President Nixon's April 3 statement on abortion, which "I can't square with my personal belief in the sanctity of human life—including the life of the yet unborn." That same week, Mr. Nixon directed Calley's release from the stockade after his conviction for the My Lai massacre, and Roth laid aside his novel to write the interview between Tricky and "A Troubled Citizen" that became the first chapter of *Our Gang.* Says Roth: "The discrepancy between his attitude toward Calley's crime and his attitude toward abortion was wholly revealing of the man's gross opportunism and moral stupidity. It seemed to me to merit special indignation."

Roth didn't intend to go any further with Tricky. But when he went back to his novel, "I began to think of further episodes, and finally realized that this Tartuffe of ours was worthy of a whole book," and less than three months later, in mid-July, *Our Gang* was delivered to his publisher.

"I don't know exactly how readers will react," Roth told *Newsweek*'s Walter Clemons. "The book has teeth and claws, and not everybody likes that. Even those who share my view of him may be made uneasy by the 'assassination' chapter. But then it is designed to make the reader uneasy—in part, by making him laugh! In a letter to Pope, Swift once described his satiric intentions by saying, 'I propose in all my labors to vex the world rather than divert it.' There are readers who will be vexed. On the other hand, to see Nixon ridiculed in this way may be a small comfort to those who think as I do, that he degrades both the office he holds and the nation."

Did he make a systematic study of Mr. Nixon's rhetoric? "I read as much as I could stomach. *Six Crises* is a strange book, you know. Though it appears to be about politics, it's actually about psychology.

41

What seems to intrigue Nixon most isn't the historical or political significance of these crises, but that he managed to survive them without going to pieces. Then I reread a lot of speeches on microfilm, particularly the debates with Kennedy, and of course the priceless 'I See a Day' acceptance speech. Then I watch him on TV every chance I get. I'm particularly flattered now when he uses one of my lines."

*Our Gang* is part of a sudden spurt of anti-Nixon satire that includes Emile de Antonio's movie *Millhouse*, which uses documentary footage, Philip Guston's forthcoming folio of drawings entitled *Poor Richard,* and Gore Vidal's new play, *An Evening With Richard Nixon* (scheduled for production early next year), which takes place entirely in hell. What does Roth expect his book to accomplish? "In the way of changing things? Probably nothing. I don't think we can judge a satire like this one in terms of its political effectiveness. It's in the realm of art, not propaganda or homily. My purpose is not to bring others around to my point of view, but rather to turn my own indignation and disgust from raw, useless emotion into comic art. What does a guy in a bar expect to accomplish by cursing the President? Nothing. He's expressing his opinion, he's letting off steam. Well, this is my way of letting off steam—this is *my* opinion."

# On Satirizing Presidents
## Alan Lelchuk/1971

From *The Atlantic*, December 1971, 81–88. © 1971 by Alan Lelchuk, as originally published in *The Atlantic*, December 1971. Reprinted with permission.

My remarks here grew out of a lengthy conversation I had with a Random House executive who in 1971 was uneasy about publishing *Our Gang.* He objected to the book principally on grounds of taste; also he wondered if it might not be politically counterproductive—that is, if one could imagine it having any political effect at all. Since there would doubtless be other readers who would share the publisher's point of view, I asked Alan Lelchuk (who is the interviewer here) if he would help me to reconstruct and extend my thoughts on the subject of satire, Nixon, and *Our Gang,* so that they might appear in print in this form. (1971)

*First, is there a tradition of political satire in America to which* Our Gang *belongs?*

Yes, though it probably isn't known even to most educated Americans. Political satire isn't writing that lasts. Though satire, by and large, deals with enduring social and political problems, its comic appeal lies in the use made of the situation of the moment. It's unlikely that reading even the best satiric work of another era we feel anything like the glee or the outrage experienced by a contemporary audience. Subtleties of wit and malice are wholly lost over the years, and we're left to enjoy the broadest, least timebound aspects of the work, and to hunt through footnotes in order to make connections and draw inferences that are the teeth and claws of this sort of writing. Except for a few students of American literature and history, no one today is going to be interested in reading James Russell Lowell's satires in doggerel verse, *The Biglow Papers,* written in the middle of the nineteenth century from an abolitionist point of view, or the dialect letters of "Petroleum V. Nasby," the work of another

antislavery Northerner, David Ross Locke. Yet both are wonderful
comic inventions, as virulent and funny as the political satire of Defoe
and maybe even some of Swift. Lincoln admired the Nasby letters so
much that he is supposed to have said he would have given up the
Presidency to have been able to write them.

Another reason Americans might not realize satirical writing once
flourished here is that there's hardly any around today. People would
be surprised, not only by the imaginative richness, but by the ferocity
of the political satire that appeared in ordinary daily newspapers
throughout the country in the nineteenth century, especially during
the decades leading up to and following the Civil War. I don't believe
there's a daily newspaper in America today that would print the kind
of sustained attack that Lowell made upon General Taylor during the
campaign of 1847, or Locke made upon the Northern Democrats
during Lincoln's Administration. If you look at how American Presidents were ridiculed in the daily papers in the nineteenth century,
you have to conclude that editors and readers were a heartier bunch
a hundred years ago, far less intimidated than they appear to be
today by Emily Postish notions of respectability.

*Are there any other American writers you admire who have
worked along these lines?*

Well, Mencken. Specifically, his attack on Harding's puerile prose
style, which he called "Gamalielese." Mencken said that Harding's
style was so bad that a sort of grandeur crept into it. And there is
a poem by e. e. cummings, a sort of mock eulogy occasioned by
Harding's death, which describes President Harding as "the only
man woman or child who wrote/a simple declarative sentence with
seven grammatical/errors . . ."

*Are you suggesting a connection between Mencken's attitude
toward Harding and your own toward President Nixon in* Our Gang?

Yes and no. I don't feel much kinship with Mencken's *ideas*—
particularly his notions as to what constitutes an aristocracy rub me
the wrong way. But as a critic of American public rhetoric, he was
very funny. I think, yes, there is in my book a concern similar to his
in the essay "Gamalielese." But we approach the problem of debased political language in different ways. Where he analyzes and
evaluates Harding's prose in a journalistic essay, *Our Gang* is an

exaggerated impersonation, a parody, of Nixon's style of discourse and thought. I go about my work in the manner of a fantasist and *farceur;* Mencken uses the weapons of a literary critic.

I believe he was also more amused by Mr. Harding than I am by Mr. Nixon. The reason may be that there's been a lot of terror packed into the short space of time that separates Mencken's "Gamalielese" from George Orwell's "Newspeak"—related kinds of double-talk at which President Nixon is equally adept. Mencken might never have drawn the same conclusions from rotten political prose that Orwell did twenty-eight years later in the novel *1984.* Mencken thought it was inevitable that American democracy would produce as leaders clowns and charlatans who, along with their other disabilities, couldn't speak English. He considered what they said and the way they said it *entertainment,* rivaled only by Barnum and Bailey. It took an Orwell—and a second world war, and savage totalitarian dictatorships in Germany and Russia—to make us realize that this seemingly comical rhetoric could be turned into an instrument of political tyranny.

*You've mentioned specifically two nineteenth-century satirical works,* The Biglow Papers *and the Nasby letters, both growing out of the Civil War period, and now Mencken's essays. Any other literary works of a satiric nature that seem to you relevant to our discussion of* Our Gang?

It might be as much to the point to mention satiric works of a non-literary, or popular, nature. "Satiric" probably isn't the right word here—I mean broadly comic in the style of Olsen and Johnson, the Marx Brothers, the Three Stooges, Laurel and Hardy, Abbott and Costello, and the like. Recently I saw Abbott and Costello in a segment from an old movie of theirs, doing that famous baseball dialogue "Who's on First?" It's a marvel of punning and verbal confusion, characterized by the sort of buffoonery that I was trying for in the longest section of *Our Gang,* "Tricky Has Another Crisis." Obviously, Tricky—in contrast to either the colorless straight man Abbott or the benign fool Costello—is an old fashioned villain in the Tartuffian mold. Still, the *style* of some of Abbott and Costello's slapstick comedy seems to me suited to the monkey business that Tricky and his friends engage in in that "crisis" section.

Do you remember Charlie Chaplin and Jack Oakie as Hitler and Mussolini in *The Great Dictator?* Well, in their performances there's something, too, of the flavor I hoped to get into the more outlandish sections of *Our Gang.*

All I'm saying, of course, is that the level of comedy in *Our Gang* isn't exactly what it is in *Pride and Prejudice*—in case anybody should fail to notice. *Our Gang* is out to destroy the protective armor of "dignity" that shields anyone in an office as high and powerful as the Presidency. It was no accident, for instance, that President Nixon took it into his head a few years ago to tart up the White House police staff in the imperial garb of Junkers out of *The Student Prince.* He knows better than anybody how much he needs all the trappings of dignified authority—or authoritarian dignity. But rather than accept his "official" estimate of himself, which we see for Mr. Nixon is very regal indeed, I prefer to place him in a baggy-pants burlesque skit. It seems to me more appropriate.

Clearly, satire of this kind has no desire to be decorous. Decorum—and what hides behind it—is often just what it's attacking. To ask a satirist to be in good taste is like asking a love poet to be less personal. Is *The Satyricon* in good taste? Is *A Modest Proposal?* Swift recommends the stewing, roasting, and fricasseeing of one-year-old children so as to unburden their impoverished parents and provide food for the meat-eating classes. How nasty and vulgar that must have seemed, even to many who shared his concern for Ireland's misery. Imagine how this went down in polite society: "A Child will make two Dishes at an Entertainment for Friends; and when the Family dines alone, the fore or hind quarter will make a reasonable Dish, and seasoned with a little Pepper or Salt will be very good Boiled on the fourth Day, especially in Winter."

Now that's considered Literature. It's called "Swiftian." Back in 1729 it probably seemed, to a lot of Swift's contemporaries, bad taste, and worse. Similarly, Rabelais is no longer an obscene writer who can't resist a joke about feces, urine, or the apertures—four hundred years in the grave and he's "Rabelaisian." The trick, apparently, is to turn yourself from a proper noun into an adjective, and the best way to accomplish that is to die.

Imagine if today you were to write a satire modeled upon Swift's *Modest Proposal* about our "involvement"—nice euphemism, that—

in Southeast Asia. As it turns out, under orders from Presidents
Johnson and Nixon, our armed forces have been following Swift's
advice for some time now, boiling and fricasseeing the children in
Vietnam and Laos, and lately roasting succulent Cambodian infants.
Suppose someone were to propose in print to President Nixon that
instead of killing these Asian children for no good reason, as we
do now, we adopt a policy at once more practical and humane.
Since statistics prove that x number of children are going to die
anyway, why not slaughter them for food for the Vietnamese refu-
gees? The proposal might be written in the style of the Pentagon
Papers. This fellow named McNaughton could probably have drafted
a first-rate contingency plan on how to barbecue with napalm,
sprinkle with soy sauce, and serve—including a breakdown in Penta-
gonian percentage points of the various minimum daily vitamin
requirements fulfilled by the liver, lungs, and brains of an Asian
infant, when mixed with a bowl of rice.

We can safely conclude that few American newspapers would rush
to publish such a piece. "Swiftian" it is, if it's about what Englishmen
were doing to Irishmen in 1729; if, however, you were to employ
similar means to indict our country for what it has done to the
Vietnamese now—which is a thousand times more vicious than
anything the British could hope to do in the eighteenth century with
their limited arsenal of torture devices—you would find your satire
unpublishable in most places because of bad taste.

Which it is. All the works I've mentioned, by ordinary community
standards, or whatever the legal phrase is to describe the lowest
common denominator of social conformism, are in execrable taste.
By ordinary community standards they are shocking—just in order to
dislocate the reader and get him to view a familiar subject in ways he
may be unwilling or unaccustomed to. You know how people taking
offense will sometimes say, "Now, stop kidding around, this is serious." But in satire it is *by* kidding around that one hopes to reveal
just *how* serious. This is illustrated by the modest proposal to use
Asian infants for barbecued spareribs instead of "wasting" them as
cannon fodder.

A distinctive characteristic of shocking and tasteless satire is its high
degree of distortion. On the whole, Americans are more familiar with
distortion and exaggeration in the art of caricature than in literary

works. Newspaper readers deal with distortion every day in political cartoons, and are not only untroubled by it but easily grasp the commentary implicit in the technique. Well, the same techniques of distortion apparent in the work of Herblock, Jules Feiffer, and David Levine—or, to invoke the names of giants, in the satirical drawings of Hogarth and Daumier—are operating in prose satire. Distortion is a dye dropped onto the specimen to make vivid traits and qualities otherwise only faintly visible to the naked eye.

*You've begun to touch upon the impulses behind writing* Our Gang. *Can you be more specific about motives? Previous to this, you have written and published four books of fiction; is it clear to you why you have chosen to write political satire just now in your career?*

Well, at Bucknell University, where I went to college and edited a literary magazine in the early fifties, I spent nearly as much time writing satire as I did trying to write fiction. Then in the middle fifties I began to publish pieces in *The New Republic,* most of them ostensibly movie reviews, but with the appeal—in that they had any—of satirical comedy. I once did a parody in *The New Republic* of President Eisenhower's religious beliefs (and prose style) inspired by a Norman Vincent Peale sermon that had revealed to Reverend Peale's parishioners that Ike was on a first-name basis with Jehovah. By the way, Oliver Jensen wrote a very funny version back then of the Gettysburg Address as Eisenhower might have composed and delivered it. The first sentence went, "I haven't checked these figures, but eighty-seven years ago, I think it was, a number of individuals organized a governmental set-up here in this country, I believe it covered certain Eastern areas, with this idea they were following up based on a sort of national independence arrangement and the program that *every* individual is just as good as every other individual."

My own first book of fiction, *Goodbye, Columbus,* was described by Alfred Kazin as "acidulous," suggesting a satiric intention. To a degree that's true, but in retrospect that book seems to me very mild comedy, in turn ironical and lyrical in the way of books about sensitive upstarts in summer romances. Nothing since would seem to qualify as satire, unless you call *Portnoy's Complaint* a satirical lament.

Why have I turned to political satire? In a word: Nixon.

What triggered—that's the word for it, too—what triggered *Our Gang* was his response to the Calley conviction back in April 1971. Do you remember what the army lawyer, Joseph Welch, said to Senator McCarthy at the Senate hearings after McCarthy had gratuitously insinuated that a junior member of Welch's Boston law firm had a Communist background? "Until this moment, Senator, I think I never really gauged your cruelty or your recklessness." Well, when Nixon announced that Calley, who had been convicted of murdering four times as many unarmed civilians as Charles Manson, would not have to await his appeal in the post stockade (alongside the monsters who go AWOL and the Benedict Arnolds who get caught snoozing on guard duty) but need only be restricted to quarters until such time as Nixon (with his nose to the wind) reviewed the decision of the appeals court, I thought: Tricky, I knew you were a moral ignoramus, I knew you were a scheming opportunist, I knew you were fraudulent right down to your shoelaces, but truly, I did not think that even you would sink to something like this.

I am, like so many satirists, just a naïf at heart, Why *shouldn't* he sink to that? But what that statement of his on Calley "made perfectly clear" was that if it seemed to him in the interest of his career, he would sink to anything. If 50.1 percent of the voters wanted to make a hero out of a convicted multiple murderer, then maybe there was something in it—for him.

Look at him today [Fall 1971], positively gaga over his trip to Red China, as he used to like to call it when he was debating Kennedy. Now he says the "People's Republic of China" as easily as any Weatherman. Doesn't he stand for *anything?* It turns out he isn't even anti-Communist. He never even believed in *that*. I remember joking back in 1968 that if Rockefeller got the Republican nomination, Nixon would divorce Pat, remarry, and try again in '72. But who, even in his most cynical wisecracks, could have imagined that the Nixon who gave it to Khrushchev about "freedom" in that kitchen would one day be delirious with joy about visiting a "tyrant" who had "enslaved" eight hundred million Chinese? Talk about bad taste. Doesn't his heart bleed for "enslaved peoples" any more? Or did they take everybody's shackles off over there? If so, he neglected to mention it on his two-minute spot commercial for the

People's Republic of China. No more explanation from Nixon about
his ideological turnabout than from the rulers in *1984*, when they
interrupt news broadcasts every other day to inform the people that
their enemies are now their friends and their friends their enemies.
You would think that the people—here, not in Orwell's Oceania—
might want their Commie-chasing President to explain to them what
it is about godlessness, totalitarianism, and slavery that is less repugnant to him today than it was ten years ago, or even ten months ago.
And if it's suddenly okay with the United States for eight hundred
million people in China not to be able "to determine their own future
in free elections," why isn't it okay for a mere thirteen million more in
Vietnam? By comparison, that's only a drop in the enslavement
bucket. But nobody asks, and he doesn't tell. The liberal newspapers
even praise him for his "flexibility."

*Then you've also been inspired to write this book out of frustration
with the ways in which popular spokesmen—newspaper columnists,
TV commentators, even congressmen and senators—respond to
Nixon?*

Only to a small degree. Nixon is sufficient unto himself to make the
steam rise. Of course, the high seriousness with which "responsible"
critics continue to take his public statements does tend to increase
frustration. There is this shibboleth, "respect for the office of the
Presidency"—as though there were no distinction between the man
who holds and degrades the office and the office itself. And why all
the piety about the office anyway? A President happens to be in *our*
employ.

The best journalists I've read on Nixon are Tom Wicker, Nicholas
von Hoffman, Murray Kempton, and Gary Wills in *Nixon Agonistes*.
They don't seem to consider it a setback to the species to point up
how utterly bizarre this guy is. And then, in public life, there's the
Arkansas Traveler, Senator William Fulbright. Cross-examining Laird,
after that Terry and the Pirates raid on the POW camp in North
Vietnam, he was as beautifully droll—his timing as perfect, his assumed innocence as effective—as Mark Twain. When Fulbright
retires, he ought to go around the country, the way Twain and
Artemus Ward and Will Rogers used to, doing humorous monologues about his experiences as Chairman of the Foreign Relations

Committee. He and Eugene McCarthy could be a very dry comic duo, on the order of Lum 'n' Abner.

*Do you actually think* Our Gang *will do anything to restrain or alter Nixon's conduct? Affect his conscience? Shame him? What do you expect to accomplish by publishing a satire like this one?*

Do I expect the world to change? Hardly. True, when we all first learned about satire in school, we were told that it was a humorous attack upon men or institutions for the purpose of instigating reform, or words to that effect about its ameliorative function. Now, that's a very uplifting attitude to take toward malice, but I don't think it holds water. Writing satire is a literary, not a political act, however volcanic the reformist or even revolutionary passion in the author. Satire is moral rage transformed into comic art—as an elegy is grief transformed into poetic art. Does an elegy expect to accomplish anything in the world? No, it's a means of organizing and expressing a harsh, perplexing emotion.

What begins as the desire to murder your enemy with blows, and is converted (largely out of fear of the consequences) into the attempt to murder him with invective and insult, is most thoroughly sublimated, or socialized, in the art of satire. It's the imaginative flowering of the primitive urge to knock somebody's block off.

*Of course, you have the villainous President in your book murdered, don't you? The next-to-last chapter of* Our Gang *begins with the announcement that Trick E. Dixon has been assassinated, and for the next thirty pages or so you give us everything exuded by the television networks in the wake of that announcement. Do you think there will be readers who will accuse you of advocating or encouraging the murder of President Nixon?*

If so, it will be because they have failed to read the chapter—and the book—with even a minimal amount of comprehension. I'm not saying the chapter is in good taste. But I just can't imagine that the ludicrous manner in which Trick E. Dixon is disposed of would serve to fire the will of a would-be Presidential assassin. The President of *Our Gang* is found stuffed in a Baggie in the fetal position, so that he resembles one of those "unborn" for whose rights he speaks so eloquently throughout the book. That he meets his end in a Baggie is just satiric retribution, parodic justice.

And in the next chapter he's alive and well anyway. In Hell, admittedly, but debating the pants off Satan, whom he's running against for Devil. I subtitled that last chapter "On the Comeback Trail" to suggest that you can't hold a Trick E. Dixon down, even by stuffing him into a Baggie and turning the twister seal.

Back in 1966, Max Hayward edited and translated a chilling, depressing document that he called *On Trial.* It was the transcript of the Moscow trial of the Soviet writers Yuli Daniel and Andrei Sinyavsky, who were given five- and seven-year sentences in a forced-labor camp for "slandering" the state in their literary works. Andrei Sinyavsky's final plea to the judge, prior to the sentencing, was particularly memorable. Throughout the trial the judge had brutally chastised Sinyavsky for "lecturing the court on literature"—of all things—whenever the writer tried to explain his intentions in *The Makepeace Experiment,* a fantastic novel, or fable, in which (among other funny things) the people in a provincial Russian town eat toothpaste and think they're dining on caviar because their leader tells them it's so. The judge didn't want to hear about satire or fantasy or hyperbole or playfulness or humor or the make-believe aspect of literature; he didn't want to hear any comparison to Gogol or Pushkin or Mayakovsky—all he wanted to know was: "Why do you slander Lenin?" "Why do you slander the Russian people who suffered so in the war?" "Why do you play into the hands of our enemies in the West?" Yet, when the time came for Sinyavsky to speak his final words to the court—or to *anyone* in the outside world for a long, long time—he proceeded, with incredible determination, to say: "I want to repeat a few elementary arguments about the nature of literature. The most rudimentary thing about literature—it is here that one's study of it begins—is that words are not deeds . . ."

I hardly presume to compare myself to Andrei Sinyavsky, or my situation as a writer to his, or Daniel's, in Russia. I am wholly in awe of writers like Sinyavsky and Daniel, of their personal bravery and their uncompromising devotion and dedication to literature. To write in secrecy, to publish pseudonymously, to work in fear of the labor camp, to be despised, ridiculed, and insulted by the mass of writers turning out just what they're supposed to—it would be presumptuous to imagine one's *art* surviving in such a hostile environment, let alone coming through with the dignity and self-possession displayed by Sinyavsky and Daniel at their trial.

I use the case of Sinyavsky because it is an extreme and horrifying example of the kind of "misunderstanding" one's adversaries might wish to encourage in order to defame a work that makes fun of them. In other words, I am aware of the problem that you raise, and I don't take it lightly. I expect some readers will miss the point, clear as it seems to me. But all I can say to those who will fear for the President's life is that they would do better to lobby for a strong federal gun-control bill than to worry about the influence of *Our Gang* on potential assassins. Admittedly, it might be easier to get Attorney General Mitchell to push for a bill outlawing literature than for one making it impossible to buy a rifle through the mail for fifteen bucks, but the fact remains, more people are killed in this country every year by bullets than by satires.

*What is your purpose then in writing the chapter entitled "The Assassination of Tricky"?*

Well, to me it seems so obvious that I feel uncomfortable having to explain it . . . What's ridiculed here is the discrepancy between official pieties and the unpleasant truth. On the one hand, I have tens of thousands of people flocking to Washington to confess to assassinating Trick E. Dixon, and on the other, the television commentators who persist in describing these self-avowed killers as though they were the mourners who thronged to Washington after President Kennedy was killed—or President Charisma, as he is called in the book. It really isn't Nixon and his friends who are being mocked in this chapter so much as the platitudinous mentality of the media. (Pardon the Agnewesque rhetoric; I assure you, there's no similarity between the Vice President's attitude toward TV and my own. That he should find this utterly conformist medium, these mammoth corporations like NBC and CBS, to be heretical and treasonous is a perfect measure of his powers of social observation.) Partly, the point is that Tricky, living or dead, in the White House or in the grave, is unworthy of such tribute, but the joke in that chapter entitled "The Assassination of Tricky" is largely at the expense of network blindness. The implication is that the mass media are purveyors of the Official Version of Reality and, for all their so-called criticism of the government, can be counted on, when the chips are down, to cloud the issue and miss the point.

Lastly, the chapter is concerned with the fine art of government lying, but then so is the entire book.

*Let me press you further on "The Assassination of Tricky" with a question that some people might want to raise about it. Won't certain details about that chapter be particularly disturbing, if not repellent, to those who continue to grieve over the death by assassination of the two Kennedy brothers and Martin Luther King?*

I expect that even Mrs. Martin Luther King and Senator Edward Kennedy would agree that every time we alluded to an act of criminal brutality, such as the murder of a national leader, it is not necessary to draw a long face and make pious testimony to our abhorrence of violence.

I think, really, whatever there might be that is disturbing or unsettling here arises out of the imaginative exploration of a violent fantasy. To give an extreme and well-known literary example: what could be more unsettling than reading *Crime and Punishment?* I recently assigned it to a literature class and found those students whose habit it is to read a novel straight through the night before the class meeting in a state of anxiety that had to do with something more than just going without their sleep. Reading *Crime and Punishment* is a disgusting, if not repellent, experience, among other things; so is watching *Othello.* Even Synge's *Playboy of the Western World,* which just toys with the theme of parricide, has been known to cause audiences in Ireland to riot.

In *Our Gang,* the farcical style seems to me to work to *becalm* whatever anxiety might be aroused in the reader by a parricidal (or, I supposed, regicidal) fantasy made "real." It doesn't dilute it as much as a Bugs Bunny cartoon—where the violence is morally inconsequential because of the utter silliness of the situation—but there is a similar kind of relief felt as a result of the comedy. However, simultaneous with the pleasure taken in the harmless, make-believe, sadistic fun, the reader probably can't help remembering that Presidents of the United States *have* been assassinated—and knowing that it is possible for President Nixon to be assassinated too. So suddenly it's not so funny after all—and I think what is then most disturbing to the reader is that he has found himself *enjoying* a fantasy that he has known in reality to be terrible.

# On *The Breast*

## Alan Lelchuk/1972

From *The New York Review of Books,* 19 October 1972, 26–28. Reprinted with permission from *The New York Review of Books.* Copyright © 1972 Nyrev, Inc.

*I'd like to ask about the origins of* The Breast. *How do you account for the idea itself? Do you think this is a strange or unusual book for you to have written? Do you see any connection between* The Breast *and your previous work, or do you consider it a work really a little out of your line?*

Thinking back over my work, it seems to me that I've frequently written about what Bruno Bettelheim calls "behavior in extreme situations." Or until *The Breast* perhaps what I've written about has been extreme behavior in ordinary situations. At any rate, I have concerned myself with men and women whose moorings have been cut, and who are swept away from their native shores and out to sea, sometimes on a tide of their own righteousness or resentment. For instance, in an early story, "The Conversation of the Jews," a little Jewish boy finds himself playing God on a synagogue roof; now he may not be in such dire straits as Kepesh in *The Breast,* but he is definitely in a new and surprising relationship with his everyday self, his family and his friends. Lucy Nelson in *When She Was Good,* Gabe Wallach and Paul Herz in *Letting Go,* Alex Portnoy in *Portnoy's Complaint*—all are living beyond their psychological and moral means; it isn't a matter of sinking or swimming—they have, as it were, to invent the crawl.

Kepesh's predicament is similar—with a difference: his unmooring can't be traced (much to his dismay, too) to psychological, social, or historical causes. His longing to be at one again with his fellows and his old self is, to my mind, far more poignant and harrowing than Lucy Nelson's or Portnoy's. Those two characters, at the same time that they yearn for a more sociable and settled existence, are hell-bent on maintaining their isolation with all the rage and wildness in their arsenals. They are two very stubborn American children, locked in prototypical combat with the beloved enemy: the spirited Jewish boy pitted against his mother, the Cleopatra of the kitchen; the solemn Gentile girl pitted against her father, the Bacchus of Hometown, U.S.A. Kepesh strikes me as far more heroic than either of these two: perhaps a man who turns into a breast is the first heroic character I've ever been able to portray.

*What problems did you face while writing* The Breast? *Were there any special pitfalls you worried over while you were at work? Or did the story unfold more or less of a piece?*
One difficulty in writing this kind of story is deciding what sort of claim to make on the reader's credulity: whether to invite him to accept the fantastic situation as taking place in the recognizable world (and so to respond to the imagined actuality from that vantage point, with that kind of concern) or whether to ignore the matter of belief and move into other imaginative realms entirely—the worlds of dream, hallucination, allegory, nonsense, play, literary self-consciousness, sadism, and so on.

In "The Metamorphosis" Kafka asserts at the outset that the catastrophe is happening to his hero in the very real, believable, mundane world of families, jobs, bosses, money, and housekeepers. If you don't accept this, if you read "The Metamorphosis" as if it were Gogol's "The Diary of a Madman," and think of Samsa as someone trapped in an insane hallucination, then you will not be on the right wave length to receive the full impact of the story. Kafka doesn't go more than a dozen sentences before he tells you, point blank, "It was no dream." On the other hand, Gogol, in "The Nose," is intermittently provocative and teasing about Kovalev's misfortune. There is a playful, sadistic imagination back of the story that keeps expressing itself in farcical and satiric turns and, in that way, keeps alive and unresolved the question of the story's "reality." As Gogol says in the end, maybe it's only a cock-and-bull story anyway—then again, maybe not. Clearly he can't have it both ways, but perverse trickster that he is here (Chichikov-as-writer), *that* suits him to a T.

I refer to these masters of fantasy to illustrate possibilities, not to lay claim to similarities of accomplishment or stature. In *The Breast* my approach to the outlandish seems to me to be something like a blending of the two methods that I've just described. I want the fantastic situation to be accepted as taking place in what we call the real world, at the same time that I hope to make the reality of the horror one of the issues of the story. "Is it really happening? Can I believe this?"—the questions that Kafka settles (or suppresses) on the very first page by asserting that the metamorphosis is "no dream," and that Gogol is so prankish about at the reader's expense, are absorbed into *The Breast* by Kepesh himself. Whether it is or isn't a dream, a hallucination, or a psychotic delusion, is no small matter to my hero (or to me)—consequently, I didn't choose to render the problem unproblematical by a wave of the author's magic wand.

"The Nose" and "The Metamorphosis" are both cited by Kepesh in the story, part of his desperate struggle to make some sense out of what's happened to him. I thought it was fitting for a serious, dedicated literature professor to think of Gogol and Kafka when his own horrible transformation occurs; it also seemed a good idea not to leave it to the reader to speculate on his own about my indebtedness to "The Nose" and "The Metamorphosis," but instead to make that issue visible in the fiction. *The Breast* proceeds, in fact, by attempting to answer the objections and the reservations that might be raised in a skeptical reader by its own fantastic premise. It has the design of a rebuttal or a rejoinder, rather than a hallucination or a nightmare. Above all, I thought it would be in the story's best interest to try to be straightforward and direct about this bizarre circumstance, and for the protagonist to be no less intelligent than the reader about the implications of his misfortune. No crapola about Deep Meaning; instead, try to absorb that issue, the issue of meaning, into the story—along with the issues of literary antecedents and the "reality" of the horror.

*You say you wanted to be straightforward and direct. Yet one critic has complained that "on the metaphorical level the fantasy remains rather opaque."*

First off, that a fiction is clear and straightforward about itself on the narrative level, and opaque or difficult on the metaphorical level, is not necessarily a bad thing. To use Kafka again as an illustration—it isn't the transparency of "The Metamorphosis" that accounts for its power; Kafka's strategy (and brilliance) is to resist interpretation, even of a very high order, at the same time that he invites it. Whatever

intellectual handle you use to get a hold on a Kafka story is never
really adequate to explain its appeal; and to address yourself primarily to the "meaning" has always seemed to me the way to miss much
of his appeal.

I'm not arguing that impenetrability is itself some kind of virtue. It's
not hard, after all, for a writer to delude himself into believing he is
being deep just because he is being difficult or vague. The issue isn't
opacity or transparency anyway—it's usability. What makes an image
telling or even, if you prefer, meaningful, is not how much meaning
we can associate to it but the quality of the overall invention that it
inspires, the freedom it gives the writer to explore his obsessions and
his talent. A novelist doesn't persuade by what he is "trying to say,"
but by a sense of fictional authenticity he communicates, the sense of
an imagination so relentless and thoroughgoing that it is able to
convert into its own nonconvertible currency whatever the author has
absorbed through reading, thinking, and "raw experience."

To get back to your critic's complaint: what's frustrating him is very
like what's killing Kepesh. I wish I had thought to give Professor
*Kepesh* those words to speak: "On the metaphorical level the fantasy
remains rather opaque." What a marvelous, chilling conclusion that
would have made! What your critic senses as a literary problem
seems to me the human problem that triggers a good deal of Kepesh's ruminations. To try to unravel the mystery of "meaning" here
is really to participate to some degree in Kepesh's struggle—and to
be defeated, as he is. Not all the ingenuity of all the English teachers
in all the English departments in America can put David Kepesh
together again. For him there is no way out of the monstrous situation, not even through literary interpretation. There is only the
unrelenting education in his own misfortune. What he learns by the
end is that, whatever else it is, it is the real thing: he *is* a breast,
and must act accordingly.

Now what "accordingly" means is still another question, and the
one Kepesh raises near the end of the story, with his daydream about
becoming his own one-man, or one-breast, circus. Unlike Gregor
Samsa, who accepts his transformation into a beetle from the first
sentence, Kepesh is continually challenging, questioning, and defying
his fate, and even after he consents to believe that he has actually

become a mammary gland, his mind is alive with alternative ways of being one.

*I'm interested in the relationship between the sexual ecstasy that Kepesh discovers as a breast and his spiritual pain, his excruciating sense of exile and aloneness. Doesn't the connection you make here recapitulate, in a more extreme way, a psychological motif that was central to* Portnoy's Complaint, *where the hero feels increasingly at odds with himself and his past the more sexually adventurous he becomes?*

Yes, though with a different emphasis and implications. Speaking broadly, it's the struggle to accommodate warring (or, at least, contending) impulses and desires, to negotiate some kind of inner peace or balance of power, or perhaps just to maintain hostilities at a low destructive level, between the ethical and social yearnings and the implacable, singular lusts for the flesh and its pleasures. The measured self vs. the insatiable self. The accommodating self vs. the ravenous self. In these works of fiction, of course, the sides are not this clearly drawn, nor are they in opposition right on down the line. These aren't meant to be diagrams of conflicting "selves" anyway but stories of men experiencing the complicated economics of human satisfaction, men in whom spiritual ambitions *and* sensual ambitions are inextricably bound up with the overarching desire to somehow achieve their own true purpose.

However, I don't think of the two works simply as variations on a sexual theme. The grotesqueness of Kepesh's transformation complicates the sexual struggle to a point where it's no longer really useful to view him and Portnoy as blood brothers—or to describe his trouble as only sexual. Portnoy, for all his confusion and isolation, knows the world like the back of his own hand (to make the kind of joke that book seems to inspire). Kepesh is *lost*—somewhat the way Descartes claims to be lost at the beginning of the *Meditations:* "I am certain that I am, but what am I? What is there that can be esteemed true?" Unlike Portnoy, Kepesh is not interested in making his misery entertaining, nor is he able to bridge the gap between what he looks like and what he feels like with wild humor. If Portnoy could do that, it was because he had less territory to cover.

*Is there any implied criticism in* The Breast *of ideas about sexual freedom that are currently enjoying a vogue? When you speak of the "economics of human satisfaction," with its implications of loss as well as gain, I wonder if perhaps you may have had a satiric inten- tion—if there's a critique here aimed at the high value placed upon a "liberated" sexual life. Along this line, I'd like to ask you if you didn't also set out to criticize, or deromanticize, certain extreme but increas- ingly popular notions about madness and alienation—in particular, the idea that either is a desirable alternative to sanity and to a sense of harmony with ordinary life.*

I don't think you're describing my intentions so much as a point of view that may have stimulated my imagination along the way but that was consumed—I'd like to think—by the invention itself. For me, one of the strongest motives for continuing to write fiction is an increasing distrust of "positions," my own included. This is not to say that you leave your intellectual baggage at the door when you sit down to write, or that in your novel you discover that you really think just the opposite of what you've been telling people—if you do, you're probably too confused to be producing good work. I'm only saying that I often feel that I don't really know what I'm talking about until I've stopped *talking* about it and sent everything down through the blades of the fiction-making machine, to be ground into some- thing else, something that is decidedly *not* a position but that allows me to say, when I'm done, "Well, that isn't what I mean either—but it's more like it."

So—I intended to write a critique of nobody's ideas but my own. Not that I think that madness or alienation are glamorous or enviable conditions; being insane and feeling estranged don't accord with my conception of the good life. You correctly identify the bias, but are sniffing after a polemical objective that isn't there. I see what you mean about "deromanticizing" these "voguish" ideas, but if that happens, it happens by the way. And had I intended to write a satire, even of the most muted kind, I would have flashed a different set of signals from the coach's box to the reader.

*Do you anticipate hostile reactions to* The Breast *from voices within the women's movement? I know that there has already been discussion of the book which characterizes the hero, disapprovingly, as a man who thinks of women as existing solely for his sexual pleasure. What do you think of this sort of reading of your story?*

I think it's inaccurate and misses the point. Whatever Kepesh thinks, whether about women, art, reality, or his father, hasn't to do with his being a man but with the fact that he *isn't* one any longer, that he's all but lost touch, to quote him, with the "professor of literature, the lover, the son, the friend, the neighbor, the customer, the client, and the citizen" that he was before his transformation. What he's become has narrowed his life down to a single issue: his anatomy.

I would think that there might even be women, particularly those who have been sensitized by the women's movement, who will feel a certain *kinship* with my hero and his predicament. Surely if anybody has ever been turned totally into a "sexual object," both to himself and to others, it is David Alan Kepesh. Isn't this all-encompassing sexualization exactly what he struggles with from the moment he discovers he's an enormous female breast with a supersensitive five-inch nipple? The battle to be, not simply that shape and those dimensions, but simultaneously to be something *other*, constitutes the entire action of the book.

Of course it's an ambiguous struggle, shot through with contradiction and bewilderment, and waged with varying degrees of wisdom and success—but then it's the *confused* nature of Kepesh's battle with his own soft adipose tissue that might well strike a chord similar to women who are thoughtful about the relationships possible between their physical and their psychic selves.

*One of the surprising aspects of the book is its elegiac tone—David Kepesh mourning his predicament the way, say, Tommy Wilhelm mourns his in Bellow's* Seize the Day. *Given that the book begins with such a bizarre, freakish catastrophe, one might have expected either comedy or grotesquerie, not elegy. Can you explain why you took the approach you did?*

I'm not sure I'd call the tone elegiac. It's a sad story and Kepesh is mournful sometimes, but it's more to the point to say that there is an elegiac tone *trying* to make itself heard but held in check by the overriding (and, I think, in the circumstances, ironic) tone of reasonableness. The mood is less plaintive than reflective—horror recollected in a kind of stunned tranquility. The mood of the convalescent.

The story could have been more comic, or more grotesque, or

both. Certainly there are wonderful models for the kind of humor
that manages to be wildly funny and perfectly gruesome all at once.
"The Nose" treats mutilation as a marvelous joke, and then in *Molloy*
and *Malone Dies,* Samuel Beckett does for bodily decomposition
what Jack Benny used to do on Sunday nights for stinginess. I like
that kind of comedy, and it goes without saying that at the outset
I recognized the gruesomely comic possibilities in the idea of a man
turning into a breast.

But I resisted comedy or farce in large part because the possibility
was so immediately apparent. Since the joke was there before I even
began, perhaps the best thing was to stand it on its head by *refusing*
to take it as a joke . . . Then a certain contrariness probably figured in
my decision, a reluctance, such as I imagine any writer might feel, to
do what is supposed to be his "number."

In all, it seemed to me that if I was going to come up with anything
new (in terms of my own work), it might best be done by taking this
potentially hilarious situation and treating it perfectly *seriously*. I think
there are still funny moments in the story, but that's okay with me
too. I didn't feel I had necessarily to make myself over into William
Ernest Henley just for the sake of going against the expectations
aroused by the material or by my own track record.

# Reading Myself
## Philip Roth/1973

From *Partisan Review,* 40 (1973), 404–17. © 1973 by *Partisan Review.* Reprinted by permission.

*To begin with, how extreme a departure from your previous fiction is* The Great American Novel?

If *The Great American Novel* is an extreme departure, it's because the tendency to comedy that's been present even in my most somber books and stories was allowed to take charge of my imagination and lead it where it would. I was no less farcical, blatant, and coarse-grained in *Our Gang,* but that book, aimed at a precise target, had a punitive purpose that restricted the range of humorous possibilities. And in *Portnoy's Complaint,* though the comedy may have been what was most obvious about the novel, strains of pathos, nostalgia, and (as I see it) evocative lyricism worked to qualify the humor and to place the monologue in a reasonably familiar setting, literary and psychological; comedy was the means by which the character synthesized and articulated his sense of himself and his predicament.

In *The Great American Novel* the satiric bull's-eye has been replaced by a good-sized imaginary world more loosely connected to the actual than in *Our Gang.* And except for the Prologue and Epilogue, the comedy is not turned on and off, or on and on, by a self-conscious narrator using humor to shape your (and his) idea of himself, as in *Portnoy's Complaint.* Widening the focus, and by and large removing the comedian himself from the stage, allowed for a less constrained kind of comic invention. The comedy here is not softened or mitigated by the familiar human presence it flows through and defines, nor does the book try to justify whatever is reckless about it by claiming some redeeming social or political value. It follows its own comic logic—if one can speak of the "logic" of farce, burlesque, and slapstick—rather than the logic of a political satire or a personal monologue.

*But there is certainly satire in this novel, directed, however play-*

*fully, at aspects of American popular mythology. The comedy may not be so free of polemical intent, or even of redeeming social or moral value as you might like to think. And why would you want to think that anyway?*

The comedy in *The Great American Novel* exists for the sake of no higher value than comedy itself; the redeeming value is not social or cultural reform, or moral instruction, but *comic inventiveness*. Destructive, or lawless, playfulness—and for the fun of it.

Now, there is an art to this sort of thing that distinguishes it from sadism, nonsense, or even nihilism for the fun of it; however, a *feel* for the sadistic, the nonsensical, and the nihilistic certainly goes into making such comedy (and into enjoying it). I don't like using the word "satiric" for describing this book because the suggestion of cruel means employed for a higher purpose doesn't square with what I felt myself to be doing. "Satyric," suggesting the sheer pleasure of exploring the anarchic and the unsocialized, is more like it.

The direction my work has taken since *Portnoy's Complaint* can in part be accounted for by my increased responsiveness to, and respect for, what is unsocialized in me. I don't mean that I am interested in propagandizing for the anarcho-libidinists in our midst; rather, *Portnoy's Complaint,* which was concerned with the comic side of the struggle between a hectoring superego and an ambitious id, seems now, in retrospect, to have realigned those forces as they act upon my imagination.

*Can you explain why you are trying to come on like a bad boy— although in the manner of a very good boy indeed? Why quarrel, in decorous tones, no less, with decorum? Why insist, in balanced sentences, on libido? Why "reckless" and "anarchic" to describe one's work, rather than "responsible" and "serious" and "humane"? In "Writing About Jews," the essay you published in* Commentary *in 1963, answering charges of "self-hatred" and "anti-Semitism," your argument consisted almost entirely of an attempt to demonstrate your righteousness through the evidence of your work. Does that now seem to you so much defensive obfuscation?*

No, it expressed concerns central to the stories under attack; and my rhetoric then, far from being borrowed to obfuscate the issue, was all too close at hand, the language of a preoccupation with conscience, responsibility, and rectitude rather grindingly at the center of *Letting Go,* the novel I was writing in those years.

At that time, still in my twenties, I imagined fiction to be something like a religious calling, and literature a kind of sacrament, a sense of things I have had reason to modify since. Such elevated notions aren't (or weren't, back then) that uncommon in vain young writers; they dovetailed nicely in my case with a penchant for ethical striving that I had absorbed as a Jewish child, and with the salvationist literary ethos in which I had been introduced to high art in the fifties, a decade when cultural, rather than political, loyalties divided the young into the armies of the damned and the cadre of the blessed. I might turn out to be a bad artist, or no artist at all, but having declared myself *for* art—the art of Tolstoy, James, Flaubert, and Mann, whose appeal was as much in their heroic literary integrity as in their work—I imagined I had sealed myself off from being a morally unacceptable person, in others' eyes as well as my own.

The last thing I expected, having chosen this vocation—*the* vocation—was to be charged with heartlessness, vengeance, malice, and treachery. Yet that was to be one of the first experiences of importance to befall me out in the world. Ambitious and meticulous (if not wholly enlightened) in conscience, I had gravitated to the genre that constituted the most thoroughgoing investigation of conscience that I knew of—only to be told by more than a few Jews that I was a conscienceless young man holding attitudes uncomfortably close to those promulgated by the Nazis. As I saw it then, I had to argue in public and in print that I was not what they said I was. The characterization was ill-founded, I explained, and untrue, and yes, I maintained that Conscience and Righteousness were the very words emblazoned upon the banner I believed myself to be marching under, as a writer *and* as a Jew.

I think now—I didn't then—that this conflict with my Jewish critics was as valuable a struggle as I could have had at the outset of my career. For one thing, it yanked me, screaming, out of the classroom; all one's readers, it turned out, weren't New Critics sitting on their cans at Kenyon. Some people out there took what one wrote to *heart*—and wasn't that as it should be? I resented *how* they read me, but I was never able to complain afterward that they didn't read me; I never felt neglected.

Also, the attack from Jewish critics and readers, along with personal difficulties I was having during those years, made me begin to understand that admiration for me and my mission on earth was, somewhat to my surprise, going to be less than unanimous, and probably hardest to win closest to home. Above all, I eventually came to realize that my way of taking myself seriously was more at odds than I ever could have imagined with what others believed seriousness to be. In time (more, probably, than it should have taken) I became aware of enormous differences of *sensibility* between my Jewish adversaries and myself—a good deal of the disagreement, I realized, had to do with somewhat antithetical systems of aversion and tolerance, particularly with respect to subjects that are conventionally described as "distasteful."

In brief, the opposition was instructive—partly because opposition wasn't all that my early work aroused. However, one shouldn't conclude that a friendly, or enthusiastic, readership functions as a kind of countervailing soporific, or "ego trip," for the writer. The greatest value of an appreciative audience may even be the irritant that it provides, specifically by its collective (therefore simplistic) sense of the writer, the place it chooses for him to occupy on the cultural pecking order, and the uses it wants to make of selective, disconnected elements of his work and of his own (imagined) persona. Like antagonistic opposition, the amiable irritant is useful insomuch as it arouses whatever is stubborn, elusive, or even defiant in the writer's nature, whatever resents being easily digested. Almost invariably one's reaction *against* will exceed the necessities of one's work (certainly as they might narrowly be defined), and the relationship with an attentive audience may even come, as in the case of J. D. Salinger on the one idiosyncratic extreme, and Norman Mailer on the other, to shape one's conduct, not only as a writer, but as a friend, a husband, a citizen, a colleague, etc.

"Fame," Rilke wrote, "is no more than the quintessence of all the misunderstandings collecting around a new name." Mailerism and Salingerism are vigorous, highly conscious responses to that kind of misunderstanding: the first assaults the misunderstanding at the source, challenging its timidity and conventionality ("You think I'm bad? You don't know how bad! You think I'm a brute? Well, I'm a courtly gentleman! You think I'm a gentleman? I'm a brute!" and so on), deliberately, as it were, *exceeding* the misunderstanding in an indefatigable act of public self-realization; the second, Salingerism, refuses to be vexed by misunderstanding (and misappropriation) in any way, even, if need be, by not being published. I suspect that serious American novelists with a sense of an audience swing on a pendulum from Mailerism to Salingerism, each coming to rest at a point on the arc that appears (and needless to say, a man can be wrong) to be congruent with his temperament and nourishing to the work.

To get back to the defense I made of my own work in *Commentary* in 1963—in that essay I evoked the name of Flaubert and the example of Emma Bovary, a memorable character, I said, because of the vividness and depth with which she was presented, and not because she was necessarily representative of French middle-class women of her day; likewise, I went on, *my* characters were not intended to provide a representative sampling of Jews, though they were well within the range of Jewish possibilities.

I wish now that instead of describing my intentions—or validating them—by referring to a revered artist out of the World Literature Pantheon, I had mentioned the name of Henny Youngman, a Jewish nightclub and vaudeville comic, whose wisecracks, delivered in an offhand whine while he played atrociously on the violin from the stage of the Roxy, had impressed me beyond measure at the age of ten. But because it was precisely my seriousness, my sense of proportion and consequence, that was under attack, I did not have the nerve to appear frivolous in any way. So much the worse for me. Had I had it in me to admit, in just those circumstances, that it was to the low-minded and their vulgarity that I owed no less allegiance than I did to the high-minded with whom I truly did associate my intentions, I might at least have provided *myself* with a fuller description and explanation of the work I was doing, if a still more repugnant one to those who disapproved of me.

*Really, do you think of yourself as a disciple of Henny Youngman?*

I do now. Also of Jake the Snake H., a middle-aged master of invective and insult, and a repository of lascivious neighborhood gossip (and, amazingly, the father of a friend of mine), who owned the corner candy store in the years when I much preferred the pinball machine to the company of my parents. I am also a disciple of my older brother's friend and navy buddy, Arnold G., an unconstrained Jewish living-room clown whose indecent stories of failure and confusion in sex did a little to demythologize the world of the sensual for me in early adolescence. As Jake the Snake demythologized the world of the respectable. As Henny Youngman, whining about family and friends while eliciting laughable squeaks from the violin (the very violin that was to make of every little Jewish boy, myself included, a world-famous, urbane, poetic, dignified, and revered Yehudi), demythologized our yearnings for cultural superiority—or for superiority through culture—and argued by his shlemieldom that it was in the world of domestic squabble and unending social compromise, rather than on the concert stage, that the Jews of his audience might expect to spend their lives.

Later I also became a disciple of certain literature professors and their favorite texts. For instance, reading the *Wings of the Dove* all afternoon long in the graduate-school library at the University of Chicago, I would find myself as transfixed by James's linguistic tact and moral scrupulously as I had ever been by the coarseness, recklessness, and vulgar, aggressive clowning with which I was so taken during those afternoons and evenings in "my" booth at the corner candy store. As I now see it, one of my continuing problems as a writer has been to find the means to be true to these seemingly inimical realms of experience that I am strongly attached to by temperament and training—the aggressive, the crude, and the obscene, at one extreme, and something a good deal more subtle and, in every sense, refined, at the other. But that problem is not unique to any single American writer, certainly not in this day and age.

Back in 1939, Philip Rahv wrote a brief, incisive essay wherein he noted the opposition in American literature between "the thin, solemn, semiclerical culture of Boston and Concord" and "the lowlife world of the frontier and the big cities," and accordingly grouped American writers around two polar types he called the "paleface" and the "redskin." According to Rahv's scheme, James was a paleface, as was T. S. Eliot: "The paleface continually hankers after religious norms, tending toward a refined estrangement from reality. . . . At his highest level the paleface moves in an exquisite moral atmosphere, at his lowest he is genteel, snobbish, and pedantic." Whitman and Twain—and after them Anderson, Wolfe, Farrell, etc.—Rahv identified as redskins: their "reactions are primarily emotional, spontaneous, and lacking in personal culture. . . . In giving expression to the vitality and to the aspirations of the people, the redskin is at his best; but at his worst he is a vulgar anti-intellectual, combining aggression with conformity, reverting to the crudest forms of frontier psychology."

What happened in postwar America is that a lot of redskins—if, not to the wigwam, then to the candy store and the borscht belt born—went off to universities and infiltrated the departments of English, till then almost exclusively the domain of the palefaces. All manner of cultural defection, conversion, confusion, enlightenment, miscegenation, parasitism, transformation, and combat ensued. This is not the place to go into all that studies in English and American literature meant, in personal and social terms, to that tribe of redskins like myself, from the semiliterate and semiassimilated reaches of urban Jewish society, or all that the presence of such Jews signified to those directing their studies (what a novel that would make!). The point here is that the weakening of social and class constraints accelerated by World War II, and the cultural exchanges thus encouraged, has produced a number of writers, many now in their forties, who have to some degree reconciled what Rahv described as this "disunity of the American creative mind," though not in any way necessarily congenial to Philip Rahv, or even to the writers themselves. For what this "reconciliation" often comes down to is a feeling of being *fundamentally ill at ease in, and at odds with, both worlds,* although, one hopes, ill at ease with style, alert to the inexhaustible number of intriguing postures that the awkward may assume in public, and the strange means that the uneasy come upon to express themselves. In short: neither the redskin one was in the days of innocence, nor the paleface one could never be in a million (or, to be precise, 5,733) years, but rather, at least in my own case, what I would describe as a "redface."

To my mind, being a redface accounts as much as anything for the self-conscious and deliberate zigzag that my own career has taken, each book veering sharply away from the one before, as though the author were mortified at having written it as he did and preferred to put as much light as possible between that *kind* of book and himself.

Rahv, in his essay, reminds us that the contemporaries Paleface James and Redskin Whitman "felt little more than contempt for each other." The redface sympathizes equally with both parties in their disdain for the other, and, as it were, reenacts the argument within the body of his own work. He can never in good conscience opt for either of the disputants; indeed, bad conscience is the medium in which his literary sensibility moves. Thus the continuing need for self-analysis and self-justification.

*Let's go back to Jake the Snake. In* The Great American Novel, *your allegiance to him is obviously stronger than it is to Henry James, wouldn't you say?*

Yes, there is more of Jake the Snake in there than in *Letting Go* or in *When She Was Good.* Not that I regret now that I wasn't writing books like *The Great American Novel* all along. I don't know if I would ever have found my way to this "recklessness" if I hadn't first tried to dramatize, in a series of fictions—*When She Was Good* is one—the problematical nature of moral authority and of social restraint and regulation. Though I was not deliberate about this at all, it seems to me now that the question of who or what shall have influence and jurisdiction over one's life has been a concern in much of my work. From whom shall one receive the Commandments? The Patimkins? Lucy Nelson? Trick E. Dixon? These characters, as I imagined them, are hardly identical in the particulars of their lives, nor do they inhabit similar fictional worlds, but invariably the claim each makes to being the legitimate moral conscience of the community is very much what is at issue in the book. The degree to which irony, pathos, ridicule, humor, or solemnity permeate *Goodbye, Columbus, When She Was Good,* and *Our Gang* seems to me now to have been determined by what I took to be the dubiousness (and relative danger) of that claim.

The question of moral sovereignty, as it is examined in *Letting Go, Portnoy's Complaint,* and *The Breast,* is really a question of the kind of commandment the hero of each book will issue to himself; here the skepticism is directed inward, upon the hero's ambiguous sense of personal imperatives and taboos. I can even think of these characters—Gabe Wallach, Alexander Portnoy, and David Kepesh—as three stages of a single explosive projectile that is fired into the barrier that forms one boundary of the individual's identity and experience: that barrier of personal inhibition, ethical conviction and plain, old monumental fear beyond which lies the moral and psychological unknown. Gabe Wallach crashes up against the wall and collapses; Portnoy proceeds on through the fractured mortar, only to become lodged there, half in, half out. It remains for Kepesh to pass right on through the bloodied hole, and out the other end, into no-man's-land.

To sum up: the comic recklessness that I've identified with my old mentor, Jake the Snake, the indecent candy-store owner, apparently could not develop to its fullest until the *subject* of restraints and taboos had been dramatized in a series of increasingly pointed fictions that revealed the possible consequences of banging your head against your own wall.

*Did it help and encourage the anarchic spirit to be writing about baseball, morally a "neutral" subject, rather than about Jews, say, or sexual relations?*

Maybe; though before beginning this novel I wrote a long story, "On the Air," in which a small-time Jewish theatrical agent is put through a series of grotesque adventures, some violently sexual, that were as extreme in their comedy as anything in *The Great American Novel*. But it was only a story, and perhaps I couldn't go further with it because the dreadful comic fantasies of persecution and humiliation depicted there were, to my mind, so decidedly "Jewish."

I think one reason I finally have finished a novel about baseball is that it happens to be one of the few subjects that I know much about. If I were as familiar with forestry, music, ironmongering, or the city of Rotterdam, I am sure I would have written fiction grounded in that knowledge long ago. I have not gotten around sooner to a subject as close to me as this one because I had thought that it could not be made to yield very much, the old bugaboo once again of serious-ness, or profundity. Over the last fifty years some gifted writers had done pretty well by it, of course—Ring Lardner, Mark Harris, and Bernard Malamud particularly—but despite my admiration for their ingenuity (and the pleasure I took in baseball stories by writers as good, and as serious, as Isaac Rosenfeld and J. F. Powers), a certain snobbishness about the material held my own imagination in check.

*What changed your mind?*

The point I had reached in my own career: the confidence I had developed in my literary impulses, combined with the experience of the sixties, the demythologizing decade.

This confidence expressed itself partly in a greater willingness to be deliberately, programmatically perverse—subversive not merely of the "serious" values of official literary culture (such subversion, after all, is the standard stuff of our era, if not the new convention), but subversive of my own considerable investment (witness this interview) in seriousness.

I had been at something like this for a while—in the chapter of *Portnoy's Complaint* called "Whacking Off," in much of *Our Gang*, in "On the Air"—but I still had not come anywhere near being as thoroughgoingly *playful* as I now aspired to be. In an odd way— maybe not so odd at that—I set myself the goal of becoming the writer some Jewish critics had been telling me I was all along: irresponsible, conscienceless, *unserious*. Ah, if only they knew what that entailed! And the personal triumph that such an achievement would represent! A quotation from Melville began to intrigue me, from a letter he had sent to Hawthorne upon completing *Moby Dick*. I pinned it up along with the other inspirational matter on my bulletin board. "I have written a wicked book, and feel spotless as the lamb." Now I knew that no matter how hard I tried I could never really hope to be wicked; but perhaps, if I worked long and hard and diligently, I could be frivolous. And what could be more frivolous, *in my own estimation,* than writing a novel about sports?

If perversity, contrariness, my pursuit of the unserious helped to relax my snobbishness about baseball as a subject for my fiction, the decade we had just been through furnished me with the handle with which to take hold of it. Not that I knew that at the outset, or even, in so many words, at the conclusion; but I know it now. I'll try to explain.

Earlier I described the sixties as the demythologizing decade. I mean by this that much that had previously been considered in my own brief lifetime to be disgraceful and disgusting forced itself upon the national consciousness, loathsome or not; what was assumed to be beyond reproach became the target of blasphemous assault; what was imagined to be indestructible, impermeable, in the very nature of

American things, yielded and collapsed overnight. The shock to the system was enormous—not least for those like myself who belong to what may have been the most propagandized generation of young people in American history, our childhoods dominated by World War II, our high school and college years colored by the worst of the Cold War years—Berlin, Korea, Joe McCarthy; also the first American generation to bear the full brunt of the mass media and advertising. Mine was of course no *more* gullible than any other generation of youngsters—it's only that we had *so* much to swallow, and that it was stuffed into us by the most ingenious methods of force-feeding yet devised to replace outright physical torture. The generation known in its college years as "silent" was in actuality straitjacketed, at its most dismal bound by the sort of pieties, fantasies, and values that one might expect to hear articulated today only by a genuine oddball like Tricia Nixon.

Even to have been a dissident, highly skeptical member of that generation did not make one any better prepared than the straitjacketed to absorb the shocks and upheavals of post-Oswald America—for in retrospect the first act of demythologizing committed in the decade seems to me to have been the "demythologizing" of John F. Kennedy by Lee Harvey Oswald. The remythologizing of Kennedy began the instant the last shot had been fired, but once the President of Camelot, as they called it, was pronounced dead, the point about the vulnerability and mortality of the charismatic and indestructible had been made. It remained for Sirhan Sirhan to demythologize Bobby Kennedy, and for the lesser characters like Jackie and Teddy Kennedy to demythologize themselves, the one with Aristotle Onassis and the other with Mary Jo Kopechne, for the decade to turn completely inside out that legend of glamour, power, and righteousness.

Disorienting, shocking, all this may have been, but it did not begin to work deeply to test or alter one's ties to America; Vietnam did that. To have been trained to be a patriotic schoolchild on the rhetoric of World War II, to have developed an attachment to this country in good part on the basis of the myth (*and* reality) of that wartime America made my own spiritual entanglement with *this* wartime America probably more like Lyndon Johnson's than Jerry Rubin's. That I came eventually to despise Johnson did not mean that I was impervious, ever, to his sense, which I took to be genuine, that the America whose leader he was simply could not be on the wrong side, even if for some reason everything seemed to look that way. No, no, cried the America of World War II—"Say it ain't so, Lyndon." Instead, he went on television and said it was, in the only real way he was ever able to admit it publicly, by washing his hands of the whole hideous mess. L.B.J., the last of the decade's great demythologizers. *Après lui,* the bullshit artists once again.

All that by way of background. Here's what I'm getting at: the fierce, oftentimes wild and pathological assault launched in the sixties against venerable American institutions and beliefs and, more to the point, the emergence of a counter-history, or *countermythology,* to challenge the mythic sense of itself the country had when the decade opened with General Eisenhower, our greatest World War II hero, still presiding—it was these social phenomena that furnished me with a handle by which to take hold of baseball, of all things, and place it at the center of a novel. It was not a matter of demythologizing baseball—there was nothing in that to get fired up about—but of discovering in baseball a means to dramatize the *struggle* between the benign national myth of itself that a great power prefers to perpetuate, and the relentlessly insidious, very nearly demonic reality (like the kind we had known in the sixties) that will not give an inch in behalf of that idealized mythology.

Now, to admit to the discovery of thematic reverberations, of depth, of overtone, finally of meaning, would seem to contradict what I have said about wanting fundamentally to be unserious; and it does. Yet out of this opposition, or rather out of the attempt to maintain these contradictory impulses in a state of contentious equilibrium, the book evolved. Sustaining this sort of opposition is not simply a mechanical means of creating literary energy, either; rather, it is itself an attempt to be simultaneously as loyal to one's doubts and uncertainties as to one's convictions, of being as skeptical of the "truth" turned up by imagination as of the actuality that may have served as inspiration or model. A full-scale farce is rarely directed outward only, but takes its own measure as well; much of its inventiveness goes into calling itself into question as a statement, satiric, humane, or what have you. In this sense, the genre is the message, and the message is agnostic: "I tell you (and I tell you and I tell you), I don't know."

An early reader of my book, meaning to offer praise, told me, "This is what America is really like." I would have been happier had he said, "This is what a farce written in America is really like." Now *that* is praise. I don't claim to know what America is "really like." *Not* knowing, or no longer knowing for sure, is just what perplexes many of the people who live and work here and consider this country home. That, if I may say so, is why I invented that paranoid fantasist Word Smith—the narrator who calls himself Smitty—to be (purportedly) the author of *The Great American Novel.* What he describes is what America is really like to one like *him.*

I do not mean by this to disown the novel, or to pretend, defensively, that it is what is called a put-on. Whom would I be trying to put on? And why? By attributing the book to Smitty, I intended, among other things, to call into question the novel's "truthfulness"— to mock any claim the book might appear to make to be delivering up *the* answer—though in no way is this meant to discredit the book itself. The idea is simply to move off the question "What is America really like?" and on to the kind of fantasy (or rewriting of history) that a question so troublesome and difficult has tended of late to inspire. I would not want to argue that Smitty's is the true dream of our lives, his paranoia a wedge into the enigmatic American reality. I would claim, however, that his are not so unlike the sort of fantasies with which the national imagination began to be plagued during this last demythologizing decade of disorder, upheaval, assassination, and war.

I finally anchored this book in the investigations into Communist activities conducted by the House Committee on Un-American Activities in order to give Smitty a break, too. As far off in an American never-never land as he may sound with his story of the destruction of the imaginary Ruppert Mundys of the imaginary Patriot League, his version of history has its origins in something that we all recognize as *having taken place,* and moreover, at a level of bizarre, clownish inventiveness similar to much of the "real" American history that Smitty has obviously invented out of whole cloth. I was trying, then, at the conclusion of the book, to establish a kind of passageway from the imaginary that comes to seem real to the real that comes to seem imaginary, a continuum between the credible incredible and the incredible credible. This strikes me as an activity something like what many of our deranged countrymen must engage in every morning, reading the newspaper on the one hand and swooning over the prophetic ingenuity of their paranoia on the other. Truly, America is the Land of Opportunity—now even the nuts are getting an even break.

So, to conclude: Smitty is to my mind correct in aligning himself with Melville and Hawthorne, whom he calls "my precursors, my kinsmen." They too were in search of some encapsulating fiction, or legend, that would, in its own oblique, charged, and cryptic way, constitute the "truth" about the national disease. Smitty's book, like those of his illustrious forebears, attempts to imagine a myth of an ailing America; my own is to some extent an attempt to imagine a book about imagining that American myth.

# Philip Roth Talks about His Own Work

## Martha Saxton/1974

From *Literary Guild*, June 1974, 2. © 1974 by the Literary Guild. Reprinted by permission.

*In* My Life as a Man, *as in other books of yours, there is an important relationship between a character and his psychoanalyst. Why is that a recurring situation in your work? Of what particular interest is it to you and what uses do you put it to?*

I take it you're referring to four books: *Letting Go,* where Libby Herz, a frantic young woman in despair over her husband's increasing remoteness and gloom, spends a hapless hour with an analyst in Chicago; *Portnoy's Complaint,* a novel cast in the form of an analytic monologue by a lust-ridden, mother-addicted young Jewish bachelor; *The Breast,* in which David Kepesh, an intelligent professor of imaginative literature who has turned overnight into an enormous female breast, engages in a daily dialectic with his former analyst about his new condition; and *My Life as a Man,* in which Peter Tarnopol, a baffled writer and humiliated husband, suffers a breakdown following the collapse of a disastrous marriage and, during the long effort to make sense of what happened, struggles with his doctor over fundamental differences of opinion (and values and language), a struggle that eventually destroys their genuine, therapeutic friendship.

All of these characters, in pain and in trouble, turn to doctors because they believe psychoanalysis may help them from going under completely. *Why* they believe this is a subject I haven't the space to go into here, nor is it what I've given most thought to in these books. I've mainly been interested in the extent to which unhappy people *do* define themselves as "ill" or agree to view themselves as "patients," and in what each then makes of the treatment prescribed. The connection between patient and analyst varies considerably from one book to the next, as do the relation-

ships, say, between the lay Catholics and their priests in the stories of
J. F. Powers.

Until *My Life as a Man,* the psychoanalyst in my fiction hasn't been
much of a character, in the conventional novelistic sense. In *Portnoy's Complaint,* Dr. Spielvogel was nothing more than he for whom
Portnoy re-enacted the drama, or vaudeville skit, of his life. Much
like the priest discreetly hidden away in the confessional (or the
audience beyond the footlights), Spielvogel is silent until the last
mortifying detail (or routine) has been extracted from the babbling
sinner/showman seeking absolution/applause. Moreover, it is a highly
stylized confession that this imaginary Spielvogel gets to hear, and I
would guess that it bears about as much resemblance to the drift and
tone of what a real psychopathologist hears in his everyday life as a
love sonnet does to the iambs and dactyls that lovers whisper into
one another's ears in motel rooms and over the phone.

What I was looking for when I wrote *Portnoy's Complaint* was a
stratagem that would permit me to bring into my fiction the sort
of intimate, shameful sexual detail, and coarse, abusive sexual
language, that had largely been beside the point of my first three
books. One would just as soon not—if one has a sense of propriety,
that is—serve vodka out of a milk carton: what I wanted was the
appropriate vessel for the unpalatable stuff that I was ready to dis-
pense. And I found it, I thought, in the *idea* of the psychoanalytic
session, wherein pile driving right on through the barrier of good
taste and discretion is considered central to the task at hand. In
*Portnoy's Complaint* I did not set out to write a book "about" an
analysis, but utilized the permissive conventions of the patient-analyst
situation to get at material that had previously been inaccessible to
me, and that in another fictional environment would have struck me
as pornographic, exhibitionistic, and nothing *but* obscene.

In *The Breast,* another analyst appears, this time one who speaks,
and does so more or less in the voice of enlightened common sense.
Dr. Klinger favors the cadences and vocabulary of psychotherapeutic
demystification. The difficulty is that the affliction confronting him—
Kepesh's transformation into a human sized mammary gland—is
bottomlessly mysterious and horrifying. But to the suffering patient,
what affliction isn't? Then too, in the course of a day, a doctor in
Klinger's line of work dutifully hears out half a dozen patients who, if

they do not consider themselves to be breasts, imagine with some
degree of conviction that they are testicles, or vaginas, or bellies, or
brains, or buttocks, or noses, or two left feet, or all thumbs, or all
heart, or all eyes, or what-have-you. "I'm a prick! She's a cunt! My
partner is an asshole!" Granted, say the doctors Klinger, but nonetheless what shall you do out in the great world where you are
obliged to call yourself (and may even wish others to refer to you) by
another name?

Dr. Klinger prevails. By attending to the doctor's homely, anti-
apocalyptic, demystifying view of things ("Come off it, Mr. Kepesh,"
he has the nerve to say to the surreal sexual object), David Kepesh
manages to maintain a tenuous hold, not only on his sanity—which is
just the half of it for this former literature professor—but on his moral
dignity.

The Dr. Spielvogel who turns up as the analyst in *My Life as a Man*
has no such luck with his patient—nor does the patient (in this case
Peter Tarnopol) with his doctor. In the end there is no meeting of
minds or capitulation on either side to the other's sense of reality.
And not because Spielvogel is a fool and a tyrant—he is neither the
All-Knowing Analyst out of patient fairy tales, nor is he the Big Bad
Idiot Analyst out of anti-Freudian folklore—or because Tarnopol lacks
sympathy for the man or the method. If Tarnopol cannot agree to
see himself as Spielvogel sees him, it is partly because Tarnopol
cannot for any length of time see himself as Tarnopol sees Tarnopol
either. Tarnopol the patient finally rejects Spielvogel's version of him
and his world as so much fiction; but as a novelist who takes himself
and his personal life as his subject, so too does he reject his *own*
fictions as so much fiction.

Now, how Portnoy conceives of Portnoy is not much of an issue in
that book (at least not until the doctor delivers, at the conclusion,
his one and only line). Portnoy knows precisely how to present
himself—a good part of his complaint is that his sense of himself, his
past, and his ridiculous destiny is so *fixed*. In *The Breast*, Kepesh
must be educated to understand what he is, and very much against
the grain of his own defiant hopefulness. Only by the end of the
book does he capitulate and take the doctor's word for what has
seemed so utterly impossible all along, accepting finally both the
preposterous description of what he's become and the equally

preposterous prescription as to what now to do about it ("Tolerate it"). But for Tarnopol the presentation or description of himself is what is most problematical—and what remains unresolved. To my mind, Tarnopol's attempt to realize himself with the right words—as earlier in life he attempted realizing himself through the right deeds— is what's at the heart of the book, and accounts for my joining his fictions about his life with his autobiography. When the novel is considered in its entirety, I hope it will be understood as Tarnopol's struggle to achieve a description.

# Writing and the Powers-that-Be
## Walter Mauro/1974

From *The American Poetry Review*, July/August 1974, 18–20.
© 1974 by *The American Poetry Review*. Reprinted by permission.

*Tell us first of all about your adolescence—its relationship with the type of American society you have represented in* Goodbye, Columbus; *your rapport with your family; and if and how you felt the weight of paternal power.*

Far from being the classic period of explosion and tempestuous growth, my adolescence was more or less a period of suspended animation. After the victories of an exuberant and spirited childhood—lived out against the dramatic background of America's participation in World War II—I was to cool down considerably until I went off to college in 1950. There, in a respectable Christian atmosphere hardly less constraining than my own particular Jewish upbringing, but whose strictures I could ignore or oppose without feeling bedeviled by long-standing loyalties, I was able to reactivate a taste for inquiry and speculation that had been all but immobilized during my high school years. From age twelve, when I entered high school, to age sixteen, when I graduated, I was by and large a good, responsible, well-behaved boy, controlled (rather willingly) by the social regulations of the self-conscious and orderly lower-middle-class neighborhood where I had been raised, and mildly constrained still by the taboos that had filtered down to me, in attenuated form, from the religious orthodoxy of my immigrant grandparents. I was probably a "good" adolescent partly because I understood that in our Jewish section of Newark there was nothing much else to be, unless I wanted to steal cars or flunk courses, both of which proved to be beyond me. Rather than becoming a sullen malcontent or a screaming rebel—or flowering, as I had in the prelapsarian days at elementary school—I obediently served my time in what was, after all, only a minimum-security institution, and enjoyed the latitude and privileges awarded to the inmates who make no trouble for their guards.

The best of adolescence was the intense male friendships—not only because of the cozy feelings of camaraderie they afforded boys coming unstuck from their close-knit families, but because of the opportunity they provided for uncensored talk. These marathon conversations, characterized often by raucous discussions of hoped-for sexual adventure and by all sorts of anarchic joking, were typically conducted, however, in the confines of a parked car—two, three, four, or five of us in a single steel enclosure just about the size and shape of a prison cell, and similarly set apart from ordinary human society.

Still, the greatest freedom and pleasure I knew in those years may have derived from what we said to one another for hours on end in those automobiles. And how we said it. My closest adolescent companions—clever, respectful Jewish boys like myself, all four of whom have gone on to be successful doctors—may not look back in the same way on those bull sessions, but for my part I associate that amalgam of mimicry, reporting, kibbitzing, disputation, satire, and legendizing from which we drew so much sustenance with the work I now do, and I consider what we came up with to amuse one another in those cars to have been something like the folk narrative of a tribe passing from one stage of human development to the next. Also, those millions of words were the means by which we either took vengeance on or tried to hold at bay the cultural forces that were shaping us. Instead of stealing cars from strangers, we sat in the cars we had borrowed from our fathers and said the wildest things imaginable, at least in our neighborhood. Which is where we were parked.

"The weight of paternal power," in its traditional oppressive or restraining guises, was something I had hardly to contend with in adolescence. My father had little aside from peccadilloes to quarrel with me about, and if anything weighed upon me, it was not dogmatism, unswervingness, or the like, but his limitless pride in me. When I tried not to disappoint him, or my mother, it was never out of fear of the mailed fist or the punitive decree, but of the broken heart; even in post-adolescence, when I began to find reasons to oppose them, it never occurred to me that as a consequence I might lose their love.

What may have encouraged my cooling down in adolescence was the grave financial setback my father suffered at about the time I was

entering high school. The struggle back to solvency was arduous, and
the stubborn determination and reserves of strength that it called
forth from him in his mid-forties made him all at once a figure of
considerable pathos and heroism in my eyes, a cross of a kind
between Captain Ahab and Willy Loman. Half-consciously I wondered if he might not collapse, carrying us under with him—instead
he proved to be undiscourageable, if not something of a stone
wall. But as the outcome was in doubt precisely during my early
adolescence, it could be that my way in those years of being neither
much more nor much less than "good" had to do with contributing
what I could to family order and stability. To allow paternal power to
weigh what it *should,* I would postpone until a later date the resump-
tion of my career as classroom conquistador, and suppress for the
duration all rebellious and heretical inclinations. . . . This is largely a
matter of psychological conjecture, of course, certainly so by this late
date—but the fact remains that I did little in adolescence to upset
whatever balance of power had enabled our family to come as far as
it had and to work as well as it did.

*Sex as an instrument of power and subjection. You develop this
theme in* Portnoy's Complaint *and achieve a desecration of pornography, at the same time recognizing the obsessive character of sexual
concerns and their enormous conditioning power. Tell us in what
real experience this dramatic fable originated or from what adventure
of the mind or the imagination.*

Do I "achieve a desecration of pornography"? I never thought of it
that way before, since generally pornography is itself considered a
verbal desecration of the acts by which men and women are imagined to consecrate their profound attachment to one another. Actually I think of pornography more as the projection of an altogether
human preoccupation with the genitalia *in and of themselves*—a
preoccupation excluding all emotions other than those elemental
feelings that the contemplation of genital functions arouses. Pornography is to the whole domain of sexual relations what a building
manual is to hearth and home. Or so it would be, if carpentry were
surrounded with the exciting aura of magic, mystery, and breachable
taboo that adheres at this moment to the range of sex acts.

I don't think that I "desecrated" pornography but, rather, excised its central obsession with the body as an erotic contraption or play-thing—with orifices, secretions, tumescence, friction, discharge, and all the abstruse intricacies of sextectonics—and then placed that obsession back into an utterly mundane family setting, where issues of power and subjection, among other things, can be seen in their broad everyday aspect rather than through the narrowing lens of pornography. Now, perhaps it is just in this sense that I could be charged with having desecrated, or profaned, what pornography, by its exclusiveness and obsessiveness, does actually elevate into a kind of sacred, all-encompassing religion, whose solemn rites it ritualistically enacts: the religion of Fuckism (or, in a movie like *Deep Throat,* Suckism). As in any religion these devotions are a matter of the utmost seriousness, and there is little more room for individual expressiveness or idiosyncrasy, for human error or mishap, than there is in the celebration of the Mass. In fact, the comedy of *Portnoy's Complaint* arises largely out of the mishaps, wholly expres-sive of the individual, that bedevil one would-be celebrant as he tries desperately to make his way to the altar and remove his clothes. All his attempts to enter naked into the sacred realm of pornography are repeatedly foiled because, by his own definition, Alexander Portnoy is a character in a Jewish joke—a genre which, unlike pornography, pictures a wholly desecrated world: demystified, deromanticized, utterly dedeluded. Fervent religionist that he would be, Portnoy still cannot help but profane with his every word and gesture what the orthodox Fuckist most reveres.

I cannot track down for you any single experience, whether of the mind or the body, from which *Portnoy's Complaint* originated. Perhaps what you want to know is whether I have firsthand knowl-edge of "sex as an instrument of power and subjection." The answer is, how could I not? I too have appetite, genitals, imagination, drive, inhibition, frailties, will, and conscience. Moreover, the massive, late-sixties assault upon sexual customs came nearly twenty years after I myself hit the beach and began fighting for a foothold on the erotic homeland held in subjugation by the enemy. I sometimes think of my generation of men as the first wave of determined D-day invaders, over whose bloody, wounded carcasses the flower children subse-quently stepped ashore to advance triumphantly toward that libidi-nous Paris we had dreamed of liberating as we inched inland on our bellies, firing into the dark. "Daddy," the youngsters ask, "what did you do in the war?" I humbly submit they could do worse than read *Portnoy's Complaint* to find out.

*The relationship in your work between reality and imagination. Have the forms of power we have mentioned (family, religion, politics) influenced your style, your mode of expression? Or has writing served increasingly to free you from these forms of power?*

Inasmuch as subject might be considered an aspect of "style," the answer to the first question is yes: family and religion as coercive forces have been a recurrent subject in my fiction, particularly in the work up to and including *Portnoy's Complaint;* and the coercive appetites of the Nixon Administrative were very much to the point of *Our Gang*. Of course the subjects themselves "influence" their treatment and my "mode of expression," but so does much else. Certainly, aside from the Nixon satire, I have never written anything determinedly and intentionally destructive. Polemical or blasphemous assault upon the powers that be has served me more as a *theme* than as an overriding purpose in my work.

"The Conversion of the Jews," for instance, a story I wrote when I was twenty-three, reveals at its most innocent stage of development a budding concern with the oppressiveness of family feeling and with the binding ideas of religious exclusiveness which I had experienced first-hand in ordinary American-Jewish life. A good boy named Freedman brings to his knees a bad rabbi named Binder (and various other overlords) and then takes wing from the synagogue into the vastness of space. Primitive as this story seems to me now—it might better be called a daydream—it nonetheless evolved out of the same preoccupations that led me, years later, to invent Alexander Portnoy, an older incarnation of claustrophobic little Freedman, who cannot cut loose from what binds and inhibits him quite so magically as the hero I imagined humbling his mother and his rabbi in "The Conversion of the Jews." Ironically, where the boy in the early story is subjugated by figures of real stature in his world, whose power he for the moment at least is able to subvert, Portnoy is less oppressed by these people—who have little real say in his life anyway—than he is imprisoned by the rage that persists against them. That his most powerful oppressor by far is himself is what makes for the farcical

pathos of the book—and also what connects it with my preceding
novel, *When She Was Good,* where again the focus is on a grown
child's fury against long-standing authorities believed by her to have
misused their power.

The question of whether *I* can ever free myself from these forms of
power assumes that I experience family and religion as power and
nothing else. It is much more complicated than that. I have never
really tried, through my work or directly in my life, to sever all that
binds me to the world I came out of. I am probably right now as
devoted to my origins as I ever was in the days when I was indeed as
powerless as little Freedman and, more or less, had no other sane
choice. But this has come about only after subjecting these ties and
connections to considerable scrutiny. In fact, the affinities that I
continue to feel toward the forces that first shaped me, having with-
stood to the degree that they have the assault of imagination and the
test of sustained psychoanalysis (with all the cold-bloodedness *that*
entails), would seem by now to be here to stay. Of course I have
greatly refashioned my attachments through the effort of testing
them, and over the years have developed my strongest attachment to
the test itself.

*Our Gang is a desecration of President Nixon and it takes its theme
from a statement on abortion. In what period of your life have you
most strongly felt the weight of political power as a moral coercion
and how did you react to it? Do you feel that the element of the
grotesque, which you often use, is the only means by which one can
rebel and fight against such power?*

I suppose I most strongly felt political power as moral coercion
while growing up in New Jersey during World War II. Little was asked
of an American schoolchild, other than his belief in the "war effort,"
but that I gave with all my heart. I worried over the welfare of older
cousins who were off in the war zone, and wrote them long "newsy"
letters to keep up their morale; I sat by the radio with my parents
listening to Gabriel Heatter every Sunday, hoping upon hope that he
had good news that night; I followed the battle maps and front-line
reports in the evening paper; and on weekends I participated in the
neighborhood collection of paper and tin cans. I was twelve when the
war ended, and during the next few years my first serious political

allegiances began to take shape. My entire clan—parents, aunts, uncles, cousins—were devout New Deal Democrats. In part because they identified him with Roosevelt, and also because they were by and large lower-middle-class people sympathetic to labor and the underdog, many of them voted for Henry Wallace, the Progressive Party candidate for President in 1948. I'm proud to say that Richard Nixon was known as a crook in our kitchen some twenty-odd years before this dawned on the majority of Americans as a real possibility. I was in college during Joe McCarthy's heyday—which is when I began to identify political power with *immoral* coercion. I reacted by campaigning for Adlai Stevenson and writing a long angry free-verse poem about McCarthyism for the college literary magazine.

The Vietnam War years were the most "politicized" of my life. I spent my days during this war writing fiction, none of which on the face of it would appear to connect to politics (though there was a time when I at least associated the rhetoric employed by the heroine of *When She Was Good* to disguise from herself her vengeful destructiveness with the kind of language our government used when they spoke of "saving" the Vietnamese by means of systematic annihilation). But by being "politicized" I mean something more telling than writing about politics or even taking direct political action. I mean something akin to what ordinary citizens experience in countries like Czechoslovakia or Chile: a daily awareness of government *as a coercive force,* its continuous presence in one's thoughts as far more than just an institutionalized, imperfect system of necessary controls. In sharp contrast to Chileans or Czechs, we hadn't personally to fear for our safety and could be as outspoken as we liked, but this did not diminish the sense of living in a country with a government morally out of control and wholly in business for itself. Reading the morning *New York Times* and the afternoon *New York Post,* watching the seven and then again the eleven o'clock TV news—all of which I did ritualistically—became for me like living on a steady diet of Dostoevsky. Rather than fearing for the well-being of my own kin and country, I now felt toward America's war mission as I had toward the Axis goals in World War II. One even began to use the word "America" as though it was the name, not of the place where one had been raised and to which one had a strong spiritual attachment, but of a foreign invader that had conquered the country and with whom one refused, to the best of one's strength and ability, to collaborate. Suddenly America had turned into "them"—and with this sense of dispossession and powerlessness came the virulence of feeling and rhetoric that often characterized the anti-war movement.

I don't think—to come to your last question—that *Our Gang* uses the "element of the grotesque." Rather, it tries to objectify in a style of its own that element of the grotesque that is inherent in the moral character of a Richard Nixon. He, not the satire, is what is grotesque. Of course there have been others as venal and lawless in American politics, but even a Joe McCarthy was more identifiable as human clay than this guy is. The wonder of Nixon (and contemporary America) is that a man so transparently fraudulent, if not on the edge of mental disorder, could ever have won the confidence and approval of a people who generally require at least a *little* something of the "human touch" in their leaders. It's strange that someone so unlike the types most admired by the average voter—in any Norman Rockwell drawing, Nixon would have been cast as the fuddy-duddy floorwalker or the prissy math teacher school kids love to tease; never the country judge, the bedside doctor, or the trout-fishin' dad—could have passed himself off to this *Saturday Evening Post* America as, of all things, an *American*.

Finally: "rebelling" or "fighting" against *outside* forces isn't what I take to be at the heart of my writing. *Our Gang* is only one of eight disparate works of fiction I've written in the past fifteen years, and even there what most engaged me had to do with *expressiveness*, with problems of presentation, rather than bringing about change or "making a statement." Over the years, whatever serious acts of rebelliousness I may have engaged in as a novelist have been directed far more at my own imagination's system of constraints and habits of expression than at the powers that vie for control in the world.

# A Conversation with Philip Roth

## Joyce Carol Oates/1974

From *The Ontario Review*, 1974, 9–22. © 1974 by *The Ontario Review*. Reprinted by permission.

*Your first book,* Goodbye, Columbus, *won the most distinguished American literary honor—the National Book Award—in 1960; you were twenty-seven years old at that time. A few years later, your fourth book,* Portnoy's Complaint, *achieved a critical and popular success—and notoriety—that must have altered your personal life, and your awareness of yourself as a writer with a great deal of public "influence." Do you believe that your sense of having experienced life, its ironies and depths, has been at all intensified by your public reputation? Have you come to know more because of your fame? Or has the experience of enduring the bizarre projections of others been at times more than you can reasonably handle?*

*My* public reputation—as distinguished from the reputation of my work—is something I try to have as little to do with as I can. I know it's out there, of course—a concoction spawned by *Portnoy's Complaint* and compounded largely out of the fantasies that book gave rise to because of its "confessional" strategy, and also because of its financial success. There isn't much else it can be based on, since outside of print I lead virtually no *public* life at all. I don't consider this a sacrifice, because I never much wanted one. Nor have I the temperament for it—in part this accounts for why I went into fiction writing (and not acting, which interested me for a while in college) and why writing in a room by myself is practically my whole life. I enjoy solitude the way some people I know enjoy parties. It gives me an enormous sense of personal freedom and an exquisitely sharp sense of being alive—and of course it provides me with the quiet and the breathing space I need to get my imagination going and my work done. I take no pleasure at all in being a creature of fantasy in the minds of those who don't know me—which is largely what the fame you're talking about consists of.

For the solitude (and the birds and the trees), I have lived mostly in the country for the last five years, right now more than half of each year in a wooded rural region a hundred miles from New York. I have some six or eight friends scattered within a twenty-mile radius of my house, and I see them a few evenings a month for dinner. Otherwise I write during the day, walk at the end of the afternoon, and read at night. Almost the whole of my life in public takes place in a classroom—I teach one semester of each year. I began to earn my living teaching full time in 1956, and though I can now live on my writing income, I have stayed with teaching more or less ever since. In recent years my public reputation has sometimes accompanied me into the classroom, but usually after the first few weeks, when the students observe that I have neither exposed myself nor set up a stall and attempted to interest them in purchasing my latest book, whatever anxieties or illusions about me they may have had begin to recede and I am largely allowed to be a literature teacher instead of Famous.

"Enduring the bizarre projections of others" isn't just something that famous novelists have to contend with, of course. Defying a multitude of bizarre projections, or submitting to them, would seem to me at the heart of everyday living in America, with its ongoing demand to be something palpable and identifiable. Everyone is invited to imitate in conduct and appearance the grossest simplifications of self that are mercilessly projected upon them by the mass media and advertising, while they must, of course, also contend with the myriad expectations that they arouse in those with whom they have personal and intimate associations. In fact, these "bizarre projections" arising out of ordinary human relations were a concern of mine in *My Life as a Man*—a novel that might have been called *"Don't Do with Me What You Will."*

*Since you have become fairly well established (I hesitate to use that unpleasant word "successful"), have less-established writers tried to use you, to manipulate you into endorsing their work? Do you feel you have received any especially unfair or inaccurate critical treatment? I am also interested in whether you have come to feel more communal now than you did when you were beginning as a writer.*

No, I haven't felt, nor have I been, "manipulated" into endorsing

the work of less-established writers. I don't like to give "endorse-
ments" for advertising or promotion purposes—not because I'm shy
about my enthusiasms, but because I can't say in fifteen or twenty
words what I find special or noteworthy about a book. If I particularly
like something I've read, I write the writer directly. At times when
I've been especially taken by an aspect of some writer's work which I
think is likely to be overlooked or neglected, I've tried to help by
writing longish paragraphs for the writer's hardcover publishers, who
always promise to use the endorsement in its entirety. However,
eventually—since it's a fallen world we live in—what started out as
seventy-five words of critical appreciation seems to wind up on
the paperback-edition cover as a two-word cry of marquee ecstasy.
    Since becoming "fairly well established" I've written paragraphs
on behalf of books by five writers: Edward Hoagland (*Notes from the
Century Before*), Sandra Hochman (*Walking Papers*), Alison Lurie
(*The War Between the Tates*), Thomas Rogers (*Pursuit of Happiness*
and *The Confession of a Child of the Century*), and Richard Stern
(*1968* and *Other Men's Daughters*). In 1972, *Esquire,* for a feature
they were planning, asked four "older writers" (as they called them),
Isaac Bashevis Singer, Leslie Fiedler, Mark Schorer, and me, each
to write a brief essay about a writer under thirty-five he admired.
Singer wrote about Barton Midwood, Fiedler about Bill Hutton,
Schorer about Judith Rascoe, and I chose to write about Alan Lelchuk. I'd met him when we were both guests over a long stretch at
Yaddo, and afterwards had read in manuscript his novel *American
Mischief,* which I admired considerably. I restricted myself to a
description and a somewhat close analysis of the book, which,
though it hardly consisted of unqualified praise, nonetheless caused
some consternation among the Secret Police. One prominent newspaper reviewer wrote in his column that "one would have to go into
the Byzantine feuds and piques of the New York literary scene" to be
able to figure out why I had written my fifteen-hundred-word essay,
which led the reviewer to describe me as a "blurb writer." That I
might simply have enjoyed a new writer's novel, and like Singer,
Schorer, and Fiedler, taken *Esquire*'s invitation as an occasion to talk
about his work, never occurred to him. Too unconspiratorial.
    In recent years I've run into somewhat more of this kind of
"manipulation"—malicious hallucination mixed with childish naïveté

and disguised as Inside Dope—from marginal "literary" journalists
(the "lice of literature," Dickens called them) than from working
writers, young or established. In fact, I don't think there's been a time
since graduate school when genuine literary fellowship has been
such a valuable and necessary part of my life. Contact with writers I
admire or toward whom I feel a kinship is precisely my way out of
isolation and furnishes me with whatever sense of community I have.
I seem almost always to have had at least one writer I could talk to
turn up wherever I happened to be teaching or living. These novelists
I've met along the way—in Chicago, Rome, London, Iowa City, at
Yaddo, in New York, in Philadelphia—are by and large people I
continue to correspond with, exchange finished manuscripts with, try
out ideas on, listen to, and visit, if I can, once or twice a year. By
now, some of us whose friendships go back a ways have fallen out of
sympathy with the direction the other's work has taken, but since we
seem not to have lost faith in one another's integrity or good will, the
opposition tends to be without the mandarin superiority, or academic
condescension (or theoretical hobbyhorsing, or competitive preening,
or merciless gravity), that sometimes tends to characterize criticism
written by professionals for *their* public. Novelists are, as a group, the
most *interesting* readers of novels that I have yet come across.

In a sharp and elegantly angry little essay called "Reviewing,"
Virginia Woolf once suggested that book journalism ought to be
abolished (because 95 percent of it was worthless) and that the
serious critics who do reviewing should put themselves out to hire to
the novelists, who have a strong interest in knowing what an honest
and intelligent reader thinks about their work. For a fee the critic—to
be called a "consultant, expositor or expounder"—would meet
privately and with some formality with the writer, and "for an hour,"
writes Virginia Woolf, "they would consult upon the book in question. . . . The consultant would speak honestly and openly, because
the fear of affecting sales and of hurting feelings would be removed.
Privacy would lessen the shop-window temptation to cut a figure,
to pay off scores. . . . He could thus concentrate upon the book itself,
and upon telling the author why he likes or dislikes it. The author
would profit equally. . . . He could state his case. He could point to
his difficulties. He would no longer feel, as so often at present, that
the critic is talking about something that he has not written. . . .

An hour's private talk with a critic of his own choosing would be incalculably more valuable than the five hundred words of criticism mixed with extraneous matter that is now allotted him."

A very good idea. It surely would have seemed to me worth a hundred dollars to sit for an hour with Edmund Wilson and hear everything he had to say about a book of mine—nor would I have objected to paying to hear whatever Virginia Woolf might have had to say to me about *Portnoy's Complaint,* if she had been willing to accept less than all the tea in China to undertake that task. Nobody minds swallowing his medicine, if it is prescribed by a real doctor. One of the nicer side effects of this system is that since nobody wants to throw away his hard-earned money, most of the quacks and the incompetents would be driven out of business.

As for "especially unfair critical treatment"—of course my blood has been drawn, my anger aroused, my feelings hurt, my patience tried, etc., and in the end, I have wound up enraged most of all with myself, for allowing blood to be drawn, anger aroused, feelings hurt, patience tried. When the "unfair critical treatment" has been associated with charges too serious to ignore—accusations against me, say, of "anti-Semitism"—then, rather than fuming to myself, I have answered the criticism at length and in public. Otherwise I fume and forget it; and keep forgetting it, until actually—miracle of miracles— I *do* forget it.

Lastly: who gets "critical treatment" anyway? Why dignify with such a phrase most of what is written about fiction? What one gets, as far as I can see, is what Edmund Wilson describes as a "collection of opinions by persons of various degrees of intelligence who have happened to have some contact with [the writer's] book."

*What Edmund Wilson says is true, ideally, yet many writers are influenced by the "critical treatment" they receive. The fact that Goodbye, Columbus was singled out for extraordinarily high praise must have encouraged you, to some extent; and the critics, certainly, guided a large number of readers in your direction. I began reading your work in 1959 and was impressed from the start by your effortless (effortless-seeming, perhaps) synthesis of the colloquial, the comic, the near-tragic, the intensely moral . . . within wonderfully readable structures that had the feel of being traditional stories, while*

*being at the same time rather revolutionary. I am thinking of "The*
*Conversion of the Jews," "Eli, the Fanatic," and the novella, "Good-*
*bye, Columbus," among others.*

*One of the prominent themes in your writing seems to be the*
*hero's recognition of a certain loss in his life, along with a regret for*
*the loss, and finally an ironic "acceptance" of this regret (as if the*
*hero had to go this way, fulfill this aspect of his destiny, no matter*
*how painful it might be). Consider the young girl in* Goodbye,
Columbus *and her twin in* My Life as a Man, *both of whom are*
*eventually rejected. But the loss might have broader emotional and*
*psychological implications as well—that is, the beautiful too-young*
*girl must have represented qualities that were also transpersonal.*

1. You correctly spot the return of an old character in a new
incarnation. The *Goodbye, Columbus* heroine, inasmuch as she
existed as a character at all or "represented" an alternative of consequence to the hero, is reconstituted (reappraised?) in *My Life as a*
*Man* as Tarnopol's Dina Dornbusch, the "rich, pretty, protected,
smart, sexy, adoring, young, vibrant, clever, confident, ambitious"
Sarah Lawrence girl he gives up because she's not what the young
literary fellow, in his romantic ambitiousness, recognizes as a
"woman"—by which he means a knocked-around, on-her-own,
volatile, combative handful like Maureen.

Furthermore, Dina Dornbusch (incidental character that she is) is
herself reconstituted and reappraised by Tarnopol, in the two short
stories preceding his own autobiographical narrative (the "useful
fictions"). First in "Salad Days," she appears as the licentious,
childish, slavish, nice suburban Jewish girl whom he buggers under
her family ping-pong table, and then, in "Courting Disaster," as the
altogether attractive, astute, academically ambitious college senior
who tells Professor Zuckerman, after he has severed relations with
her—to take up with his own brand of "damaged" woman—that
under all his flamboyant "maturity" he is "just a crazy little boy."

Both these characters are called Sharon Shatzky, and together
stand in relation to Dina Dornbusch as fictional distillations do to their
models in the unwritten world. These Sharons are what can happen
to a Dina when a Tarnopol sets her free from his life to play the role
such a woman does in his personal mythology. This mythology, this
legend of the self (the useful fiction frequently mistaken by readers

for veiled autobiography), is a kind of idealized architect's drawing for what one may have constructed—or is yet to construct—out of the materials actuality makes available. In this way, a Tarnopol's fiction is his *idea* of his fate.

Or, for all I know, the process works the other way around and the personal myth meant to *reveal* the secret workings of an individual destiny actually makes even *less* readable the text of one's own history. Thereby increasing bewilderment—causing one to tell the story once again, meticulously reconstructing the erasures on what may never have been a palimpsest to begin with.

Sometimes it seems to me that only the novelists and the nuts carry on in quite this way about living what is, after all, only a life—making the transparent opaque, the opaque transparent, the obscure obvious, the obvious obscure, etc. Delmore Schwartz, from "Genesis": " 'Why must I tell, hysterical, this story/And must, compelled, speak of such secrecies?/ . . . Where is my freedom, if I cannot resist/ So much speech blurted out . . . ?/How long must I endure this show and sight/Of all I lived through, all I lived in: Why?' "

2. ". . . loss, along with a regret for the loss, and finally an ironic 'acceptance' of this regret." You point to a theme I hadn't thought of as such before—and that I'd prefer to qualify some. Of course Tarnopol is relentlessly kicking himself for his mistake, but it is just those kicks (and the accompanying screams) that reveal to him how strongly determined by character, how characteristically Tarnopolian, that mistake was. He is his mistake and his mistake is him. "This me who is me being me and none other!" The last line of *My Life as a Man* is meant to point up a harsher attitude toward the self, and the history it has necessarily compiled, than "ironic 'acceptance' " suggests.

To my mind it is Bellow, in his last two pain-filled novels, who has sounded the theme of "loss . . . regret for the loss, and . . . ironic 'acceptance' of the regret"—as he did early on (and less convincingly, I thought) at the conclusion to *Seize the Day,* whose final event I always found a little forced, and then further schmaltzed-up with its sudden swell of *Urn-Burial* prose to elevate Tommy Wilhelm's misery. I prefer the conclusion of "Leaving the Yellow House," with its moving, ironic *rejection* of loss—no "sea-like music" necessary there to make the elemental human feeling felt. If there is an ironic acceptance of anything at the conclusion of *My Life as a Man* (or even along the way), it is of *the determined self*. And angry frustration, a deeply vexing sense of characterological enslavement, is strongly infused in that ironic acceptance. Thus the exclamation mark.

I have always been drawn to a passage that comes near the end of *The Trial*, the chapter where K., in the cathedral, looks up toward the priest with a sudden infusion of hope—that passage is pertinent to what I'm trying to say here, particularly by the word "determined," which I mean in both senses: driven, resolute and purposive—yet utterly fixed in position. "If the man would only quit his pulpit, it was not impossible that K. could obtain decisive and acceptable counsel from him which might, for instance, point the way, not toward some influential manipulation of the case, but toward a circumvention of it, a breaking away from it altogether, a mode of living completely outside the jurisdiction of the Court. This possibility must exist, K. had of late given much thought to it."

As who hasn't of late? Enter Irony when the man in the pulpit turns out to be oneself. If only one *could* quit one's pulpit, one might well obtain decisive and acceptable counsel. How to devise a mode of living completely outside the jurisdiction of the Court when the Court is of one's own devising? It is the ironic acceptance of the loss that follows *that* struggle that I would point to as a theme of *My Life as a Man*.

*Was it you, or someone more or less imitating you, who wrote about a boy who turned into a girl . . . ? How would that strike you, as a nightmare possibility? (I don't mean* The Breast: *that seems to me a literary work, rather than a real psychological excursion, like other writings of yours.) Could you—can you—comprehend, by any extension of your imagination of your unconscious, a life as a woman?—a writing life as a woman? I know this is speculative but had you the choice, would you have wanted to live your life as a man, or as a woman (you could also check "other").*

Answer: Both. Like the hero-heroine of *Orlando*. That is, sequentially (if you can arrange it) rather than simultaneously. It wouldn't be much different from what it's like now, if I weren't able to measure the one life against the other. It would also be interesting not to be Jewish, after having spent a lifetime as a Jew. Arthur Miller imagines the reverse of this as a "nightmare possibility" in *Focus,* where an anti-Semite is taken by the world for the very thing he hates. However, I'm not talking about mistaken identity or skin-deep conversions, but magically becoming *totally* the other, all the while retaining knowledge of what it was to have been one's original self, wearing one's original badges of identity. In the early sixties I wrote (and shelved) a one-act play called *Buried Again,* about a dead Jewish man who, when given the chance to be reincarnated as a goy, refuses and is consigned forthwith to oblivion. I understand perfectly how he felt, though, if in the netherworld I am myself presented with this particular choice, I doubt that I will act similarly. I know this will produce a great outcry in *Commentary,* but alas, I shall have to learn to live with that the second time around as I did the first.

Sherwood Anderson wrote "The Man Who Turned Into a Woman," one of the most beautifully sensuous stories I've ever read, where the boy at one point sees himself in a barroom mirror as a girl, but I doubt if that's the piece of fiction you're referring to. Anyway, it wasn't I who wrote about such a sexual transformation, unless you're thinking of *My Life as a Man,* where the hero puts on his wife's undergarments one day, but just to take a sex *break.*

Of course I have written *about* women, some of whom I identified with strongly and, as it were, imagined myself into, while I was working. In *Letting Go,* Martha Reganhart and Libby Herz; in *When She Was Good,* Lucy Nelson and her mother; and in *My Life as a Man,* Maureen Tarnopol and Susan McCall (and Lydia Ketterer and the Sharon Shatzkys). However much or little I am able to extend my imagination to "comprehend . . . life as a woman" is demonstrated in those books.

I never did much with the girl in *Goodbye, Columbus,* which seems to me apprentice work and weak on character invention all around. Maybe I didn't get very far with her because she was cast as a pretty imperturbable type, a girl who knew how to get what she wanted and how to take care of herself, and as it happened, that didn't arouse my imagination much. Besides, the more I saw of young women who had flown the family nest—just what Brenda Patimkin decides *not* to do—the less imperturbable they seemed. Beginning with *Letting Go,* where I began to write about female vulnerability, and to see this vulnerability not only as it determined the lives of the women—who felt it frequently at the center of their being—but the men to whom they looked for love and support, the women became characters my imagination could take hold of and enlarge upon. How this vulnerability shapes their relations with men (each vulnerable in the style of *his* gender) is really at the heart of whatever story I've told about these eight woman characters.

*In parts of* Portnoy's Complaint, Our Gang, The Breast, *and most recently in your baseball extravaganza,* The Great American Novel, *you seemed to be celebrating the sheer playfulness of the artist, an almost egoless condition in which, to use Thomas Mann's phrase, irony glances on all sides. There is a Sufi saying to the effect that the universe is "endless play and endless illusion"; at the same time, most of us experience it as deadly serious—and so we feel the need, indeed we cannot not feel the need, to be "moral" in our writing. Having been intensely "moral" in* Letting Go *and* When She Was Good, *and in much of* My Life as a Man, *and even in such a marvelously demonic work as the novella "On the Air," do you think your fascination with comedy is only a reaction against this other aspect of your personality, or is it something permanent? Do you anticipate (but no: you could not) some violent pendulum-swing back to what you were years ago, in terms of your commitment to "serious" and even Jamesian writing?*

Sheer Playfulness and Deadly Seriousness are my closest friends; it is with them that I take those walks in the country at the end of the day. I am also on friendly terms with Deadly Playfulness, Playful Playfulness, Serious Playfulness, Serious Seriousness, and Sheer Sheerness. From the last, however, I get nothing; he just wrings my heart and leaves me speechless.

I don't know whether the works you call comedies are so egoless. Isn't there really more *self* in the ostentatious display and assertiveness of *The Great American Novel* than in a book like *Letting Go*, say, where a devoted effort at self-removal and self-obliteration is necessary for the kind of investigation of self that goes on there? I think that the comedies may be the most ego-ridden of the lot; at least they aren't exercises in self-abasement. What made writing *The Great American Novel* such a pleasure for me was precisely the self-assertion that it entailed—or, if there is such a thing, self-pageantry.

(Or will "showing off" do?) All sorts of impulses that I might once have put down as excessive, frivolous, or exhibitionistic I allowed to surface and proceed to their destination. When the censor in me rose responsibly in his robes to say, "Now look here, don't you think that's just a little too—" I would reply, from beneath the baseball cap I often wore when writing that book, "Precisely why it stays! Down in front!" The idea was to see what would emerge if everything that was "a little too" at first glance was permitted to go all the way. I understood that a disaster might ensue (I have been informed by some that it did), but I tried to put my faith in the fun that I was having. *Writing as pleasure.* Enough to make Flaubert spin in his grave.

I don't know what to expect or anticipate next. *My Life as a Man,* which I finished a few months ago, is a book I'd been writing, abandoning, and returning to ever since I published *Portnoy's Complaint.* Whenever I gave up on it I went to work on one of the "playful" books—maybe my despair over the difficulties with the one book accounted for why I wanted to be so playful in the others. At any rate, all the while that *My Life as a Man* was simmering away on the "moral" back burner, I wrote *Our Gang, The Breast,* and *The Great American Novel.* Right now nothing is cooking; at least none of the aromas have as yet reached me. *For the moment* this isn't distressing: I feel (again, for the moment) as though I've reached a natural break of sorts in my work, nothing nagging to be finished, nothing as yet pressing to be begun—only bits and pieces, fragmentary obsessions, bobbing into view, then sinking, for now, out of sight. Book ideas usually have come at me with all the appearance of pure accident or chance, though by the time I am done I can generally see how what has taken shape was spawned by the interplay between my previous fiction, recent undigested personal history, the circumstances of my immediate, everyday life, and the books I've been reading and teaching. The shifting relationship of these elements of experience brings the subject into focus, and then, by brooding, I find out how to take hold of it. I use "brooding" only to describe what this activity apparently looks like; inside I am actually feeling very Sufisticated indeed.

# Talk with Philip Roth

## Sara Davidson/1977

From *The New York Times Book Review,* 18 September 1977,
1, 51. © 1977 by The New York Times Company. Reprinted
by permission.

*Philip Roth lives in southern New England. When I called to request
an interview, he suggested that he drive into New York and we talk
for several hours, after agreeing on ground rules. I asked if I could
come to his home. "I'm not going to go through your trash cans."*

*He said he preferred New York. "I'll bring you a trash can."*

*We met at my place, in the heat of August. Roth was wearing a red-
and-white checkered shirt with short sleeves, loose khaki trousers,
loafers and metal frame glasses. His manner was serious, courteous,
careful.*

**Q.** The characters in *The Professor of Desire* are the same characters
you wrote about in *The Breast,* only the action takes place several
years before. It's fairly common to write a sequel, but not so common to write an antecedent. How did this happen?

**A.** *The Breast* came out in 1972. About two years later I did have
an idea for a sequel, though *The Professor of Desire* isn't it. I wrote
some 80 pages, maybe more, but I couldn't bear working on it. The
character was still a man who'd turned into a breast, and I was being
driven a little crazy by spending five hours a day thinking about his
imprisonment. I had read somewhere that Igor Kipnis gets his harpsichord to concerts around the country in the back of a van fitted out
with giant seat belts and foam rubber cushioning, and so that's how I
had the breast get to his house in the country on weekends. I was
writing about his eminence really, and the wonderful opportunities
that come his way after he gets out of the hospital: scientific studies of
his transformed carcass, the Johnny Carson Show, etc. When I saw
that I could invent social humiliations for him until the cows came
home, I gave it up. Writing about the brutal claustrophobic predicament wearied me and troubled me terribly, and the events them-

selves were piling up to no interesting purpose I could see. The question I then put to myself was, "Who is this fellow, anyway?"—or rather, who was he before he became a breast? And who is the young woman who is willing to live with a breast and love a breast and drive him around like a harpsichord? And what about the mountainside resort hotel where he is supposed to have been raised? And the two Swedish girls with whom he is said to have lived in London, did he really have that adventure—if so, what would it have been like? And what about the Helen he is said to have married and divorced? Who is she?

The details that had formed the simple realistic underpinnings of a very surreal story seemed to me now to be begging to be brought to life, only this time on their own terms. At first all this was still part of an attempt to flesh things out so that I could in time come back more knowingly to the sequel. But soon that concern dropped away. The result is a book that doesn't really bear a necessary relationship to *The Breast*. Each can live in the world without the other—and so, in that sense, *The Professor of Desire* is neither a sequel *nor* an antecedent. There are a number of motifs from the earlier book that I picked up and transformed in the later one, but doing that was a form of play, really, and I never expected it to be anybody else's business, or pleasure, but my own.

At the very conclusion of *The Professor of Desire*, Kepesh, the hero, awakens from bad dreams of loss and affliction, and, as he reports, "sucks in a desperate frenzy" at his mistress's breast. It was probably in part because of the book's origins that this struck me as the right ending. It may have been the expression of my gratitude for what, at the outset, had nourished me.

**Q.** When I went back and read *The Breast* after *The Professor of Desire*, *The Breast* seemed like a prophecy of what's going to happen to Kepesh, what his punishment will be.

**A.** Well, maybe it's his fate imagined in an uglier, more nightmarish way, his dream of erotic enchantment come true with a vengeance. I'm not sure that I want to draw any direct connections. I'd prefer to say that at most the two books bear a potential relationship to each other, and leave it at that. Call them companion pieces. *The Breast* wasn't just about entrapment in the flesh and the horrors of desire, it was also inspired by some thinking I'd had to do about fame, notoriety and scandal. When the idea for the book first came to me, I had myself only recently become an object of curiosity, believed by some to be very much the sexual freak and grotesque.

**Q.** Could you talk about what that experience was like for you—fame and notoriety?

**A.** Now that the virulent stage is behind me, it's easier to talk about my life as a notorious personality. But when *Portnoy's Complaint* was published in 1969 it was hard for me to make sense out of it all right off. I wasn't really that experienced back then in being notorious. Beforehand I had been somewhat excited by the prospects for the book. There were requests for interviews with me, for articles about me, and I was rather enjoying it. Then, a few months before the book came out, I began to sense that something was wrong. I hadn't just written a book, it seemed, but had become somebody who stood for something. What I realized was that in the popular imagination, and in the media, Roth and Portnoy were about to be fused into the same person.

**Q.** You never expected people to make that assumption?

**A.** This may sound overly innocent, but I didn't. I certainly never expected it to become practically all that seemed to matter. For one thing, I never expected a readership quite so large, a readership that would encompass so many of those people who will, of course, make that assumption about any book told in the first person. True, in the book I had drawn heavily upon life in Newark, where I was raised, but I drew upon that, not so as to invite a simplistic identification of author and character, but because that world seemed to me to be so rich with fictional possibilities. I had thrown Newark away, really, in *Goodbye, Columbus*. I simply didn't appreciate what it was I had there, and in fact I had blurred the edges rather deliberately. But 10 years later, these real places I had known so well as a boy—the city, the high school, the neighborhood—struck me suddenly as a gift bestowed by the muse (who doesn't bestow that many gifts). You know, when you're at your typewriter, you don't worry whether people are going to think, "My God, that must be Roth himself—how beastly!" You've got other things to worry about, rather more to the point of what you're doing, which is trying to write convincing *fiction*.

**Q.** Could we talk about the relationship between your personal experience and your fiction? Many of the situations you write about are similar to experiences you've had. Like Tarnopol in *My Life as a Man* you were born in New Jersey, you received a prize in 1959, you've seen an analyst, you spent time in a writer's colony. Probably there are ever more telling similarities of experience than these. Do you ever feel that by writing about these things, you're putting them to rest?

**A.** No, not putting them to rest, but using them to get me going. What you take directly from life gives your imagination something to shoot for. You're challenging the imagination, saying to it, "All right, let's see *you* do as well." What's taken directly from life helps to place and fix a book's level of reality; it provides something against which to measure what you make up, so that in the end the invented experience and the real experience will have the same kind of life, be equally persuasive and affecting. Of course, for everything in my fiction that connects to something I've known personally, there are a hundred- things that have no connection, or connections of only the roughest and vaguest sort. But along the way you *are* sticking these hooks of direct experience into the work, hooks to hang on to as you move forward over everything that's as yet unknown to you.

That there are readers who themselves get stuck on these hooks, who want to hang on to them and nothing else, well, that's too bad for those readers. If someone cared only about whether this or that in *David Copperfield* had really happened to Dickens, he would miss much of the charm of that book.

**Q.** When I read an author, say D. H. Lawrence, I think about what his life must have been like and whether his concerns were similar to concerns of his characters.

**A.** Sure that's interesting. I'm also interested in reading biographies of writers whose fiction I like. That isn't what I'm talking about. I'm talking about a primary satisfaction that seems to reside in knowing whether the author is really like this, really did this, really said this, knowing if this character is *really* so-and-so, and so on. It's such a primitive response and has so little to do with the genuine pleasures I associate with reading novels. The writer does try to cast a spell, after all, and it's annoying—as it is, say, if you're telling a story to a child—to be constantly interrupted by a little voice asking, "But did that really happen, daddy?"

**Q.** I used to ask that question, actually.

**A.** (*A burst of laughter.*) Well, you were a journalist even as a child. It seems to me a question, when it is asked repeatedly by adults, and to the exclusion of practically every thing else that *might* be interesting, to have more to do with the magic realms of gossip than the magic realms of fiction.

**Q.** *The Professor of Desire* is written in the present tense. Did you have a reason for that?

**A.** No, not a "profound" reason. It just provided me with a sound that I liked in the beginning, something new for me in the tone. I don't know what it does to readers, if anything.

**Q.** It creates a sense of immediacy?

**A.** Does it? That's what people say about it. I don't really know whether it does. I think readers feel just as immediately the novels written in the past tense. Communicating a sense of immediacy comes primarily from the raw strength with which you take hold of your material, not from fiddling with the tenses. I wouldn't make too much of the present tense here, other than to say that it gave the prose a tone and melody that pleased me. It just sounded right.

**Q.** What about writing in the first person, are you most comfortable with that?

**A.** I seem to be doing it mostly. It's for me a way of gaining stylistic freedom. I'm able to use conversational tones and rhythms that give great expressive value and appeal for me. I can turn the volume up and down within a single sentence. I can slip in and out of the kind of colloquial talk and the kind of formal talk I'm partial to. And of course it's the "I" who can be most *intimate,* who speaks in confidence, who tells us secrets—sexual secrets, hate secrets, love secrets, family secrets, tribal secrets, the stuff of shame, embarrassment, humiliation and disgrace. If I said to you, as shame-ridden adults and small children sometimes do, "I have this friend, and a strange thing happened to him on 42nd Street last night, and now he says he needs to see a doctor," you might or might not pay attention to the plight of my dear friend. But if I say, "Look, Sara, we don't know each other too well, but something rather strange happened to me last night on 42nd Street, and I've got to tell somebody . . ." well, I think I'd be in business.

Of course using the first person in this way obviously accounts for the confusion in some of my readers as to just whose experience I'm talking about and where I would like their attention to be focused. I have been told that I ought really to be flattered to be taken for the speaker instead of the ventriloquist. But suppose you were Edgar Bergen and you went out into the street and somebody tried to drive a nail into your head because they thought you were Charlie McCarthy and your head was made of wood. You wouldn't like it.

**Q.** Do you see yourself writing over and over about the same character?

**A.** I see myself writing, in *The Breast* and *The Professor of Desire,* and earlier in *Portnoy's Complaint,* about what has been called "the great and maddening" subject of desire. It's a large enough pie, I think, for me to have cut three slices out of.

**Q.** *When She Was Good* seemed about a totally different subject.

**A.** *When She Was Good* is about a young woman's brutal disappointment in the weaknesses and failings of her father and her husband, and the rage in her to make them better men. It's about extreme moral ambitiousness and its pitfalls—so, in its own way, is *Letting Go* though in that novel it's the two male heroes who sadly discover the limitations of their power and their virtue. Tarnopol in *My Life as a Man* gets an education on that subject as well. *When They Were Good* might stand loosely as the title for those three books taken together. *And When They Were Bad,* I suppose, for the books cut from the desire pie.

**Q.** How do you feel when people tell you they like your work, it's meant a great deal to them? How do you feel about criticism, and charges made in the press, such as that you're a misogynist?

**A.** A misogynist? The rabbis used to tell me I was an anti-Semite, and an old-line American patriot from Manhattan's West Side has suggested in print that I am really anti-American, and recently a letter about *The Professor of Desire* from a homosexual accused me of "fag-baiting" and of writing "heterosexual trash." I guess you can't fool all the people all of the time. Someone cagey out there is always going to see through to what kind of son of a bitch you really are.

I've largely lost touch with what's said about my work in print. I haven't read the reviews of my books since 1972, and I usually make it my business to be out of the country when a book appears. I find the best place to be when a book comes out—at least for a Western writer—is behind the Iron Curtain. I've celebrated the publication of several recent books of mine in Prague, dining out with my writer friends there, upon whom the ironies of the situation are not wasted, by the way. I spent some 10 or 12 years paying attention to criticism and charges made in the press, and that seems to me to be enough. I think I've gotten the idea by now.

**Q.** Do you feel you need an objective outsider's opinion on a work in progress?

**A.** When I've finished what looks to me like the last draft of a novel, I give a copy of the manuscript to five or six people to read, my friend and editor Aaron Asher, and other friends whose literary judgment and taste I respect. Obviously I don't want to finish a book and then drop it into the void without hearing what *anyone* makes of it. These people read it, and then I go with a pencil and a pad and listen for two or three hours to what each of them has to say. Because the book is still in manuscript form they tend to be more candid and direct than they might be if I confronted them with a bound volume which I could no longer rework. What they give me is not only their criticism, but along the way they *describe* the book to me, and that is really the best of it—hearing words *unlike* those with which you have been describing the book to yourself as you went along, finding out how it registers upon an intelligence that's not your own.

Now these sessions may not help to make the book any better, but they certainly answer the deep need—that otherwise generally goes begging—for a patient, serious and reasoned response. And that does more for me than what comes with publication. For me it takes the place of publication. After I've made the changes that seem warranted from what I heard altogether in these sessions, I hand the book over to the publisher and begin to wash my hands of it.

**Q.** Are you ever not working?

**A.** No, mostly I work. Probably about 340 days out of the year. I don't enjoy traveling more than three weeks or so a year, and that's the only sustained activity other than writing than can keep me from getting fidgety. And even then I get fidgety.

**Q.** Don't you feel tired when you've finished a book?

**A.** No, I feel elated. The problem is starting, not finishing. When you begin something new it's so crude and unformed and unfocused, and that experience is in such sharp contrast to the last six months of finishing a book, when everything you touch turns out right. Oh, it's lovely when everything is coming together like that, and everything you read and everything you do or hear or say seems somehow to feed directly into the next day's work. But to go from that to the crude beginnings of something else, where everything you do is wrong—well, it's not pleasant. My own way seems to be to write six months of trash—heterosexual trash usually—and then to give up in despair, filing away a hundred pages or so that I can't stand, to find 10 pages or so that are actually alive, and then to try to figure out what it is that's going on there that *makes* for the life—and then to run with that. Often in the first few months after finishing one book, I find that whatever I begin is really only my old departed pal returned in a sheet from the grave. It's awfully hard to cut loose from a way of perceiving things and a way of presenting things that has taken so much work to establish in the first place. But I find that if I just keep going, some six or eight months later, I will somehow have laid the ghost to rest and be ready to write something new.

**Q.** Why do you like to teach?

**A.** It gets me out of the house (and out of writing) one day a week. Also a college classroom is the best place I've found yet to talk in any sustained way about the books I read. If I don't study a book and think about it in order to talk about it in class, then by and large the book is lost to me; teaching a book is the way I have of taking hold of it and getting the most out of it. Then, too, I like the students. Whatever they may lack in the way of experience, is more than compensated for by all the ways in which they are still uncorrupted. They read fiction as though it mattered.

**Q.** You seem to take yourself and your work very seriously.

**A.** So I do.

**Q.** What do you find pleasurable, besides writing?

**A.** Living in a place that I find beautiful; living with somebody I love; having close friends; keeping friendships; knowing my parents are all right; listening to music; reading. They are simple things, but the sort of things I think most of us cherish.

Okay, I've got to go now—back to the beautiful place. Thank you. It was painless.

# A Visit with Philip Roth

## James Atlas/1979

From *The New York Times Book Review,* 2 September 1979, 1, 12–13. © 1979 by The New York Times Company. Reprinted by permission.

Far from the Newark of Nathan Zuckerman, Alexander Portnoy and Neil Klugman, their creator dwells in the rural splendor of a secluded Connecticut estate, the sort one reads about in a Cheever story. Its resident, however, would be more likely to show up in one of his own novels. Tall, energetic, alert, he wears the standard uniform of summer camps on the New Jersey shore—shorts, a T-shirt and sandals—and rejects any suggestion of a resemblance between Saul Bellow and the novelist Felix Abravanel, a minor character in *The Ghost Writer,* by noting that the physical description applies to himself: "The rug dealer's thinning dark hair, the guarded appraising black eyes, and a tropical bird's curving bill."

Philip Roth's informality is in curious contrast to the impeccably kept grounds, the austere 18th-century gray house, the freshly mown meadows that surround his property. "The living room he took me into was neat, cozy, and plain," Roth writes in his new novel of young Zuckerman's visit to the country home of E. I. Lonoff: "A large circular hooked rug, some slip-covered easy chairs, a worn sofa, a long wall of books, a piano, a phonograph, an oak library table systematically stacked with journals and magazines." To produce this description, he had only to look around him. The aura of literary vocation is everywhere: in the lithographs by the Polish writer Bruno Schulz; the framed jackets of Roth's own books, blown up to poster size; the file cabinets and typewriters in every room. One opens the guest closet to find row upon row of foreign editions: *Lamento di Portnoy, Portnoy et Son Complexe.*

"Purity. Serenity. Simplicity. Seclusion." Thus Zuckerman characterizes Lonoff's life. In Roth's, there is another dimension: Discordant, manic, ebullient, he has the verve of a Borscht-circuit comedian and a genius for mimicry; his imitation of the late Philip Rahv's tirades against "swingers," intoned in a guttural Slavic voice, is incomparable, and he is just as good on the Elizabethan doggerel spoken by Shakespeare's fools. Raucous banter dominates his conversation. Splashing about in the Franklin Library Memorial Swimming Pool—named for a publishing house that paid him a substantial sum to sign his name several thousand times to a limited edition of *Goodbye, Columbus*—he invokes the name of a critic who has been hard on his work, and crows: "Does Irving Howe have this?" Serving an elegant luncheon of cold veal, he blurts: "What'd Updike give you, a Big Mac?"

When conversation turns to his own work, though, Roth becomes earnest. Like Gabe Wallach in *Letting Go* or Peter Tarnopol in *My Life as a Man,* he approaches literature with the zealous humility of a graduate student, eager to discourse on "moral speculations" and "matters of conscience"; he has no patience for speculation about the resemblance between his characters and living people. "New York City, where you happen to live and work," he admonishes, "is interested in the scandalous side of literature—which is the most reductive and least interesting."

Still, it is worth noting that Lonoff and Bernard Malamud are nearly the same age, live in rural New England and teach at local liberal arts colleges—and in both *The Ghost Writer* and *Dubin's Lives,* Malamud's most recent novel, a 56-year-old writer yearns to escape the constriction of a durable but unrewarding marriage. Both dream of going off to Italy with a younger mistress—a wish only Dubin realizes. Roth's account of Lonoff's work, moreover, could serve as a shrewd appraisal of Malamud's: "To me," he writes, "it was as though the hallucinatory strains in Gogol had been filtered through the humane skepticism of Chekhov to nourish the country's first Russian writer."

For Roth, Lonoff and Malamud represent the type of novelist who is "deeply skeptical of the public world"—a category to which he himself has belonged since he fled New York a decade ago, after *Portnoy's Complaint* made him a celebrity and a millionaire. "I was astonished to discover that fame and fortune—the things everyone thinks they want—should have their imprisoning side. Now I lead a nearly perfect Lonoff life. I write all day, take a walk at the end of the afternoon and usually read at night."

Since 1976 he has lived with the British actress Claire Bloom,
spending a part of each year in London. They have few visitors in
Connecticut, and last month, when Miss Bloom was away for three
weeks in Oxford, playing Lady Marchmain in the BBC production of
Evelyn Waugh's *Brideshead Revisited,* Roth saw virtually no one
apart from occasional weekend guests. "By and large, I don't get
anything from being in the literary world and I don't get anything
from living in New York City. There you pay for there, and here you
pay for here. But the price for Lonoff is isolation, loneliness, solitude—all the writer's occupational hazards pushed further along. He
maintains a sense of artistic purity—but at tremendous expense."
What is the alternative? The flamboyant public life of Abravanel, with
his "beautiful wives, beautiful mistresses, alimony the size of the
national debt . . . five-hundred-page novels every third year, and still
time and energy left over for all that self-absorption." Zuckerman is
in search of "a way to live as a writer," Roth says, "and he sees
Lonoff's way and Abravanel's way—and the consequences of each."
     This notion of "consequences" is crucial to Roth's interpretation
of *The Ghost Writer*—a novel, he has written elsewhere, that illus-
trates "the unreckoned consequences of art." The questionnaire
Judge Wapter submits to Zuckerman, inviting him to defend a short
story about a crude, unscrupulous Jewish family in Newark, "is
obviously drawn from my own experience," he says. Roth was only
23 when he published one of his first short stories in *The New Yorker,*
awaited praise and found himself widely attacked by Jews for encouraging anti-Semitism. The story, "Defender of the Faith," which
concerns a Jewish Army officer who responds to the cringing behavior of a Jew under his command by sending him off to war, seems
innocuous compared to Roth's later work. But it was from that
experience, he recalls, that he learned about the deadly serious
nature of art: "No matter what they say in the classrooms, people
read novels and make of them what they make of them."
     In *The Ghost Writer,* Zuckerman suffers the same ordeal. "To
associate yourself with literature," Roth observes, "is, in Nathan's
mind, to associate yourself with a kind of morally unchallengeable
position." But when his parents implore him to answer the judge's
philistine queries, he finds himself confused by the disparity between

Lonoff's approval and his own people's incomprehension. "They're his past, a source of strength—and his material."

To achieve a sort of parity, Roth conjured up his own Jewish myth in the form of Amy Bellette, the young woman who is Lonoff's assistant and who in Zuckerman's imagination becomes Anne Frank. "Anne Frank is a Jewish saint," Roth says, "a Jewish ghost. I had wanted to write about her for years, incorporate her into my imaginative life." His opportunity came when he saw that Anne Frank could be appropriated for Zuckerman's literary and moral uses to redress Judge Wapter's misappropriation of his story. That Anne Frank is a fantastic idea rather than a literal character has escaped a number of critics; but for Roth that subtle transmutation is one of the "narrative pleasures."

Besides, being misunderstood, Roth says, is among the "unreckoned consequences of art." "My obsession for the last seven or eight years has been the uses to which literature is put in this country. The writer in his isolation publishes a book, the book goes out into the world, and the strangest things begin to happen. Some of them are wounding. Some of them are interesting. Some of them are bizarre. Some of them are remarkable and deeply satisfying. You can never predict its fate. What I write has a particular purpose and use for me, but I've learned that what it means to me isn't what it means to others. When you publish a book, it's the world's book. The world edits it." This phenomenon is the subject of the novel Roth is working on now: a farcical account of the effects of sudden fame on a novelist who will be familiar to readers of *Portnoy's Complaint*.

Over the last decade, he has encountered a very different problem: the suspicion that he is *not* being read. "When I got that strong response"—to both *Goodbye, Columbus* and *Portnoy's Complaint*— "I knew that I was being read, or at least misread. But then, that's part of being read. I don't know about my readers now. I'm not sure who they are."

What troubles Roth is less the diminished audience for his work since *Portnoy* than the objections of certain critics that he has failed to develop as a novelist. "I see my last three books this way: *My Life as a Man* is about the surprises that manhood brings; *The Professor of Desire* is about the surprises that desire brings; and *The Ghost Writer* is about the surprises that the vocation of writing brings." He claims not to read his reviews, but one critic in particular—Irving Howe—appears to have had the same adverse effect on Roth that Judge Wapter had on Nathan Zuckerman. Brandishing a folder with two of Howe's articles, he hands me a 1959 review that acclaims his "unique voice" and a dour estimate of his subsequent career that appeared in *Commentary* six years ago. "Not that he's the only reader in the world," the novelist says wistfully. "But he was a real reader."

I was reminded of an observation Roth had made about Zuckerman: "The irony of his predicament is that he knows—through his intelligence, his education, his feelings and his moral intuition—that his father and the judge are wrong to condemn his work, but their moral judgment is inescapable; and dealing with it has become a part of his vocation."

# Philip Roth: Should Sane Women Shy Away from Him at Parties?
## Ronald Hayman/1981

From *The London Sunday Times Magazine,* 22 March 1981, 38–42. © 1981 by *The London Times.* Reprinted by permission.

*Portnoy's Complaint* was the first novel to make masturbation into comedy. There it was, the little act that no-one admitted, dragged into the centre of the stage. And masturbation on a heroic scale. Alexander Portnoy dedicated himself to his pursuit with inexhaustible energy and considerable resourcefulness in improvising variations. No English novelist could have produced such a book—partly because of inhibition but also because of language. The American vernacular affords a rich vocabulary to deal with Portnoy's obsession.

When the book was published, in 1969, some critics were exuberantly enthusiastic, others fiercely hostile. Hardback sales came to about 800,000, paperback to nearly three million. The furore of publicity did not obscure the fact that Philip Roth had written a novel which was extremely funny, liberating and important. It annexed for fiction a territory that had not previously been available. But it was easy for readers to be distracted from the seriousness of what was being said about the difficulties of launching into adult life: "Mother, I'm 33. . . . Good Christ, a Jewish man with parents alive is a 15-year-old boy, and will remain a 15-year-old boy till they die. . . ."

Philip Roth was then 36, and his parents were still alive. He had warned them, before the book was published, that life was liable to become rather unpleasant for them: not all of the American Jewish community was likely to be grateful.

*Goodbye, Columbus,* which Philip Roth had completed by the age of 25, contains a novella and five stories, wittily looking askance at American Jewish lifestyles. The novella—from which the 1969 film *Goodbye, Columbus* was made—shows Roth's precocious satirical accuracy in picking out give-away detail and in reproducing dialogue.

How is it that Roth—far from remaining a 15-year-old boy—had come of age as a writer so young? There was an extraordinary assurance in his style, which could not have been achieved without personal self-confidence. He grew up in Newark, New Jersey, which he describes as having then been "a medium-sized industrial and port city, populated largely by Irish, Italians, Germans, Jews and blacks." This meant that there was no need for a Jewish boy to feel inferior to other boys—other young members of competing minorities. His grandparents had come from Eastern Europe, and he had heard about pogroms and persecution, but his own experience had been much more secure. "I lived in a heavily Jewish neighbourhood and went to public schools where the student body was 95 per cent Jewish."

In fact the racially heterogeneous America Roth grew up in was quite different from the much WASPier America he saw in movies and read about in the books of such authors as Sinclair Lewis, Sherwood Anderson and Mark Twain. He graduated from high school when he was 16, and by then he was tremendously curious about that other America—"it was very nearly as mythical to me as it had been to Franz Kafka. I was, at 16, strongly under the sway of Thomas Wolfe and his lyrical sense of ordinary American life, also of the populist rhetoric that had risen out of the Depression of the 1930s and been transformed by the patriotic fervour of World War Two into the popular national myth about the 'vastness' of the land and the 'rich diversity of the people.' "

It had become so important to Roth to find this other America that it determined his choice of university. So in preference to Harvard, he opted to read English Literature at Bucknell University, which is situated in a beautiful farming valley in central Pennsylvania. "I went to chapel once a week with the Christian boys and girls who were my classmates. They were youngsters from conventional backgrounds with predominantly philistine interests. But my attempt to throw myself wholeheartedly into the traditional college life of that era only lasted about six months. Chapel I could never stomach: I made a habit of reading Schopenhauer conspicuously in my pew during the sermon. The others seemed to be enjoying everyting enormously. I felt like a Houyhnhnm who had strayed on to the campus from *Gulliver's Travels*." If Roth had the impression of belonging to a different species from the other undergraduates, this must have been a crucial phase in the development of his satirical vision.

Afterwards he wanted to do post-graduate work on English Literature. For this he went to Chicago: "A big roaring city, a lively university full of renegade types, a lake that looked as big and rough as an ocean—and what was more, a city that meant something to American literature. Anderson, Dreiser, Hemingway, Fitzgerald, Sandburg, Willa Cather, Sinclair Lewis, Frank Norris—they were all mid-Westerners."

Enlisted into the army, Roth did a stint of working in the Public Information Office at the Walter Reed Army Hospital in Washington, D.C., writing press releases. When he was demobilised he went back to Chicago as a lecturer, teaching English composition. "It was awful reducing all those co-eds to tears because of their comma faults, but it was a living." He had begun writing stories, but without expecting much income from them. He was earning $3200 a year from teaching, but received a total of only $100 for the novella *Goodbye, Columbus* and two short stories when they were published in the *Paris Review*. He did make an attempt to give up teaching in the summer of 1958, when his publisher paid him an advance of $1200 for the collection of stories. He settled in Manhattan.

"I hated it—it wasn't the centre of writing, it was the centre of publishing." He married in 1959, the same year that *Goodbye, Columbus* was published, and the marriage lasted until 1962.

It was a Guggenheim award that enabled him to leave New York. Each year the Guggenheim Foundation awards several hundred fellowships to artists and academics. Roth applied, and on the strength of his early stories he was given $4000. This financed a year in Rome for him and his wife and he was there when the news came through that *Goodbye, Columbus* had won the National Book Award, which was then the major literary award in the U.S. Previously the book had sold 8000 copies but hadn't gone into paperback; now, of course, it did, and it made his name.

Returning from Rome, he taught for two years at the University of Iowa in the Writers' Workshop—a graduate programme in creative writing and literary studies.

His next two novels were *Letting Go* (1962) and *When She Was*

*Good* (1967). But neither of these won any prizes, and when, at the age of 33, Roth started on *Portnoy's Complaint*, he not only didn't know he was writing a best-seller, he didn't know whether he'd find a publisher for it. In fact he didn't at first know that he was writing a novel. He began with a story called 'A Jewish Patient Begins His Analysis', which *Esquire* published in 1967.

"There was nothing obscene about it—probably nothing even very novel about the relationship of mother and son. What was new for me wasn't the story, but the form I'd found to tell it in—the psychoanalytic monologue."

The main advantage of pushing the narrator down on a couch is that this frees him from all social proprieties. The more uninhibited he can be about revealing shameful secrets, the more he will please the doctor. For Philip Roth it was not so much a matter of overcoming inhibitions as of finding a new technique: "I felt freed from the constraints of conventional narrative—it wasn't a matter of saying the unsayable or speaking the unspeakable, but of finding in the form the *justification* for saying the unsayable."

After "A Jewish Patient" Roth wrote a sequel, a kind of aria on the subject of adolescent masturbation entitled "Whacking Off." "I couldn't publish it anywhere. It wound up about as far from best-sellerdom as you can get, in a high-brow quarterly, *The Partisan Review*. If I remember correctly they paid me $125."

But by now the novel was under way. "I'd come to understand the enormous freedom there was for me in the situation I'd established: the patient talking—and talking and talking and talking—and the doctor silently listening. The freedom to be raucous, abrasive, aggressive, obscene, satiric, fantastical, beastly—but all of it with a point. A psychoanalytic hour was in session."

The result was *Portnoy's Complaint*. It was written at the right moment. "Ten years earlier I'd have been slapped down, I'm quite sure, by the same moralisers who later embraced the ethic of candour and self-expression and soon began moralising about that; but at the time I was writing, the sixties were becoming the Sixties. In '66, '67, '68, the decade was at its most volatile, and inspiring just about everyone to try a hand at performing in new roles. I was another of those performers. *Portnoy's Complaint* ssemed to me at the time very much a performance, a comedy act, an impersonation."

Unfortunately for Roth, the impersonation was taken by the public for a confession. "That accounted for a good deal of the excitement surrounding the book's publication. If you remember, in 1969 much was being made of 'letting it all hang out.' I was thought to be letting more hang out than most, and was rewarded by being raised to the American equivalent of knighthood: In 1969 I was made a Celebrity of the Realm. But despite the book's enormous success and the pleasure that gave me, I was somewhat disheartened by what often seemed to be the source of that appeal: namely, that it was Roth 'spilling his guts out.' "

The success of *Portnoy's Complaint* affected Roth's development as a novelist in two ways. One is that, having discovered his talent for comic exaggeration, he wanted to find out how far it could be pushed in other directions, and in the next four years he published three comic novels, each as different from the others as from *Portnoy: Our Gang* (1971), a political satire on Nixon's regime, *The Great American Novel* (1973), a mock saga about big-league baseball, and *The Breast* (1972), a nightmarish comic novella in which Roth's *alter ego,* David Kepesh, describes the process of being transformed into a mammary gland six feet in length, rounded at one end like a watermelon and terminating at the other in a five-inch nipple.

Roth says that the fantasy of *The Breast* came to him in part because of his fame since *Portnoy.* "I felt myself locked, suddenly, into this image of me as a sexual beast. I ran into that response frequently on the streets of Manhattan. People stepped right up to tell me what they thought of a monster like myself. I distinctly noticed women shying away from me at parties—the sane women shying away, those less sane edging close. Men I'd known as decent, hard-working fathers confessed all kinds of horrendous things to me over lunch."

The aftermath of *Portnoy* was unnerving, and it led to a new and disheartening awareness of literature as something that could be used in ways that have nothing to do with the writer's intentions. Watching television chat-shows, Roth was liable to hear jokes about his sexual propinquities; he also found that he was being used in newspaper advertisements to sell beer: a patient on a couch was talking to his psychiatrist, à la Portnoy, but about a certain brand of beer. Roth must have found having to sit back and let this happen extremely unpleasant, but to a good novelist unpleasant experiences are generally more useful than pleasant ones, and Roth also found himself wanting to make the uses of literature into a theme. This is a way of regaining control over something that has got out of control.

Four or five months after the publication of *Portnoy's Complaint,* Philip Roth moved out of New York to settle in the New England countryside, two hours' drive to the north. This is where his home still is. He likes visiting England, but he has not explored the countryside. "I only know London. That's where my friends are. I've recently completed a revision of the David Magarshack translation of *The Cherry Orchard* for the opening of Patrick Garland's Chichester Festival Theatre season. [It will star Claire Bloom, with whom he has lived for some years.] I'll be down there to sit in on the rehearsals. So I'll see something of Sussex, I suppose." Habitually he works hard. "I write from about 10 till six every day, with an hour out for lunch and the newspaper. In the evenings I usually read. That's pretty much it."

Philip Roth's novels have mostly been underrated in England, but perhaps the new anthology, which he has selected and arranged himself, will lead to a revaluation of his work. *A Philip Roth Reader* contains many of the best episodes from his best novels. *My Life as a Man* is well represented with a chapter about a writer's diastrous marriage and a sequence about the much more peaceful affair that follows. Also included are two pieces devoted to Kafka, a writer who has exerted a deep influence on Roth, an excerpt from *Portnoy's Complaint, The Breast* (in a revised version), and extracts from three other novels.

In the introduction to the new anthology Martin Green makes out a case for regarding Roth as "the most gifted novelist now writing, at least if one puts a stress on tradition." Indeed, it will be hard for anyone to read the *Reader* without being impressed by Philip Roth's versatility and his unfailing readability. He is one of the best living storytellers, and his sharpness of observation joins forces with his ability to screw up the pitch of tension in the confrontations between his characters. Becoming passionate, if not hysterical, in their self-justification, they strip themselves, and each other, emotionally naked.

But underneath the drama there is always a moral undercurrent: What exactly is wrong with their lives? What changes should they be trying to make? Roth never fails to be entertaining, but he is never just an entertainer.

# The Ghosts of Roth
## Alan Finkielkraut/1981

From *Esquire*, September 1981, 92–97. © 1981 by Alan
Finkielkraut. Reprinted by permission.

*Before* Portnoy's Complaint, *you had become a well-known writer.*
*Portnoy made you famous all over the world, and in America you*
*became a star. I even read that, while living in seclusion in the*
*countryside, you were reported in the press to be going around*
*Manhattan with Barbra Streisand. What does it mean to be a celeb-*
*rity in a media-dominated country like the United States?*

For one thing, it's likely to mean that your income is going to go
up, at least for a while. You may have become a celebrity just
because your income has gone up. What distinguishes the merely
famous from a celebrity or a star has usually to do with money, sex,
or, as in my case, with both. I was said to have made a million
dollars, and I was said to be none other than Portnoy himself. To
become a celebrity is to become a brand name. There is Ivory soap,
Rice Krispies, and Philip Roth. Ivory is the soap that floats; Rice
Krispies the breakfast cereal that goes snap-crackle-pop; Philip Roth
the Jew who masturbates with a piece of liver. And makes a million
out of it. It isn't much more interesting, useful, or entertaining than
that, not after the first half hour. The elevation to celebrity that's
thought to bring a writer a wider readership is just another obstacle
that most readers have to overcome to achieve a direct perception of
his work.

*In the late sixties, sex was being touted as the thing: the heart of*
*life, the redeemer, et cetera. Portnoy's Complaint, with its obscene*
*language and erotomaniacal candor, appeared to many to be in*
*sympathy with that viewpoint. But then, in subsequent works, you*
*have seemed to withdraw from this "advanced" position. Instead of*
*Sade or Bataille you refer in essays and interviews to such sexually*
*restrained authors as James, Chekhov, Gogol, Babel, Kafka. Do you*

120

*mean to disappoint sex worshipers or to regain credibility in respectable society?*

I haven't withdrawn from any position because I never held any position. I would never have written a book as farcical as *Portnoy's Complaint* if I had any devotion to the cause of sex; causes don't thrive on self-satire. Causes expel you for self-satire. Nor was I a soldier in the cause of obscenity. Portnoy's obscenity is intrinsic to his situation, not to my style. I have no case to make for dirty words, in or out of fiction—only for the right of access to them when they seem to the point.

Three years after *Portnoy's Complaint,* I published a novella about a man who turns into a female breast. I imagined scenes more lurid and less lighthearted than anything in *Portnoy's Complaint* but not necessarily to the satisfaction of "sex worshipers." *The Breast* has even been read as a critique of sexual salvationism.

*Several of your novels are written in the first person. And their heroes have a lot in common with you. Portnoy is brought up in Newark, much as you were; David Kepesh in* The Professor of Desire *is a professor and teaches the same literature courses that you have taught at the University of Pennsylvania. Your recent book* The Ghost Writer *begins some twenty years ago with a young writer's search for a spiritual father who will validate his art. This young writer, Nathan Zuckerman, has just published a group of stories that remind us necessarily of your first work,* Goodbye, Columbus. *Does all this mean that we should read your books as confession, as autobiography barely disguised?*

You should read my books as fiction, demanding the pleasures that fiction can yield. I have nothing to confess and no one I want to confess to. Nor has anyone asked me to make a confession or promised forgiveness if I do so. As for my autobiography, I can't begin to tell you how dull it would be. My autobiography would consist almost entirely of chapters about me sitting alone in a room looking at a typewriter. The uneventfulness of my autobiography would make Beckett's *The Unnamable* read like Dickens.

This is not to say that I haven't drawn heavily from my general experience to feed my imagination. But this isn't because I care to reveal myself, exhibit myself, or even express myself. It's so that I can invent myself. Invent my selves. Invent my worlds. To label books like mine "autobiographical" or "confessional" is not only to falsify their suppositional nature but, if I may say so, to slight whatever artfulness leads some readers to think that they must be autobiographical. You don't create the aura of intimacy by dropping your pants in public; do that and most people will instinctively look away.

These words *confessional* and *autobiographical* constitute yet another obstacle between the reader and the work—in this case, by strengthening the temptation, all too strong in a distracted audience anyway, to trivialize fiction by turning it into gossip.

Not that this is anything new. Rereading Virginia Woolf these last few months, I came across this passage of dialogue in *The Voyage Out,* her 1915 novel. The words are spoken by a character who wants to write books. "Nobody cares. All you read a novel for is to see what sort of person the writer is, and, if you know him, which of his friends he's put in. As for the novel itself, the whole conception, the way one's seen the thing, felt about it, made it stand in relation to other things, not one in a million cares for that."

"L'art, c'est une idée qu'on exagère," *said Gide. One exaggeration gave birth to Portnoy, and we know his destiny: this character has become an archetype. Another exaggeration produced Maureen, the majestically deranged woman, the Fury of jealousy and paranoia in* My Life as a Man. *But it is as if* Portnoy *had exhausted the curiosity of the reader in France.* My Life as a Man, *a book of yours that I much admire, is virtually unknown here. How was it received in America—for instance, by women's lib?*

I can only tell you that a few years after the appearance of *My Life as a Man,* a front-page article by a woman activist appeared in the influential Manhattan weekly *The Village Voice,* bearing this two-fisted headline: WHY DO THESE MEN HATE WOMEN? Beneath were photographs of Saul Bellow, Norman Mailer, Henry Miller, and me. *My Life as a Man* was the most damaging evidence brought against me by the prosecution.

Why? Because in 1974 the world had just recently discovered that women were good and only good, persecuted and only persecuted, exploited and only exploited, and I had depicted a woman who was not good, who persecuted others and who exploited others—

and that spoiled everything. A woman without conscience, a woman who misused every power, a vindictive woman with limitless cunning and wild, unfocused hatred and rage—and to depict such a woman was contrary to the new ethics and to the revolution that espoused them. It was antirevolutionary. It was on the wrong side of the cause. It was taboo.

*Of course,* My Life as a Man *is more than a challenge to feminist piety. In one scene Maureen buys a sample of urine from a pregnant black woman in order to pass the rabbit test and trick Peter Tarnopol into marriage. In another scene—their last brutal fight—when beaten by him, Maureen defecates in her pants, thus depriving them both of tragedy at the most painful moment of their marriage. Surely this novel is intended as a challenge to the pieties of American culture in general, to the moralizing and corny sentimentality so pervasive there. Do you agree with this interpretation?*

That it was intended, conceived, realized, as a challenge? No. I am more ambitious than that. You may be further describing the way it was received, however. The book was reviewed harshly, sold poorly, and went out of print in a mass paperback edition shortly after it was published, the first book of mine ever to disappear like that. It isn't for me to speculate in public on why that should have happened. I leave that to Tocquevilles like you. If it's any comfort to you as a Frenchman, the book is almost as unknown in my country as in yours.

*You seem deeply concerned with the obstacles that our society places between a work of art and its readers. We have talked about fame and the media's distortion of the writer's purpose. We have talked about gossip, the middlebrow distortion that reduces reading to voyeurism. We have talked about piety, the activist distortion that would exploit literature as propaganda. But there is yet another obstacle, is there not? The structuralist cliché, which is criticized in his introductory lecture by David Kepesh, your professor of desire: "You will discover (and not all will approve) that I do not hold with certain of my colleagues who tell us that literature, in its most valuable and intriguing moments, is fundamentally non-referential. I may come before you in my jacket and tie, I may address you as madam and sir, but I am going to request nonetheless that you restrain yourself*

*from talking about 'structure,' 'form,' and 'symbols' in my presence."
What makes the principles of the literary avant-garde so pernicious?*

I don't think of the words *structure, form,* and *symbol* as the
property of the avant-garde. In America they are usually the stock-in-
trade of the most naive high school literature teachers. When I teach,
I am not so gentle as my professor of desire, Mr. Kepesh: I *forbid*
my students to use those words, on pain of expulsion. This results in
a charming improvement in their English and even, sometimes, in
their thinking.

As for structuralism: It really hasn't played any part in my life. I'm
afraid I can't satisfy you with a vituperative denunciation.

*I was not expecting a vituperative denunciation. I was just inter-
ested in what your idea of reading is.*

I read fiction to be freed from my own suffocatingly narrow perspective on life and to be lured into imaginative sympathy with a fully
developed narrative point of view not my own. It's the same reason
that I write.

*How would you assess the sixties now? Was it a decade of libera-
tion that gave permission to write as one felt and to live the life
one wanted, or an era of arrogance, of narrow new dogmas to which
you had better pay tribute if you didn't want to get into trouble?*

I have no judgment to make of something so colossal as ten years
of world history. As an American citizen I was appalled and mortified
by the war in Vietnam, frightened by the urban violence, sickened by
the assassinations, confused by the student uprisings, sympathetic to
the libertarian pressure groups, delighted by the pervasive theatrical-
ity, disheartened by the rhetoric of the causes, excited by the sexual
display, and enlivened by the general air of confrontation and
change. During the last years of the decade, I was writing *Portnoy's
Complaint,* a raucous, aggressive, abrasive book whose conception
and composition were undoubtedly influenced by the mood of the
times. I don't think I would or could have written that book in that
way a decade earlier, not only because of the social, moral, and
cultural patterns that prevailed in the fifties but because, as a young
writer still strongly involved with literary studies, I had pledged my
loyalty to a more morally earnest line of fiction.

But by the mid-sixties I had already written two indisputably earnest books—*Letting Go* and *When She Was Good*—and was dying to turn my attention to something else, something that would call into play a more playful side of my talent. I now had the confidence to reveal that side in my fiction, in part because I was into my thirties and no longer had to work quite so hard as I did in my twenties at establishing my maturity credentials, and in part because of the infectious volatility of a moment that was inspiring feats of self-transformation and self-experimentation in virtually everyone.

*You are known to us here in France as an American-Jewish writer—even as a member (along with Bellow and Malamud) of a so-called New York-Jewish school. Do you accept this label?*

It's a journalistic cliché almost wholly devoid of content and inaccurate in the bargain. To begin with, only Malamud, of the three of us, comes from New York and spent his childhood there, in a poor neighborhood in Brooklyn. Virtually all of Malamud's adult life has been spent far away from New York, teaching at colleges in Oregon and Vermont. Bellow was born in Montreal and has lived almost all of his life in Chicago, eight hundred miles west of New York, a city as different from New York as Marseilles is from Paris or Manchester is from London. The book that brought him his first popular recognition, *Adventures of Augie March,* doesn't begin "I am a Jew, New York-born" but "I am an American, Chicago-born."

I was born in Newark, New Jersey, in my childhood an industrial port city of 150,000, mostly white and working class and, during the thirties and forties, still very much the provinces. The Hudson River, separating New York from New Jersey, could as easily have been the channel separating England from France—the anthropological divide was nearly that great, at least for people in our social position. I lived in a lower-middle-class Jewish neighborhood in Newark until I was seventeen and went off to a small college in rural Pennsylvania that had been founded by Baptists in the mid-nineteenth century and still required of its students weekly attendance at chapel services. You couldn't have gotten further from the spirit of New York or of my Newark neighborhood. I wanted to find out what the rest of "America" was like. America in quotes—because it was still almost as much of an idea in my mind as it had been in Franz Kafka's. I was, at sixteen and seventeen, strongly under the sway of Thomas Wolfe and his lyrical sense of ordinary American life. I was still under the sway of the populist rhetoric that had risen out of the Depression and had been transformed by the patriotic fervor of World War II into the popular national myth about the "vastness" of the "land," the "rich diversity" of the "people." I'd read Sinclair Lewis and Sherwood Anderson and Mark Twain, and none of them led me to think that I would find "America" in New York City or even at Harvard. I could get a good education at Harvard, but secretly that wasn't what I was looking for.

So I chose an ordinary college in a pretty little town in a beautiful farming valley in central Pennsylvania, where I went to chapel once a week with the Christian boys and girls who were my classmates, youngsters from conventional backgrounds with predominantly philistine interests. My attempt to throw myself wholeheartedly into the traditional college life of that era lasted about six months, though chapel I could never stomach and I made it a habit conspicuously to be reading Schopenhauer in my pew during the sermon. I quickly took on the role of a Houhynhnm who had strayed onto the campus from *Gulliver's Travels*.

I spent the year after college in graduate school at the University of Chicago, then went to Washington, D.C., where I served my stint in the Army. In 1956 I returned to Chicago to teach at the university for two years. I began to write the stories that were collected in my first book, *Goodbye, Columbus*. When the book was accepted for publication in the summer of 1958, I resigned my job at the university to move to Manhattan to live the life of a young writer instead of a young professor. I lived on the Lower East Side for about six months, quite unhappily: I didn't like the "literary" scene; I wasn't interested in the publishing world; I couldn't master the styles of sexual combat in vogue there in the late fifties; and as I wasn't employed in merchandising, manufacturing, or finance, I didn't see much reason to stay. In the years that followed I lived in Rome, London, Iowa City, and Princeton. When I returned to New York in 1963, it was to get away from a marriage fifty miles south in Princeton, where I was teaching at the University, and then, later, to be psychoanalyzed. When the analysis was over—and the sixties were over—I left for the countryside, where I've lived ever since.

*So New York is wrong. But the Jewish background is a major*

*source of inspiration in your work. And what strikes me, from* Goodbye, Columbus *to* The Ghost Writer, *is that as a novelist you are
drawn to the Jewish world for all the comic possibilities it offers you,
but not for the tragic ones, as might be expected. How do you
explain that?*

By my biography.

Like Bellow and Malamud, I was born to Jewish parents and raised
self-consciously as a Jew. I don't mean that I was raised according to
Jewish traditions or raised to be an observant Jew but that I was born
into the situation of being a Jew, and it did not take me long to be
aware of its ramifications.

I lived in a predominantly Jewish neighborhood and attended
public schools where about 90 percent of the pupils and the teachers
were Jewish. To live in an ethnic or cultural enclave like this wasn't
unusual for an urban American child of my generation. Newark is
now a predominantly black city in a nightmarish state of decay, but
until the late fifties it was demographically divided up like any number of American industrial cities that had been heavily settled in the
late nineteenth and early twentieth centuries by waves of immigration
from Germany, Ireland, Italy, Eastern Europe, and Russia. As soon as
they could climb out of the slums where most of them began in
America, more or less penniless, the immigrants formed neighborhoods within the cities where they could have the comfort and
security of the familiar while undergoing the arduous transformations
of a new way of life. These neighborhoods became rivalrous, competing, somewhat xenophobic subcultures within the city; each came
to have an Americanized style of its own, and rather than dissolving
when immigration virtually ceased, with the onset of World War I,
they were transformed by their own growing affluence and stability
into a permanent feature of American life.

My point is that my America in no way resembles the France or the
England I would have grown up in as a Jewish child. It was not a
matter of a few of us and all of them. What I saw was a few of
*everyone*. Rather than growing up intimidated by the monolithic
majority—or in defiance of it or in awe of it—I grew up feeling a part
of the majority composed of the competing minorities, no one of
which impressed me as being in a more enviable social or cultural
position than our own. By the time I was ready for college, it was no

wonder that I chose as I did: I had never really known at first hand any of these so-called Americans who were also said to be living in our country.

However, I had simultaneously been surrounded from birth with a *definition* of the Jew of such stunning emotional and historical proportions that I couldn't but be enveloped by it, contrary though it was to my own experience. This was the definition of the Jew as sufferer, the Jew as an object of ridicule, disgust, scorn, contempt, derision, of every heinous form of persecution and brutality, including murder. If the definition was not supported by my own experience, it surely was by the experience of my grandparents and their forebears, and by the experience of our European contemporaries. The disparity between this tragic dimension of Jewish life in Europe and the actualities of our daily lives as Jews in New Jersey was something that I had to puzzle over myself, and indeed, it was in the vast discrepancy between the two Jewish conditions that I found the terrain for my first stories and later for *Portnoy's Complaint.* Being a Jew in New Jersey was comical just because it was somehow bound up with these ghastly events.

And let me say something about "school," the last word in that useless label. One more nail in the coffin, then we'll be done with it.

Obviously, Bellow, Malamud, and I do not constitute a New York school of anything. If we constitute a Jewish school, it is only in the odd sense of having each found his own means of transcending the immediate parochialism of his Jewish background and transforming what once had been the imaginative property of anecdotal local colorists—and of apologists, nostalgists, publicists, and propagandists—into a fiction having entirely different intentions, but which nonetheless remains grounded in the colorful specificity of the locale. And even this similarity amounts to little when you think about all that must follow from our differences in age, upbringing, regional origin, class, temperament, education, intellectual interests, moral ideologies, literary antecedents, and artistic aims and ambitions.

*Of course,* The Ghost Writer *is not only about Jews. One of its subjects is what you have called "writing about Jews": young Nathan is accused, at the very outset of his career, of informing, of collaborating with the enemy, the anti-Semite. What makes writing about Jews so problematical?*

What makes it problematical is that Jews who register strong objections to what they see as damaging fictional portrayals of Jews are not necessarily philistine or paranoid. If their nerve endings are frayed, it is not without cause or justification. They don't want books that will give comfort to anti-Semites or confirm anti-Semitic stereotypes. They don't want books that will wound the feelings of Jews already victimized, if not by anti-Semitic persecution in one form or another, by the distaste for Jews still endemic in pockets of our society. They don't want books that offend Jewish self-esteem and that do little, if anything, to increase the prestige of Jews in the non-Jewish world. In the aftermath of the horrors that have befallen millions of Jews in this century, it isn't difficult to understand their concern. In fact, it's the *ease* with which one understands it that presents a problem of conflicting loyalties that's difficult to solve. For however much I may loathe anti-Semitism, however enraged I may be when faced with the slightest real manifestation of it, however much I might wish to console its victims, my job in a work of fiction is not to offer consolation to Jewish sufferers or to mount an attack upon their persecutors or to make the Jewish case to the undecided. My Jewish critics, and in America there are many, would tell you that I bend over backward not to make the Jewish case. After more than twenty years of disagreement with them on this subject, I can only say that that is the way they see it and not the way I see it. It's a fruitless discussion—which is exactly what makes it so problematical to write about Jews.

*Having read* The Ghost Writer *before our talk, I took it for granted that you were the younger writer Nathan Zuckerman and that Lonoff—the austere, ascetic older writer Zuckerman so much admires—was an imaginary amalgam of Malamud and Singer. But I see now that, not unlike Lonoff, you live like a semi-recluse in New England; you seem to write and read most of the time—in other words, to spend most of your life, in Lonoff's self-descriptive phrase, "turning sentences around." Are you Lonoff? Or, to put it less bluntly: Do you share the ideal of the writer as hermit, a self-ordained monk who must remain secluded from life for the sake of art?*

Art is life too, you know. Solitude is life, meditation is life, pretending is life, supposition is life, contemplation is life, language is life. Is

there less life in turning sentences around than in manufacturing
automobiles? Is there less in reading *To the Lighthouse* than in
milking a cow or throwing a hand grenade? The isolation of a literary
vocation—the isolation that involves far more than sitting alone in a
room for most of one's waking existence—has as much to do with
life as accumulating sensations, or multinational corporations, out in
the great hurly-burly. It seems to me that it's largely through art that I
have a chance of being taken to the heart at least of my *own* life.

Am I Lonoff? Am I Zuckerman? Am I Portnoy? I could be, I
suppose. I may be yet. But as of now I am nothing like so sharply
delineated as a character in a book. I am still amorphous Roth.

*You seem to me to be made particularly rebellious by the strain of
sentimental moralizing in American culture. At the same time, you
strenuously claim your American heritage. My last question is very
simple, if not simplistic: What does America mean to you?*

America allows me the greatest possible freedom to practice my
vocation. America has the only literary audience that I can ever
imagine taking any sustained pleasure in my fiction. America is the
place I know best in the world. It's the *only* place I know in the world.
My consciousness and my language were shaped by America. I'm an
American writer in ways that a plumber isn't an American plumber or
a miner an American miner or a cardiologist an American cardiologist. Rather, what the heart is to the cardiologist, the coal to the
miner, the kitchen sink to the plumber, America is to me.

# A Meeting of Arts and Minds
## Cathleen Medwick/1983

From *Vogue,* October 1983, 530–31, 603–04. Courtesy *Vogue.* Copyright © 1983 by The Condé Nast Publications, Inc.

It is a soft, breezy day in northwestern Connecticut. There is an old farmhouse, fronted by a sea of tall grass; beyond that, deep woods. Philip Roth walks quietly in his meadow . . .

Philip Roth? In his meadow? The writer who gave us Portnoy and Zuckerman, those anguished urbanites—Roth, the kid from Newark, strolling now alongside stone fences, his sneakers wet with dew? Roth, whom critics insist on confounding with his characters— narcissistic men with embarrassing "complaints"—this same Philip Roth, it turns out, has been living a pastoral idyll for eleven years. True, he spends some time in London; but this eighteenth-century dairy farm is home. While Nathan Zuckerman was bruising his soul in Chicago (in *The Anatomy Lesson,* the final volume in Roth's just-completed trilogy), Roth was curling up before the fireplace in his grey shingled house. "In the winter," he says fondly, "the smoke curling from the chimney looks like a child drew it."

A simple life, but not a solitary one. Roth lives here with British actress Claire Bloom, a friend for many years—another worldly, displaced spirit, although, unlike Roth's, her fame has never verged on infamy. If anything, she has had to battle the world's vision of her as "the English rose"—a dark, delicate beauty who seemed born to play Ophelia, or Juliet, but has bared her thorns in roles ranging from Blanche DuBois, in *A Streetcar Named Desire,* to Lady Marchmain in *Brideshead Revisited.* In January, Bloom appears as a New England woman married to a famous and temperamental author in a BBC/PBS co-production of Roth's novel *The Ghost Writer*—a role she felt supremely competent to play.

"I was so rich, you know. I knew so much. . . . It was, in a way, our house—not our happiness, but our quiet life, recreated out there in Vermont. Very strange. But I'd lived it. I knew what to do in the

131

kitchen, and I knew the attitude of a writer when he doesn't want to be disturbed by the telephone. . . . And then, I'd had the advantage of talking to Philip about it. . . ."

Claire Bloom is sitting on the long wicker sofa in a room of the house that was converted from a woodshed and is now a sort of sunporch. She looks decorously exotic here: the way she is dressed—in a flowing cotton skirt striped with burgundy, blue, and black; and her jewelry—amber beads from Marrakesh (a gift from Philip), silver bracelets and rings. She is always quietly moving and twisting her hands in her lap as she speaks. Her legs are perfectly still.

She is one of those women who can imperceptibly enter or leave a room: part discipline, part grace. She is never obvious. When she brings the coffee and tea, you never hear the cups clink, and you can't remember how she got past you and sat down.

Philip Roth, on the other hand, is rather sudden—he can move fast. No hurry; he just seems to like getting from one point to another, like any good administrator. He shows the house, pointing out this added-on window, that original roof; that cartoon on the wall of his study (he also writes in a log cabin on the grounds), a friend's drawing of a writer knifing a rotund and prostrate critic; the custom-made writing board that the author uses on plane trips. Not pointed out (no need): the poster of Kafka; the photos of Claire—as the Queen in *Richard II,* and with Chaplin; the large picture of Tolstoy; the alphabetized books; the paperback edition of *Portnoy et Son Complexe.*

Roth seems to take pleasure in his house and grounds, which he describes as "manageable." He is not playing the gentleman farmer: no puttering in the garden, no tilling of the soil. He is here to write. When Philip and Claire sit outside, in a screen-enclosed dome, it is not to commune with nature—or with each other. They both bring books and, explains Roth, "I say *ssh* a lot."

Right now, he is making his way past the yellow daisies, past the chorus of crickets in the meadow, toward the old house. He is laying some ground rules for the interview—everything's under control. He is also making jokes, for his own amusement: he is a man who likes to laugh. You would also guess that he likes to brood. He especially enjoys punting questions (Interviewer: "How did you and Claire meet?" Roth: "At the senior prom. Claire was there with another

guy, but I had the car.") He has an uncommonly distinctive profile—
you would know him immediately in silhouette—suggesting some
bird of prey, an eagle. He is probably amused by his looks.

The television version of *The Ghost Writer* is Roth's first attempt at
translating his fiction into film. He wrote the script. He also suggested
Claire Bloom for the role of Hope. Beyond that, Roth says, he had
little influence. "Once the writing was finished, I was sent off to
pasture. People were very courteous to me. I was treated like a nice
old gent. 'Put Mr. Roth into a taxicab. Be sure he doesn't fall.' "
Expendable—and that was, perhaps, a new experience for Philip
Roth.

"The point about being a novelist is that you're absolutely in
charge. You're the director, and you're the casting director, and
you're the cast. I think I prefer that."

*The Ghost Writer,* the first novel in Roth's trilogy, is the story of
Nathan Zuckerman, a rising young writer who has come on a sort of
pilgrimage to the isolated rural home of E.I. Lonoff, an aging literary
giant who has removed himself from his admiring public in order to
write. As Zuckerman learns, Lonoff's noble vocation is a torture to
his wife, Hope, a white-haired Boston aristocrat, and an inspiration to
one Amy Bellette, an enchanting girl-woman who helps Lonoff
organize his work with a passion that distresses Hope still more. But
who is Amy, where is she from? She has an accent ("from the
country of Fetching," as Lonoff cavalierly remarks). For Nathan, she
becomes a fantasy: She is Anne Frank, miraculously alive and in
her late twenties, hiding herself from the world in order to keep her
legend intact.

When this scenario evolved in Philip Roth's brain, it made one
kind of sense. Onstage—that was another matter. Roth: "When you
write a book, no matter how much you 'see' it, you don't see it—the
force of actuality is not present." For example, the character of
Hope—she turned out to be rather stronger in person than she did
on the page. Stronger than Roth knew.

"When Philip wrote about her," says Bloom, "one saw her as a
rather passive, beaten-down woman, interesting because of her
relationship to her husband. I didn't realize that she was interesting in
herself. But when you, as an actress, start to bring her to life, she's
not at all passive. Things happen in your acting, you don't plan it."

Did Bloom bring a lot of herself to the role of Hope?

"I don't know how you play anything that you don't bring a lot of yourself into, frankly. I know there are supposed to be great character actors who play roles totally away from their personalities—and in that case, I'm not one. That's all. When I read a script, my immediate reaction is yes or no—but immediate. And nearly always right. Not that I haven't made mistakes, obviously. But the first feeling is that something connects with what I've experienced, or might have experienced, or could experience. Hope is quite a familiar face.

"She is a very interesting woman, independent and strong. Independent in a dependent environment, really."

And Roth (dare we ask the question of any novelist?) does he bring much of himself to the characters he creates?

Well, yes—and no.

"The difference between a writer and someone who doesn't write is that the writer has something beyond self, which is imagination. I find that when certain people read books of mine, they say, 'Well, did that happen to you?' And I say, 'No.' Then they'll say, 'Well, we don't believe you,' and I'll say to them, 'Don't you see that what separates me from you is I can make things up? That's how I earn my living.' Tolstoy said you can see a street fight and write *War and Peace*—you know, you don't have to see a great battle to understand what combat is. You need something, some juice to get you going. If you had only the self, you wouldn't be a writer, you'd be something else. But you have this other thing that, for lack of a better word, is called imagination.

"Let's take the case of Lonoff, who is fifty-seven years old. I'm not fifty-seven years old now, and I was even younger when I wrote this book, but I certainly can project myself into that situation, and that's an act of imagination. I don't have to have lived it. If I had to live everything I wrote about, I'd be stuck."

Not to mention, exhausted. . . .

Roth: "Well, you do what your temperament requires. Hemingway had to go to Africa and shoot lions; and Chekhov didn't go anywhere, really, except finally to that prison camp in Siberia, and he never wrote fiction about it. When he finally did go off in search of experience, as it were, he couldn't make fiction out of it. He could make fiction only out of what flowed through his own life. What you're doing in those little rooms where you sit by yourself as a writer is not reconstructing your life—you're taking those germs and letting them sprout, aren't you?"

Bloom agrees—that is what she was saying. "I mean," she laughs, "what I tried to say, but not as well."

She goes on: "I suppose, in a way, an actor is more caged than a writer because as an actor you're limited by your body . . . but, even so, what dictates the range of your work is what you are capable of imagining yourself doing. You don't have to murder a Duncan to play Lady Macbeth. But you do have to think that you are capable of doing such a thing."

Can Philip Roth see himself as an actor?

"Not since I was in school. I just wanted to stand on the stage. In the light. No, no, I couldn't begin to do it. I remember picking Claire up at night after she'd been in a play in London. She'd be dressing, and I'd walk out onstage and stand there, just—terrified." (To Claire): "Do you ever feel that way?"

Bloom: "God, yes."

Roth: "I'd stand there on the stage and think, how does she dare do this? No one was there, and my heart was pounding."

About two years ago, Roth adapted a translation of Chekhov for a television production of *The Cherry Orchard* in which Bloom appeared. That was when he first had occasion to watch actors at work, in rehearsal, making the most awful mistakes and correcting them— much the way writers did, in fact.

"The experience of writing is mostly saying, 'This is wrong. This word is wrong, this sentence is wrong, this page is wrong.' Actors have to do all that in front of people, be wrong all the time—that's mostly in rehearsal. . . ."

(Bloom, quietly): "Not only in rehearsal."

Roth: "Well, but in rehearsal you get the first draft. That's where it's really happening.

"I think being a director is like being a writer. I do it quietly to my page, to myself. You keep saying, 'This isn't right, no, no, no, no, the other way. You talk to yourself, I think, the way a good director probably talks to actors. And that is sometimes very sweetly and gently, and sometimes saying, 'Look, take a walk, this stinks.' "

In her autobiography *Limelight and After,* Claire Bloom talks about

actors' failings—how they signal that they are in trouble with a role:
"It's a professional affliction that almost no one escapes . . . I have a
little gesture that's an obvious sign of tension—the arm is straight
down and I raise my wrist so my hand is parallel to the ground. . . .
It's like something you might do out of nervousness at a cocktail
party. You put on some kind of face or voice, some act that . . . you
hope will get you by until you can get the hell out of there and on to
something else."

Where did she get the nerve to expose a secret like that?

"Ah, well, I thought I'd give a lot of people an ax to hit me over
the head with. . . . I found that a very difficult part of the book to
write, because I knew I would be giving things away. I tried to be
specific about how one acts. And it's a very mysterious and peculiar
process altogether, but it's interesting to try to pin it down."

An urge to pin down the mystery is apparently what enables Claire
Bloom to speak frankly about her abilities and limitations—the
difficulty she had in being both a good mother and a good actress:
the reasons for her failure to become a grand-scale Hollywood
star ("In films, I fear I was a lady, and that is just fatal to anybody").
She is a woman who appears to have sacrificed certain illusions for
the sake of emotional clarity.

The frustrations of being an actress:

"I have to rely on other people, on things and ideas that are not
mine. And it's too late now; that's what I chose to do, and that's the
world that I live in. I hesitate to say it, but I think my world is much
more difficult than any other. It's chancy; and for the kind of person I
am, that's not a particularly good way to live. I'm someone who likes
to be in control, but I can't."

For Roth, of course, it is otherwise: "I don't need anyone else.
That's probably why I chose to do what I do. And she needs a whole
world."

But he is also—surprisingly—philosophical about an artist's limitations:

"As you go on in a career in the arts, what do you learn? You learn
what you can't do. And that's exactly what happens over ten, twenty,
thirty years. You know what you can't do. Others may accept it as
your style or your trademark, your appeal. It may be the very thing

that's most appealing, which is what others may call your 'vision.'
You yourself may feel it as your limitation, your boundary."

In a sense, much of Roth's fiction is about the artist and his
limitations. Lonoff is a case in point—his great limitation being that
he is so thoroughly an artist. And then there is Nathan Zuckerman
who, in the course of three novels, discovers what he is not.

"I wanted to take this writer through three stages of his career, the
beginning, the middle—and the middle. And so the first book is
about the enthusiasm, and the conflict, and the obsession. Then the
next book [*Zuckerman Unbound*] is about his strange success. The
last book is about Zuckerman's exhaustion in his forties, his exhaustion and his growing distaste for his own vocation—if not hatred of
it—and his attempt to leave it.

"In *The Anatomy Lesson*, there are other consequences which
appear to be physical—the ruin of his body, the toll that's been taken
by his career. He decides to leave Manhattan and his life there, and
become a doctor. There's nothing more different from being a writer
than being a doctor. People actually need doctors—they don't need
writers. But there's more to it than that. Zuckerman winds up in the
hospital as a patient rather than as a doctor. In short, for him, there's
no way out."

There is a scene in *The Ghost Writer* in which Hope, frustrated by
Lonoff's relentless nobility, his faithful marriage to his profession,
screams at him, "I cannot take any more moral fiber in the face of
life's disappointments."

That sounds like a line either Philip Roth or Claire Bloom might
have said.

Roth laughs. "I don't know what it means. I go completely blank
when I hear it." (To Bloom): "Do you know?"

"I think it means she's had it up to here."

"She's talking about Lonoff," explains Roth, "Not giving in to his
yearning for Amy, and not giving in to the monotony and
boredom. . . ."

". . . and being," continues Bloom, "such an endlessly honorable
man. Whereupon, Hope says, 'I'll go to Boston, I'll go to the end of
the world. I'll go anywhere. Just let me out of this.' "

" 'Let me out of the prison of your decency' "—Roth is getting
into the spirit now. "But it's complicated because the prison of his

decency may well keep her together. Who knows? Lonoff is, as Claire says, a bottomlessly honorable man who has this fiendish dignity that she feels as a prison. . . . I did write it. I didn't say it."

Bloom laughs now. "And I said it. I didn't write it."

# "The job," says Roth,
# "was to give pain its due."
## Jonathan Brent/1983

From *The Chicago Tribune,* 6 November 1983, 36, 38. © 1983 by Jonathan Brent. Reprinted by permission.

Philip Roth lives with actress Claire Bloom in a large wood-frame farmhouse built in 1790 and set on 40 wooded acres in the secluded Connecticut countryside. When not in England, where they spend varying amounts of time each year, Roth writes seven days a week, six to eight hours a day, in a small nearby guest house, which has been converted to a studio. The majority of our conversation took place in the studio before the large stone fireplace. Asked about his present living arrangements and plans for the future, Roth said: "I love this house. I've lived here for 10 years. The only thing I've had more than 10 years is my writing. This place represents permanence in a life that's known a lot of flux. It would kill me to move, yet, as you see, this is nowhere. I envy Saul Bellow several things aside from his great gift. One is Chicago—living where he grew up. Most writers I know live far from where they began, deliberately mind you—but when you consider Bellow and Faulkner, you wonder if there isn't a good case to be made for staying put. You know who's in power and how they got there. You know who isn't and why. There are people around you went to school with. You run into them on the street, you talk, you keep track of them. To be without easy access to the world that's yours—yours and nobody else's—is a handicap for a writer like me."

**JB:** In your case, of course, the decision has been your own. No one's forcing you.

**PR:** True. It sure is my decision not to live in Newark. I thought of making my home in Philadelphia during the years that I was teaching at the University there, but the city didn't mean anything to me. I didn't get it. You can't will this closeness, you know. New York?

When I lived there I never understood why. Totally foreign to me. I was just a wanderer where other people were on the go.

Now it seems to me that what I've had instead of Newark or Chicago or Mississippi or Philadelphia has been the human body. There's my terrain—and in more books than this one. When I was writing *The Anatomy Lesson* I made a list of novels about illness and disease. It was a short list. *Cancer Ward* and *The Magic Mountain.* If you want to stretch it, you can toss in *Malone Dies.* There is no great body of literature on this strain of misery. Astonishing, isn't it? All those great books about adultery and none about diabetes. There's *Philoctetes, The Plague,* "The Death of Ivan Ilych"—but pain, the physical pain, remains peripheral. Even in *The Magic Mountain* the pain is peripheral. All that philosophy and all that snow reminds Zuckerman of the University of Chicago.

While I was writing this book I would say to myself that when I finished I wanted someone who'd suffered chronic pain to read it and say, "Yes. That's it." I wanted a writer to be able to say the same thing, "Yes—that's the life." If Zuckerman weren't in physical pain, he wouldn't care about Milton Appel, his mother's ghost wouldn't appear at his bedside, he wouldn't decide to become a doctor and fly back as he does to enroll at Pritzker. The pain is the fire at the heart of the book.

**JB:** But unlike in some other books I can think of, the interesting thing is that the pain in *The Anatomy Lesson* isn't in the service of anything. It serves no worthwhile purpose.

**PR:** So Zuckerman learns. "It's not interesting," he says, "and it has no meaning—it's just plain stupid pain, it's the opposite of interesting." The book is a comedy, remember. Not that pain is funny or that I would want to pretend that it is. The job was to give pain its due while at the same time rendering accurately the devastation it wreaks upon reason, dignity, pride, maturity, independence— upon all of one's human credentials. You generally wait in vain for the ennobling effects.

**JB:** Zuckerman wants to become a doctor because, with the destruction of Newark, the death of his parents and the estrangement from his brother, he says he's lost his subject. Have you lost yours?

**PR:** No. Luckily Zuckerman's subject isn't my subject. Zuckerman, who's lost his subject, is my subject.

**JB:** Something I've been struck by in all these Zuckerman books is how beautifully formed they are. I wouldn't know precisely how to describe the forms, but I can sense this in them.

**PR:** Because of the constant shifting of mood and tone and rhythms, I frequently thought of this book in musical terms.

**JB:** It seems to gain speed until it comes abruptly to a halt in the cemetery scene and then there's no coda.

**PR:** Each book has its own pace and speed, which explains why I decided on the three rather than on one long sustained narrative. I wanted those sharp divisions. I've always liked juxtaposing sharply contrasting blocks of material. I also like the movement between the chapters: those long running broad jumps. So many of my pleasures are narrative pleasures. How to tell the story: This is my greatest source of confusion and my greatest source of pleasure.

**JB:** Did you know in advance where the three Zuckerman books were headed?

**PR:** Yes and no. Each book contained a big surprise. In *The Ghost Writer,* Amy was going to claim to Lonoff that she was indeed Anne Frank. What I couldn't figure out was how Zuckerman would come to know that. What I discovered was that he knew it because he made it up: Her claim to be Anne Frank was his own invention. In the second book, *Zuckerman Unbound,* the surprise was the death of the father. Everything in the book was pointing toward the father's death, and the deathbed rebuke of Zuckerman, as its conclusion. But stupidly I didn't see that for months and months. In *The Anatomy Lesson,* the breakthrough came when I realized that I was taking it easy on Zuckerman, protecting him by casting him again in the role of the observer. That was all right for books one and two, but now he had to act. The aspiring 23-year-old from *The Ghost Writer,* who yearned to be a saintly writer like the great literary puritan E.I. Lonoff, must now go over the top and passionately pretend, in his own words, to be a "kike-pornographer."

That's what I discovered writing this book.

**JB:** You mentioned Saul Bellow before. What kind of effect did he have on your work?

**PR:** I don't think there's an American writer between 40 and 55 who hasn't, over the years, been stunned by Bellow and what he's done with what he knows. I was surprised recently to learn how

much John Updike felt he owed to Bellow. There's Dick Stern,
obviously. And me. Writers who in their work bear little or no
resemblance to each other, or even to Bellow—except that Bellow
was inspiring to them all. Stanley Elkin too, I would think: his verbal
fun, the outsize characters, the shady deals, the brilliant, loony,
not-so-loony monologues. Morandi points to a little thing like a bottle
and says: "Bottles are art. Art is bottles." And proves it. That's the
history of art, no? Someone comes along and says, "Put that in too."
"That? That—stuff?" "Precisely. Put it in." That's what Mark Twain
did, that's the American energy in Melville. "I'll put whales in. Every
last thing about whales." Well, that's Bellow: He put the whale in,
and everything there is to know about them. He's big. A big contemporary. That's bracing for everybody.

   **JB:** Could you talk a little bit about when you lived in Chicago?

   **PR:** I came to the University of Chicago in 1954 from a good but
provincial little college in Pennsylvania. The change was terrific. I was
21 and had a great year there as a graduate student—bibliography
by day, women by night. That was the Byronic dream, anyway. I
came back to teach in the college from 1956 to 1958. When Esquire
gave me $300 for a short story—a quarter of my annual university
salary—I resigned my job and went off to New York to live in a
basement and write a novel. I could have written a novel in a
basement in Hyde Park; there were plenty of basements around,
going begging, but I thought I had to free myself from schools and
school friends, and I was also washing my hands of a hectic romance.
I missed Chicago afterwards. I've never felt as close to any other city
I've lived in. But maybe that's because it was my first real city after
leaving home.

   **JB:** Who was important during those years?

   **PR:** I suppose my greatest supporter was Napier Wilt, who was
then dean of humanities, and one of my first teachers in the graduate
school. I liked his offhand way with literature.

   There was also a lot of young talent around. That was important,
too. The competition, the ambition, the stimulation, the talk. The
novelist Tom Rogers was teaching freshman English with me, and the
critic and editor Ted Solotaroff, who was then fighting the 14th
round with his Ph.D., became a close friend. I owe "Goodbye,
Columbus" to Dick Stern, who had just arrived from Iowa in 1955.

We had lunch one day at the University Tavern, which used to stand at the corner of 55th and Ellis. Over our hamburgers I was telling Dick stories about the New Jersey Jewish country club set into which I had not been fortunate enough to be born. Dick got a kick out of the stories. "Why don't you write that down?" he said. My head was so full of *The Golden Bowl,* I thought he was having me on. But when I went home, I did it. What I owe Dick is that he helped me to see that what was in front of my nose, though not so resounding as Conrad or as convoluted as James, qualified as fiction. That's what I learned in Hyde Park: how to talk back to all those great books.

# Zuckerman Found? Philip Roth's One-Man Art Colony

## Jesse Kornbluth/1983

This article was originally published in *House and Garden*, December 1983, 127, 213–214. © 1983 by Jesse Kornbluth. Reprinted by permission.

At 23, Nathan Zuckerman is primed for success. He has published four stories, had his picture in the *Saturday Review,* and been welcomed at the Quahsay Colony. All he lacks, as he sees it, is "the magical protection" of a mentor—and who better for the job than E.I. Lonoff, the immigrant child who grew up to write like Chekhov, marry the scion of an old New England family, and live "in the *goyish* wilderness of birds and trees"? So Zuckerman contacts Lonoff. Lonoff responds. And, on a December afternoon in 1956, with the light falling and his anxiety peaking, Zuckerman makes his way up an unpaved road in the Berkshires to Lonoff's shingled home.

Literary sponsorship may be Zuckerman's purpose, but as he enters the two-hundred-year-old clapboard farmhouse, Lonoff's bookshelves aren't what he first notices. For Lonoff's "neat, cozy, and plain" living room is more of a writer's fantasy than anything a decorator—or Zuckerman—could dream up. The sofa is worn, the walls are almost bare, the view of dark maples and fields of snow is framed by primly tied cotton curtains. "Purity. Serenity. Simplicity. Seclusion. All one's concentration and flamboyance and originality reserved for the grueling, exalted, transcendent calling," Zuckerman rhapsodizes. And he makes a pledge to himself: "This is how I will live."

It is a commonplace among Philip Roth's readers and critics to hold that Nathan Zuckerman—the young careerist of *The Ghost Writer,* the notorious best-selling novelist of *Zuckerman Unbound,* and now the written-out obsessive of *The Anatomy Lesson*—is nothing more than a stand-in for his creator. The joke's on them. For although Nathan Zuckerman can be found, as *The Anatomy Lesson* opens, writhing in pain on a plastic-covered mat in his New York apartment, Philip Roth has been living in Connecticut's second-smallest municipality in a house almost exactly like Lonoff's since 1972, well before he began the Zuckerman trilogy. And if Roth, like Zuckerman, is full of complaints about his profession, he also takes deep comfort in a home that, like Lonoff's, gives him nature as "a backdrop to my thoughts."

A Jewish writer from Newark living with a beautiful English actress in the most fashionable corner of rural Connecticut is a character whose magnificent contradictions would greatly amuse Roth-the-novelist. But Roth-the-man hadn't met Claire Bloom when he moved to Connecticut, nor was he lured to the country by a weekend house-party. His reason for embracing the Lonovian ideal is, he says, so simple and obvious it requires no apology—he came for his work.

"I lived in New York, mostly in a brownstone, from 1963 to 1970," he explains. "Everybody would go out in the morning, and there I'd be—alone, trying to keep the city at bay. I put double-glazing on the windows and complained about stereos across the courtyard, but even then there were sounds I couldn't stand: a dog upstairs scratching on the floor, a door slamming. I couldn't go out to lunch because that too was a distraction, and I didn't stay out late in the evening because I wanted to get started in the morning. All in all, I knew why I was living there—I was alone—but I didn't know why I was *writing* there."

New York was even more of a negative environment whenever Roth compared it to his favorite artists' colony. "I began going to Yaddo in 1963," he recalls. "The first time I went I stayed six months. I loved sleeping in the old Victorian Palace, walking to my bare studio with my workman's lunchpail, working until I got stuck and then taking a solitary walk around Saratoga." By 1970, the contrast between the prodigious bouts of writing he did at Yaddo—usually in the winter, when only a dozen people tended to be there—and the difficulty he experienced working in New York drove him to rent a house in Woodstock.

Roth liked the one-man writer's colony he created for himself in Woodstock and intended to stay in that area. But at a party given by Random House editor Jason Epstein, he heard the painter Cleve

Gray and his writer wife, Francine du Plessix Gray, talking about a
house for sale in their corner of Connecticut. Roth drove over one
afternoon—and discovered that this was a very unusual house
indeed. "In the twenties, the owners paid the town to move the road
from the front to out back of the apple orchard," he explains. "And
this is what appealed to me when I first saw it: the house was facing
nowhere."

Those privacy-minded owners went on to enlarge the kitchen and
attach a barn to the house as a "summer room." And then, thank-
fully, they stopped. As a result, almost two hundred years after its
construction, the house remains so true to its origins that it has never
been painted. Every few years, to Roth's delight, a man comes and
stains it with linseed oil.

For his part, Roth has not been quick to alter the house's design or
mood. He would like to have a more efficient heating system, but
that would require six-inch-high baseboards along the walls. "It
would look like a motel," Roth says, "and I just couldn't do that to
the house." The changes he has made are extremely modest: a
sauna where the downstairs bath used to be, a stone floor and sliding
glass doors in the summer room, larger kitchen cabinets.

Roth has been only slightly less reverential in his remake of the
smallest building on his forty acres—the studio. "I wanted the kind of
environment where working made sense," he says, and so he refur-
bished the studio's kitchen and bath, shored up a floor, ordered a
phone that doesn't take incoming calls, and had a typing table
custom-built so his long legs wouldn't bang against it every time he
wheeled his posture chair to his Selectric. Then he hung some
drawings by his friend Philip Guston and the Czech writer Bruno
Shulz, set several photographs on his desk ("That's me in Prague,
walking toward the building where Kafka's father had his office"),
dragged in some file cabinets—and went to work.

"From 1971 to 1975, I published a book a year," Roth says,
swiveling in his standard-issue leather Eames chair to contemplate
the empty desk where most of those books were wrestled into being.
"That's largely because of this place and the discipline it imposes. *My
Life as a Man,* for instance—I owe that book to this place. It was
begun in 1969, but I didn't publish it for years. I'd write, make no
headway, go off and do something else. I was unhappy, really steely

miserable. But there was no way around it, not here. There's a
tremendous amount of drive I pick up from this place. It sharpens my
single-mindedness, intensifies the monomania."

"Megalomania?"

"Monomania," Roth says, quick with the correction. "If you're a
megalomaniac, you can't make it out here. The trees and the birds
aren't interested. But if you're a monomaniac—or a mythomaniac, or
a graphomaniac—you're in business."

Like Flaubert, who was said by Henry James to have "felt of his
vocation almost nothing but the difficulty," Roth's greatest apparent
pleasure lies in the alchemical conversion of frustration into literature.

"Problem solving is what I do." Roth says. "It's what the activity is,
all day, sometimes a sentence, sometimes a whole book. My satisfactions come from solving those problems. It's work, just endless work.
There isn't time for any bullshit. I just have to work all the time, very
hard, and cut everything else out."

No matter how it's going, Roth comes to the studio at 9:30 each
morning, plays music on the radio for a few minutes, and starts
writing. When that palls, he walks, counting the time spent striding
through nature as doubly profitable if he comes back to his desk with
one usable sentence. He lunches alone, returns to the studio, and
sits over his typewriter again until "the frustration that drips in my
system like water from a leaking tap" forces him outside once more.

Roth usually works like this for twenty months straight. Then,
inevitably, there is a crisis. "No writing," he reports. "Just sitting at
my desk. And then suddenly, very simply, after all that wrongness,
the book virtually writes—or rights—itself. So the two years it generally takes to write a book means a long running start to get to the
pitch, and then the leap of the last three or four months. And I come
out here nights then, or I'm taking a shower and halfway through I
have an idea and rush off in my bathrobe to come back out here and
have yet another go at the book. Those last months are wonderful."

This is, of course, not a novel way of working. Flaubert longed "to
live in a place where no one loves me or knows me, where the sound
of my name causes only indifference," and even in the first heat of
his affair with Louise Colet, he saw her only six times in eighteen
months. Kafka went even further: "The best mode of life for me
would be to sit in the innermost room of a spacious locked cellar with

my writing things and a lamp. Food would be brought and always put down far away from my room, outside the cellar's outermost door. The walk to my food, in my dressing gown, through the vaulted cellars, would be my only exercise."

Roth too believes he has to be entombed to write well, but his, he says, is "a benign prison." Considering that his days are devoted to writing and his nights to reading, that he doesn't like to cook or play the host, and that he's "as savage over my dinner alone as anybody else, tearing things with ten fingers while I read the paper," it is not immediately clear how his style differs from Flaubert's or Kafka's. At this point, however, the critical difference appears at the door.

"Yes?"

Claire Bloom steps into the office. "Don't open the door," she announces. "You'll kill me."

Roth has already pointed out an inner room in the studio, replete with a chinning bar, a contraption for sit-ups, and an exercise bicycle. Bloom, who wears a simple skirt, Pendleton shirt, cardigan sweater, and pearls, is on her way there. "There's a chinning bar on the door," she says, "and there's no lock. . . ."

"And there's a big picture of it on the cover of House & Garden," Roth says, instigating a burst of laughter from all involved.

Bloom closes the door behind her, but her presence lingers. "You have to be with someone to live out here," Roth says. "That goes without saying." It also goes without saying that Bloom—who has lived with Roth for almost seven years—doesn't have the vocational luxury of spending all her time in Connecticut. She endured her first winter here, using the isolation to write a book, but since then has accepted work that takes her from the farmhouse for weeks at a time.

Bloom's influence, though nowhere overt, can be felt in the softening of the house's Puritan edges and the mellowing of her lover's rage and frustration. Since her arrival, two modified geodesic domes have been erected near the house, allowing the couple to spend time in bug-free nature under a sky of mesh. The glossy-white bedroom that, to Roth, is the manifestation of Rilke's desire to sleep up among the trees is humanized by Bloom's needlepoint pillows. From the kitchen comes the smell of new potatoes in a skillet. In this context, even the terrible clang of the antique bell that Bloom uses to summon the writer to dinner has ironic appeal.

So complete is their commitment to this life that Roth and Bloom make the tedious two-hour drive to New York no more than once a month. They entertain equally infrequently. "There's the tofu run, the fish run, the veal run, the bread run, the fresh fruit and vegetable run—and they're all in different directions," Roth notes. "If we're having guests, Claire puts 125 miles on the car."

Despite their isolation, the only dark cloud over the Connecticut retreat hangs over Roth's studio. "Ordinarily, by the time I've finished a book and it's about to be published, I've started another," he says. "This is the first time in twenty years that I haven't. I was really beat—I'd had frustration up to here—and didn't even know how beat I was. I've made one page of notes for a new book but fortunately I lost it."

Were Roth really Zuckerman—a writer crying out against his "solitary confinement," declaring himself "sick of raiding my memory and feeding on the past"—this unprecedented lapse in production might easily be the harbinger of silence. Certainly, a number of critics and not a few readers will be inclined to think so. But at the end of the Zuckerman series, when Zuckerman gives up his wild plan to become a doctor, he returns to his New York brownstone—alone, "a man apart." In Connecticut, though, Philip Roth is standing in mid-meadow and announcing, without irony, "Life is the two of us." Nathan Zuckerman would give anything to say that.

# Conversations with Philip: Diary of a Friendship

## David Plante/1984

From *The New York Times Book Review*, 1 January 1984, 3, 30–31. © 1984 by David Plante. Reprinted by permission.

David Plante is an American writer from Providence, R.I., who has lived abroad since 1966. His recent books include *The Woods,* a novel, and *Difficult Women,* a memoir of his friendships with Jean Rhys, Sonia Orwell and Germaine Greer. He met the novelist Philip Roth in 1975 in London, where Mr. Roth and the actress Claire Bloom live half the year. Mr. Plante, who lives there with the Greek poet Nikos Stagos, is collaborating with Mr. Roth in adapting the Jean Rhys section of *Difficult Women* for film; they would like Miss Bloom to play the role of Jean Rhys. What follows are excerpts from David Plante's diary that record his friendship with Philip Roth.

**June 6, 1981**  Philip telephoned today to say he's back in London. I hadn't known he'd gone—suddenly, because his mother died.

He says he couldn't look at her body. He didn't want that meaningless image to obliterate all the images that matter.

During the two weeks he spent with his father after the funeral he took notes. He's still taking notes.

I said, "What kind of people are we? We don't even stop taking notes at a funeral."

"Good enough."

"Are we?"

**August 23, 1981**  Connecticut. On the outside, Claire is still, then a quick gesture, like taking a hand from the steering wheel and passing it through her hair, will reveal all her inside movement. Her eyes calm, her bright black hair seems to swing of itself.

She turned off a country road and through an apple orchard to a dark gray clapboard house shaded by big, old maples. Philip appeared with his father, Philip tall and lean, his father shorter and squarer, both wearing straw hats. Claire disappeared.

When Philip smiles, he presses his lips together as if barely suppressing his amusement, and you don't quite know what his amusement is. It occurs to me that he is always trying to contain his expressions, large and on the point of going off in peculiar directions, so his face and even his body are kept composed. He says, "So the New England boy is back," but you feel he could have said a hundred other things, and what he *could* have said, but didn't, amuses him. A spark in his eyes, behind his rectangular, gold-framed glasses, is like a spark off his amusement.

I said, "Me? I'm just a Canuck."

I was sure he wanted to say more, but he pressed his smiling lips together. He didn't say, as I wanted him to, that he was just a boy from Newark, New Jersey.

He told me I would stay in his study, which he pointed to across a lawn—a gray cottage with a screened-in porch.

Philip left me with his father, who waited while I changed into a bathing suit, then, linking his arm in mine, guided me to the pool. He asked, "Are you married, Dave?" I said I wasn't. "You should be," he said. "You should have a girl like Claire, a nice fellow like you." He continued to talk as I swam back and forth in the pool. As I climbed out, he ran for a towel to hold it open and wrap it around me. I told him I was sorry about the death of his wife. "A wonderful woman," he said, "a really wonderful woman, Dave," and he turned away as his face gave way to his grief. He is much more expressive than his son. He is 80, was married for 54 years.

He, Philip and I sat in the living room. Claire did not want help in the kitchen.

Philip said, "I just finished reading Updike's *Rabbit Is Rich* in proof. He knows so much, about golf, about porn, about kids, about America. I don't know anything about anything. His hero is a Toyota salesman. Updike knows everything about being a Toyota salesman. Here I live in the country and I don't even know the names of the trees. I'm going to give up writing."

His father said, "Bess and I always said we were proud of Philip's writing. Anyone ever called us up, we'd say, 'We're very proud of our son,' that's all."

After supper, Mr. Roth went into another room to watch television, and Philip, Claire and I talked about giving up our careers to become, as Philip insisted, doctors. Claire wanted to be a pediatrician. Philip said, "I'm going to be an obstetrician." I'd be a gynecologist.

On my way back to the cottage, Philip said, with his smile, that I could look through the papers on his desk, in his files. "Love letters under L." Alone, I looked around carefully, thinking: I must recall all this—the photograph of Kafka, the drawing by Philip Guston of Philip (Roth, that is) with black beard stubble. Perhaps he did mean that I could look through his papers, and yet perhaps not. Without touching them, I studied the pages of yellow foolscap on his desk; most sentences were crossed out, and all were illegible. There was only one I could make out alone on a sheet: "How many Jews can dance on the head of a pin?" Then I turned to his large metal files, and a curious self-consciousness came over me—not only that of a younger writer in the study of an older (not that much older) and renowned writer, but that of the younger writer having *read* in one of that renowned writer's novels a scene similar to the one in which the younger writer finds himself. Did Philip think of this when he put me in his study? What was odd was that I enjoyed this self-consciousness—enjoyed it without thinking I was being false, because the scene was already made real, made true, by its appearance in "The Ghost Writer."

At breakfast, Philip's father talked a lot about friends in Newark—who'd married, who'd had babies, who'd died. Claire was quiet. I asked questions. Philip brought to the table a long, rolled-up photograph and spread it out; his father held one side, I the other, and Philip, standing, pointed to the members of a family convention at a hotel in Boston in 1948, where about 200 people were sitting around tables in a paneled dining room with chandeliers and Turkish carpets, and all the people were facing the camera and smiling. Philip didn't make jokes, as he usually does; he spoke with a quiet seriousness. At the very back were his father and mother, she with a long, white, beautiful face. Philip was not present.

Claire quietly left the room.

I said to Philip, "You've got to work."

"I do," he answered matter-of-factly.

He came with me to his study, where I'd left my bag. "Let's talk a while," he said. On the screened porch, we looked out on a wall of gray, lichen-covered boulders and birch trees beyond.

He said, "If you were with my father a month, he'd have you married. He'd find even you a girl, David. You'd have to fight her off."

"I'm sure your father knows the right thing for me."

We talked about our families, openly and in great detail. Philip said to me that people are too easily shocked. "A little less shock, a little more curiosity."

Back in the kitchen, Claire was making out a shopping list. Philip's father went out. Philip and Claire argued about the shopping. They were silent for a moment, then they finished the list together.

Before I left for New York, Claire and I had a walk along the river. She wore a red dress with green and yellow Mexican embroidery and a straw hat. I asked her about her life. Sometimes we stopped on the path to watch the river. She said that before she met Philip she was incapable of protecting herself because since she was 17 everything was taken care of by others—agents, lawyers, producers, etc. Then suddenly she found that some of those who had been taking care of her had taken her for a ride. She was very low. Philip changed her life, saved her—toughened her up.

She asked me about Nikos.

I felt close to her, and at the bus stop, I embraced her with a kind of understanding closeness.

The fact is, I don't know Claire and Philip.

**February 10, 1982**   Philip and I were standing on a corner in Notting Hill, by a red mailbox, I saw an Englishman I know come toward us in a crowd, but he didn't see us and passed us by. Philip was talking, leaning toward me.

He has been talking a lot about his mother's death.

When he is keen, his nostrils contract. He stops talking, and his eyebrows, too, contract. I always take the first step to get us going. As we walk, he talks, much more than I do, and much more intensely.

**February 21, 1982**   The last time we met, Philip talked of real stuff in writing and gave me this, written on a torn sheet of paper, to think about:

"You must so change that in broad daylight you could crouch

down in the middle of the street and, without embarrassment, undo your trousers."

I forget now where the quotation is from, some 19th-century German author, I think.

Philip added: "The emphasis is on the word *could*. Not that you would, because you wouldn't. But you should be *capable* of doing it."

**March 25, 1982**   In his study, Philip said, "Updike and Bellow hold their flashlights out into the world, reveal the real world as it is *now*. I dig a hole and shine my flashlight into the hole. You do the same."

I said that I long to write about the moment I'm living in, as in my diaries. In my fiction, I'm still an adolescent, learning about a world that's now 20 years old.

We went out to supper in a restaurant with white tablecloths and white napkins peaked on white plates. He asked me if I think often of death.

"For some reason," I said, "death reassures me. It can't be faked."

"Oh, no," he said, "you can't be reassured by that."

"I shouldn't be."

"Yet I'm sure of the final doom," Philip said with that quiet seriousness I got used to. "The nuclear holocaust is well on its way."

"And that reassures my dark soul."

"What is your dark soul?" he asked brusquely.

"My sense that what is true is that everything is fated for destruction and there is nothing we can do about it."

"There is a devil, isn't there?"

I laughed.

"Now I've become rather dark myself," he said.

"I'm sorry."

"Can you write when you're in a dark state?"

"Yes, I can."

"I can't. I have to write from a lively state."

Oh yes, this: we mixed up sexual obsession in our talk about doom. I said I was less and less obsessed, and it is a relief. He said, "I'll be obsessed when I'm 80 exactly as I was when I was 18."

**April 6, 1982**   A few days ago I telephoned Philip to invite him and Claire to dinner. He said they couldn't make it, and I was relieved—I suppose because I am self-conscious when with them. But I went on saying how much I wanted to see him and Claire.

After I hung up, Nikos said, "You were utterly false. Utterly insincere."

I groaned. "I know."

"Your niceness toward Philip was completely unconvincing."

"To him?"

"I know what you try to do—you try to show him you're open to admitting anything about yourself, whatever it is. Well, you've got to be open, but not because you think he's only interested in you if you are. I thought you'd reached a point where you could be bold with people."

"What shall I do?"

"Be aware. You're intimidated by Philip."

"I am."

**May 10, 1982**   Philip and I often go to a cafeteria in Mayfair. It has small tables with shaded lamps hanging low over them, so the upper halves of our faces are in darkness, the lower halves bright, and to see one another we have to bend our necks.

I gave him a long story, what might be the first chapter of a novel, to read and comment on, and he gave me the typescript of his latest novel, *The Anatomy Lesson.*

I said, "Your commenting on my writing terrifies me."

"Why? Because you've got to start taking yourself seriously as a writer?"

I said, "If, five years ago, I fantasized about having a respected writer comment on my writing, he'd never have been you. Your writing is so different from mine."

"It is," he said. "I think you're a dreamy kind of writer and I'm a realistic writer, concerned with the hard facts of life; yet the opposite is true, and I'm the dreamy writer, always trying to invent a world in which all my nightmares will come true."

"And I'm a realist?"

"Yes, you are. When you're not writing about those damn trembling rhomboids of sunlight. That's the easy stuff, David. Circles, squares, triangles of light. It's the other kind I'm talking about. Providence. Your brothers. The machine shop. The priest. You're in the real world in that."

"But *that's* the kind of writing that's easy for me. I just put down what happened."

"I know."

"I'm not even sure it's fiction."

"It's the best fiction. It's not just pretty sentences—it's *stuff.*"

I felt a little thrill up my spine, as if allowed to do anything I want.

We talked, as always, autobiographically.

He described how he, from his childhood, felt a foreigner in America wondering what America was, and then he realized that it was exactly this that made him an American.

After lunch, we went to a bookshop. He turned to the entry on him in a new dictionary of American writers, read it, and held it out to me. "Cliches," he said. "The same old stupid cliches." He slammed the book shut before I could read and slotted it back. Then he left.

**May 20, 1982**   Philip sat at his desk with the typescript of *The Anatomy Lesson* and I sat on a chair before him with a copy on my lap, and as I turned the pages to read my comments, he turned his pages. I said I thought the first simile about the pain being like an upside down menorah was very powerful in its reference, and that all the similes in the rest of the book would, I thought, be read as equally intentional in their references; that was why I was worried, later on, by the tumor "the size of a lemon." Also, in a novel with so many references to other worlds of literature, I was worried by Zuckerman taking his mother to see *Barefoot in the Park,* which seemed to me to have no relevance. I had 10 or 12 queries like this. He wrote down my comments, with page and line numbers, in a notebook. The novel expands in many, many different directions, like Philip's smile, but whereas his smile contains the directions but doesn't reveal them, the novel reveals them all—sometimes going off very far in one direction, as with the character of the Chicago pornographer, who is a great fecund bulge in the book. I am still too intimidated to tell Philip all this.

When you talk to Philip, he, attentive, nods and says, "a-hun, a-hun." I think he listens to be able, after, to talk at much greater length than he has been attentive.

Is it odd that I feel nothing competitive toward Philip, as I do

toward other writers? I think this has to do with Philip's own attitude
toward other writers. He is not a jealous man.

Also, he is remarkably unguarded.

He and Claire are going to America for some months.

**March 1, 1983**   Philip gave me another draft of *The Anatomy
Lesson*. He has shortened it, reduced the number of characters and
made Zuckerman himself the pornographer, *possessed* by the pornographer as by a truly shocking spirit.

Shortly after I called him about it, he called back to ask if we could
have lunch. He said, "You know how it is—you can never hear
enough about your work."

We met at a restaurant in Covent Garden and were the last
customers to leave. He does not know what he'll write next. One
thing is for sure, he's done with his past.

"Not me," I said.

He laughed. "Well, maybe not me, either."

He warned me about the pared-down writing I am trying now:
"My mother used to say that, in dressing to go out, one could wear
two plains and one fancy—but never one plain and two fancies—and
certainly not three fancies—and never three plains."

"I know what you're telling me," I said.

"Get something fancy in there."

He thinks I'm odd. When he was a kid and got a new mitt and
ball, he asked his father to play catch with him. His father, wearing
his suit and tie and hat and carrying his briefcase of insurance
ledgers, was going out to work, but went with Philip into the street to
play catch. I said I had never played baseball, never went to baseball
games, wasn't interested in baseball. He said he was shocked.

**May 4, 1983**   Philip said he wouldn't mind, would rather like, to
have someone write about him, to see what it felt like to be someone
else's subject. He has a very amorphous and blurry self-image, he
says, even of his body. Sometimes he sees himself as tall and rising
upward and sometimes he sees himself as pushing downward.

I see him as stretched taut.

He said, "You long to see yourself from without, but the more you
look, the more you see yourself from within."

We were having tea in our favorite cafeteria. Suddenly, looking at him, I said, "I'd like to do a portrait of you. You know I write about you in my diary. Why shouldn't I publish it?"

He was silent, as if he could not think of anything to say, which I had never seen happen to him. Then he said, "Sure. Do it. It'll be interesting to see how you screw up the self-satire."

"I'll have to try hard."

"You don't know me. So fine, do it."

"I can invent what I don't know."

"It'll all be fiction anyway, David." He offered me a pen. "Why don't you take notes as we talk?"

"I'll remember the important things. You can count on me."

Looking at me from an angle, he said, "You wouldn't hurt a virtuous, innocent man like me, would you, David?"

I raised my hand and made a wide gesture, as if canceling out something, and said, "Oh, no."

"You bastard," he said. "You really are totally untrustworthy. You're worse than I am. It's true about you, you're not a nice boy at all."

I laughed.

"You want another cup of tea?" he asked.

I realized my laugh was forced.

While he was at the counter getting the tea, it came over me that I'd made a mistake. I thought: This is really going to make me self-conscious, and perhaps it'll be the end of our friendship. I tried to laugh again when he came back, as if nervously anticipating something he'd say that would make me laugh.

He served me the cup of tea and said, "Here. Anything you want." He sat. "I'm going to spend a lot of time now showing you how generous I can be. Have I never told you about my admirable acts of generosity and kindness? You want a piece of cake with your tea?"

His joking made me laugh in earnest, and he became completely unguarded. I wondered if it was *because* he knew I wanted to write down everything he told me that he was so open.

Writing, sex, teaching are all playgrounds, all play, he says. The thing is, they're serious games. If they were just played for fun, they'd be boring. And if you *took* writing, sex, teaching seriously, they'd be boring.

He's never wanted a baby, a family. No one has ever convinced
him that a family could be a playground.

He asked, "Why can't I take it easy now that I've finished a novel?
Why can't I enjoy myself? Museums, theaters, restaurants, *Frivolous*
games."

"Don't you think we're strange," I said, "because, for some
reason, we have to write down everything we do, think, feel?"

"*You're* strange," he said. "I'm straight."

**May 15, 1983**   Philip is a man completely devoid of femininity,
of sexual ambiguity.

He said to me today, "You should call your portrait of me 'Straight
Man.' "

He often says to me, "Between you, me and the diary." We are
enjoying ourselves.

He said, "I've always been intrigued by the Other. Why did I go to
a nice Christian college? Not because I wanted to be like them, but
because I wanted to find out what they were like. Now, after being
away for so long, America is becoming *other.*"

We were in the R.A.C., the club on Pall Mall where he goes to
swim every morning. He's taken a room there to write—just for a
while, for the change. It was a Saturday morning, and the vast public
rooms were empty. We stopped outside the billiard room and looked
in through the little windows in the brass-studded, leather doors.

"My guests are playing," he said.

**May 20, 1983**   Philip told me about the two and a half years
when agonizing pain in his shoulder reduced his life to practically
nothing.

I thought, Then you don't invent everything, as you say, and
Zuckerman's pain is yours.

"I hit bottom," he said.

"What saved you?"

"Claire did."

He said, as if discovering something, that there is *so* much physical
suffering in his books, that so many of his characters are in pain. He
frowned deeply when he said this.

**September 10, 1983**   Yesterday, I sat on a little, hard, wooden
chair before Philip's desk. As he turned on his desk lamp and sat, he
asked, "Are you ready for this?"

I laughed.

I had given him my last novel. He said he'd only had time so far to read the first chapter. Everything I'd cut (crossed out lightly so he could read underneath) he said I should put back in.

"It's interesting," he said, "all the information about where the narrator comes from. But otherwise, David, these pages are lifeless. I've been thinking about your writing: sensations without associations. My work is all associations."

I knew what he meant. His work refers at all times to the world outside, and mine doesn't.

I said, "I feel I'm a person entirely without associations. If, say, I mention World War Two, I have to create the war *in* my book, as if no one *outside* the book has ever heard of it."

Philip put his hand to the side of his mouth and whispered, "Let me tell you: We've all heard of World War Two."

"But I'm not sure my characters have. The only way I can trust myself in my writing is if I reduce all the thoughts and feelings to nothing but sensations."

"I understand," he said. "I can only trust my thoughts, my feelings, my ideas in my writing when I can turn them into comedy. You've got to trust yourself more. Trust your confusion."

"Don't you think about the shape of the novel?"

He said, firmly, "Don't use that word again—O.K?" Then he smiled. "Stop constraining yourself so. Who're you writing for? Your professor?"

"Of course I want life in my writing, but I'm really terrified that all the life I want in it will appear fake, so I reduce the writing to the lowest vibration. I repeat words over and over."

"I don't like your repetitions. It's a boring device. Not repetitions—but the *opposite*: variety, surprise, the *unexpected*."

"I'll tell you the truth about repetitions. If I write, say, 'desperate' three times—and this most often happens with abstract words—I feel I've at least got it down, even though I still don't quite know what it means. I was brought up without any real language."

"And you think I was? I come from nowhere, too, my friend. I had to learn out of *nothing*. Even now, in conversation, I'll find the most ordinary word will suddenly put me in doubt. 'Is this really what I mean—is this English?' I stop short and wonder if it's 'instinct' I mean

or do I mean 'intuition'? We're hicks. We're real hicks. It's just
because we're such hicks that we've all become so sophisticated.
Look at John Updike. Shillington, Pennsylvania. John's the biggest
hick of us all, and he's the best writer of us all."

As I was leaving, he said, "I hope I haven't been too hard on
you."

I stepped toward him and, I felt, he drew back a little, as if startled.

"No," I said. "I don't know how or why, but you reassure me."

Later, at home, I rang him to ask what the two words are that he
can't distinguish, and he said, "You're not writing that down, are
you? To show what an illiterate I am? To reveal the truth about my
verbal skills? Oh, David, you really are a bastard."

**October 5, 1983**    Claire and Philip have gone to America. He
left me with a proof copy of *The Anatomy Lesson,* which I've read
again. I imagine telling him this:

"You know, you're *not* Nathan Zuckerman. From time to time I
thought you were. The fact is, you're too far removed from yourself
to write about yourself as you really are. You think you can't see
outside yourself, but you do, you see this thin, dark man whom you,
from your distance, describe as incapable of seeing outside himself.
What I keep forgetting about you, and shouldn't, is that when you
talk about yourself digging a hole and shining a flashlight into it
you're talking just to try it on for five minutes to see what it looks like,
then you decide it doesn't really suit you, but some man who exists
in your scrutiny of him. You're not, with each novel, getting in closer
to yourself so that you can't see yourself, you're drawing further and
further away to see someone else. And in *The Anatomy Lesson,* I
think you're drawn so far away you've left Zuckerman at that zero
point where he's entirely on his own, and I feel compassionate
toward him for simply surviving your looking at him."

After all, I don't imagine telling Philip this. I imagine him picking up
a magazine and reading it.

# The Art of Fiction LXXXIV:
# Philip Roth

## Hermione Lee/1984

*I met Philip Roth after I had published a short book about his work for the Methuen Contemporary Writers Series. He read the book and wrote me a generous letter. After our first meeting, he sent me the fourth draft of* The Anatomy Lesson *which we later talked about, because, in the final stages of writing a novel, Roth likes to get as much criticism and response as he can from a few interested readers. Just after he finished* The Anatomy Lesson *we began the Paris Review interview. We met in the early summer of 1983 at the Royal Automobile Club in Pall Mall, where Roth occasionally takes a room to work in when he's visiting England. The room had been turned into a small, meticulously organized office—IBM golfball typewriter, alphabetical file holders, anglepoise lamps, dictionaries, aspirin, copyholder, felt tip pens for correcting, a radio—with a few books on the mantlepiece, among them the recently published autobiography by Irving Howe,* A Margin of Hope, *Erik Erikson's* Young Man Luther: A Study in Psychoanalysis and History, *Leonard Woolf's autobiography, David Magarshak's* Chekhov, *John Cheever's* Oh What A Paradise It Seems, *Fordyce's* Behavioural Methods for Chronic Pain and Illness *(useful for Zuckerman), Claire Bloom's autobiography* Limelight and After, *and some Paris Review interviews. We talked in this businesslike cell for a day and a half, pausing only for meals. I was looked after with great thoughtfulness. Roth's manner, which matches his appearance—subdued, conventional clothes, gold-rimmed spectacles, the look of a quiet professional American visitor to London, perhaps an academic or a lawyer—is courteous, mild, and responsive. He listens carefully to everything, makes lots of quick jokes, and likes to be amused. Just underneath*

*this benign appearance there is a ferocious concentration and mental*
*rapacity; everything is grist for his mill, no vagueness is tolerated,*
*differences of opinion are pounced on greedily, and nothing that*
*might be useful is let slip. Thinking on his feet, he develops his ideas*
*through a playful use of figurative language—as much as a way of*
*avoiding confessional answers (though he can be very direct) as of*
*interesting himself. The transcripts from this taped conversation were*
*long, absorbing, funny, disorganized, and repetitive. I edited them*
*down to a manageable size and sent my version on to him. Then*
*there was a long pause while he went back to America and* The
Anatomy Lesson *was published. Early in 1984, on his next visit to*
*England, we resumed; he revised my version and we talked about*
*the revision until it acquired its final form. I found this process*
*extremely interesting. The mood of the interview had changed in the*
*six months between his finishing a novel and starting new work; it*
*became more combative and buoyant. And the several drafts in*
*themselves displayed Roth's methods of work: raw chunks of talk*
*were processed into stylish, energetic, concentrated prose, and the*
*return to past thoughts generated new ideas. The result provides an*
*example, as well as an account, of Philip Roth's presentation of*
*himself.*

*How do you get started on a new book?*
   Beginning a book is unpleasant. I'm entirely uncertain about the
character and the predicament, and a character in his predicament is
what I have to begin with. Worse than not knowing your subject is
not knowing how to treat it, because that's finally everything. I type
out beginnings and they're awful, more of an unconscious parody of
my previous book than the break-away from it that I want. I need
something driving down the center of a book, a magnet to draw
everything to it—that's what I look for during the first months of
writing something new. I often have to write a hundred pages or
more before there's a paragraph that's alive. Okay, I say to myself,
that's your beginning, start there; that's the first paragraph of the
book. I'll go over the first six months of work and underline in red a
paragraph, a sentence, sometimes no more than a phrase, that has
some life in it, and then I'll type all these out on one page. Usually it
doesn't come to more than one page, but if I'm lucky, that's the start

of page one. I look for the liveliness to set the tone. After the awful
beginning come the months of freewheeling play, and after the play
comes the crises, turning against your material and hating the book.

*How much of a book is in your mind before you start?*
What matters most isn't there at all. I don't mean the solutions to
problems, I mean the problems themselves. You're looking, as you
begin, for what's going to resist you. You're looking for trouble.
Sometimes in the beginning uncertainty arises not because the
writing is difficult, but because it isn't difficult enough. Fluency can be
a sign that nothing is happening; fluency can actually be my signal to
stop, while being in the dark from sentence to sentence is what
convinces me to go on.

*Must you have a beginning? Would you ever begin with an end-ing?*
For all I know I *am* beginning with the ending. My page one can
wind up a year later as page two hundred, if it's still even around.

*What happens to those hundred or so pages that you have left
over? Do you save them up?*
I generally prefer never to see them again.

*Do you work best at any particular time of the day?*
I work all day, morning and afternoon, just about every day. If I sit
there like that for two or three years, at the end I have a book.

*Do you think other writers work such long hours?*
I don't ask writers about their work habits. I really don't care. Joyce
Carol Oates says somewhere that when writers ask each other what
time they start working and when they finish and how much time
they take for lunch, they're actually trying to find out "Is he as crazy
as I am?" I don't need that question answered.

*Does your reading affect what you write?*
I read all the time when I'm working, usually at night. It's a way of
keeping the circuits open. It's a way of thinking about my *line* of work
while getting a little rest from the work at hand. It helps inasmuch as
it fuels the overall obsession.

*Do you show your work-in-progress to anyone?*

It's more useful for my mistakes to ripen and burst in their own good time. I give myself all the opposition I need while I'm writing, and praise is meaningless to me when I know something isn't even half finished. Nobody sees what I'm doing until I absolutely can't go any further and might even like to believe that I'm done.

*Do you have a Roth reader in mind when you write?*
No. I occasionally have an anti-Roth reader in mind. I think, "How he is going to hate this!" That can be just the encouragement I need.

*You spoke of the last phase of writing a novel being a "crisis" in which you turn against the material and hate the work. Is there always this crisis, with every book?*
Always. Months of looking at the manuscript and saying, "This is wrong—but what's wrong?" I ask myself, "If this book were a dream, it would be a dream of what?" But when I'm asking this I'm also trying to *believe* in what I've written, to forget that it's writing and to say, "This *has* taken place," even if it hasn't. The idea is to perceive your invention as a reality that can be understood as a dream. The idea is to turn flesh and blood into literary characters and literary characters into flesh and blood.

*Can you say more about these crises?*
In *The Ghost Writer* the crisis—one among many—had to do with Zuckerman, Amy Bellette, and Anne Frank. It wasn't easy to see that Amy Bellette *as* Anne Frank was Zuckerman's own creation. Only by working through numerous alternatives did I decide that not only was she his creation, but that she might possibly be her own creation too, a young woman inventing herself *within* Zuckerman's invention. To enrich his fantasy without obfuscation or muddle, to be ambiguous *and* clear—well, that was my writing problem through one whole summer and fall. In *Zuckerman Unbound* the crisis was a result of failing to see that Zuckerman's father shouldn't already be dead when the book begins. I eventually realized that the death should come at the conclusion of the book, allegedly as a consequence of the son's blasphemous best-seller. But, starting off, I'd got the thing back to front, and then I stared at it dumbly for months, seeing nothing. I knew that I wanted the book to veer away from Alvin Pepler—I like to be steamrolling along in one direction and then to

spring my surprise—but I couldn't give up the premise of my earliest drafts until I saw that the novel's obsessive concern with assassinations, death threats, funerals, and funeral homes, was leading up to, rather than away from, the death of Zuckerman's father. How you juxtapose the events can tie you in knots and rearranging the sequence can free you suddenly to streak for the finish line. In *The Anatomy Lesson* the discovery I made—having banged the typewriter with my head far too long—was that Zuckerman, in the moment that he takes flight for Chicago to try to become a doctor, should begin to impersonate a pornographer. There had to be willed extremism at either end of the moral spectrum, each of his escape-dreams of self-transformation subverting the meaning and mocking the intention of the other. If he had gone off solely to become a doctor, driven only by that high moral ardor, or, if he had just gone around impersonating a pornographer, spewing only that anarchic and alienating rage, he wouldn't have been my man. He has two dominant modes: his mode of self-abnegation, and his fuck-'em mode. You want a bad Jewish boy, that's what you're going to get. He rests from one by taking up the other; though, as we see, it's not much of a rest. The thing about Zuckerman that interests me is that everybody's split, but few so openly as this. Everybody is full of cracks and fissures, but usually we see people trying very hard to hide the places where they're split. Most people desperately want to heal their lesions, and keep trying to. Hiding them is sometimes taken for healing them (or for not having them). But Zuckerman can't successfully do either, and by the end of the trilogy has proved it even to himself. What's determined his life and his work are the lines of fracture in what is by no means a clean break. I was interested in following those lines.

*What happens to Philip Roth when he turns into Nathan Zuckerman?*

Nathan Zuckerman is an act. It's all the art of impersonation, isn't it? That's the fundamental novelistic gift. Zuckerman is a writer who wants to be a doctor impersonating a pornographer. I am a writer writing a book impersonating a writer who wants to be a doctor impersonating a pornographer—who then, to compound the impersonation, to barb the edge, pretends he's a well-known literary critic. Making fake biography, false history, concocting a half-imaginary existence out of the actual drama of my life *is* my life. There has to be some pleasure in this job, and that's it. To go around in disguise. To act a character. To pass oneself off as what one is not. To *pretend.* The sly and cunning masquerade. Think of the ventriloquist. He speaks so that his voice appears to proceed from someone at a distance from himself. But if he weren't in your line of vision you'd get no pleasure from his art at all. His art consists of being present *and* absent; he's most himself by simultaneously being someone else, neither of whom he "is" once the curtain is down. You don't necessarily, as a writer, have to abandon your biography completely to engage in an act of impersonation. It may be more intriguing when you don't. You distort it, caricature it, parody it, you torture and subvert it, you exploit it—all to give the biography that dimension that will excite your verbal life. Millions of people do this all the time, of course, and not with the justification of making literature. They *mean* it. It's amazing what lies people can sustain behind the mask of their real faces. Think of the art of the adulterer: under tremendous pressure and against enormous odds, ordinary husbands and wives, who would freeze with self-consciousness up on a stage, yet in the theater of the home, alone before the audience of the betrayed spouse, they act out roles of innocence and fidelity with flawless dramatic skill. Great, great performances, conceived with genius down to the smallest particulars, impeccably meticulous naturalistic acting, and all done by rank amateurs. People beautifully pretending to be "themselves." Make-believe can take the subtlest forms, you know. Why should a novelist, a pretender by profession, be any less deft or more reliable than a stolid unimaginative suburban accountant cheating on his wife? Jack Benny used to pretend to be a miser, remember? Called himself by his own good name and claimed that he was stingy and mean. It excited his comic imagination to do this. He probably wasn't all that funny as just another nice fellow writing checks to the U.J.A. and taking his friends out to dinner. Céline pretended to be a rather indifferent, even irresponsible physician when he seems in fact to have worked hard at his practice and to have been conscientious about his patients. But that wasn't interesting.

*But it is. Being a good doctor is interesting.*

For William Carlos Williams maybe, but not for Céline. Being a devoted husband, an intelligent father, and a dedicated family physician in Rutherford, New Jersey, might have seemed as admirable to Céline as it does to you, or to me for that matter, but *his* writing drew its vigor from the demotic voice and the dramatization of his outlaw side (which was considerable), and so he created the Céline of the great novels in somewhat the way Jack Benny, also flirting with the taboo, created himself as a miser. You have to be awfully naive not to understand that a writer is a performer who puts on the act he does best—not least when he dons the mask of the first-person singular. That may be the best mask of all for a second self. Some (many) pretend to be more lovable than they are and some pretend to be less. Beside the point. Literature isn't a moral beauty contest. Its power arises from the authority and audacity with which the impersonation is pulled off; the belief it inspires is what counts. The question to ask about the writer isn't "Why does he behave so badly?" but "What does he gain by wearing this mask?" I don't admire the Genet that Genet presents as himself any more than I admire the unsavory Molloy impersonated by Beckett. I admire Genet because he writes books that won't let me forget who that Genet is. When Rebecca West was writing about Augustine, she said that his *Confessions* was too subjectively true to be objectively true. I think this is so in the first-person novels of Genet and Céline, as it is in Colette, books like *The Shackle* and *The Vagabond.* Gombrowicz has a novel called *Pornografia* in which he introduces himself as a character, using his own name—the better to implicate himself in certain highly dubious proceedings and bring the moral terror to life. Konwicki, another Pole, in his last two novels, *The Polish Complex* and *A Minor Apocalypse,* works to close the gap between the reader and the narrative by introducing "Konwicki" as the central character. He strengthens the illusion that the novel is true—and not to be discounted as "fiction"—by impersonating himself. It all goes back to Jack Benny. Need I add, however, that it's hardly a disinterested undertaking? Writing for me isn't a natural thing that I just keep doing, the way fish swim and birds fly. It's something that's done under a certain kind of provocation, a particular urgency. It's the transformation, through an elaborate impersonation, of a personal emergency into a public act (in both senses of that word). It can be a

very trying spiritual exercise to siphon through your being qualities
that are alien to your moral makeup—as trying for the writer as
for the reader. You can wind up feeling more like a sword-swallower
than a ventriloquist or impersonator. You sometimes use yourself
very harshly in order to reach what is, literally speaking, beyond you.
The impersonator can't afford to indulge the ordinary human instincts which direct people in what they want to present and what
they want to hide.

*If the novelist is an impersonator, then what about the autobiogra-
phy? What is the relationship, for example, between the deaths of the
parents, which are so important in the last two Zuckerman novels,
and the death of your own parents?*

Why not ask about the relationship between the death of my
parents and the death of Gabe Wallach's mother, the germinating
incident in my 1962 novels, *Letting Go?* Or ask about the death and
funeral of the father, at the heart of my first published story, "The
Day It Snowed," which appeared in the *Chicago Review* in 1955? Or
ask about the death of Kepesh's mother, wife of the owner of a
Catskill hotel, which is the turning point in *The Professor of Desire?*
The terrible blow of the death of a parent is something I began
writing about long before any parent of mine had died. Novelists are
frequently as interested in what hasn't happened to them as in what
has. What may be taken by the innocent for naked autobiography is,
as I've been suggesting, more than likely mock-autobiography or
hypothetical autobiography or autobiography grandiosely enlarged.
We know about the people who walk into the police station and
confess to crimes they haven't committed. Well, the false confession
appeals to writers, too. Novelists are even interested in what happens
to other people and, like liars and con men everywhere, will pretend
that something dramatic or awful or hair-raising or splendid that
happened to someone else actually happened to them. The physical
particulars and moral circumstances of Zuckerman's mother's death
have practically nothing to do with the death of my own mother. The
death of the mother of one of my dearest friends—whose account of
her suffering stuck in my mind long after he'd told me about it—
furnished the most telling details for the mother's death in *The
Anatomy Lesson.* The black cleaning woman who commiserates with

Zuckerman in Miami Beach about his mother's death is modeled on
the housekeeper of old friends in Philadelphia, a woman I haven't
seen for ten years and who never laid eyes on anybody in my family
but me. I was always entranced by her tangy style of speech, and
when the right moment came, I used it. But the words in her mouth I
invented. Olivia, the black eighty-three-year-old Florida cleaning
woman, *c'est moi.*

As you well know, the intriguing biographical issue—and critical
issue, for that matter—isn't that a writer will write about some of what
has happened to him, but *how* he writes about it, which, when
understood properly, takes us a long way to understanding *why* he
writes about it. A more intriguing question is why and how he writes
about what hasn't happened—how he feeds what's hypothetical or
imagined into what's inspired and controlled by recollection, and
how what's recollected spawns the overall fantasy. I suggest, by the
way, that the best person to ask about the autobiographical relevance
of the climactic death of the father in *Zuckerman Unbound* is my
own father, who lives in Elizabeth, New Jersey. I'll give you his phone
number.

*Then what is the relationship between your experience of psychoa-
nalysis and the use of psychoanalysis as a literary strategem?*

If I hadn't been analyzed I wouldn't have written *Portnoy's Complaint* as I wrote it, or *My Life as a Man* as I wrote it, nor would
*The Breast* resemble itself. Nor would I resemble myself. The experience of psychoanalysis was probably more useful to me as a writer
than as a neurotic, although there may be a false distinction there. It's
an experience that I shared with tens of thousands of baffled people,
and anything that powerful in the private domain that joins a writer to
his generation, to his class, to his moment, is tremendously important
for him, providing that afterwards he can separate himself enough to
examine the experience objectively, imaginatively in the writing clinic.
You have to be able to become your doctor's doctor, even if only to
write about patienthood, which was, certainly in part, a subject in *My
Life as a Man.* Why patienthood interested me—and as far back as
*Letting Go,* written four or five years before my own analysis—
was because so many enlightened contemporaries had come to
accept the view of themselves as patients, and the ideas of psychic

disease, cure, and recovery. You're asking me about the relationship between art and life? It's like the relationship between the eight hundred or so hours that it took to be psychoanalyzed, and the eight or so hours that it would take to read *Portnoy's Complaint* aloud. Life is long and art is shorter.

*Can you talk about your marriage?*
It took place so long ago that I no longer trust my memory of it. The problem is complicated further by *My Life as a Man*, which diverges so dramatically in so many places from its origin in my own nasty situation that I'm hard put, some twenty-five years later, to sort out the invention of 1975 from the facts of 1959. You might as well ask the author of *The Naked and the Dead* what happened to him in the Philippines. I can only tell you that that was my time as an infantryman, and that *My Life as a Man* is the war novel I wrote some years after failing to receive the Distinguished Service Cross.

*Do you have painful feelings on looking back?*
Looking back I see these as fascinating years—as people of fifty often do contemplating the youthful adventure for which they paid with a decade of their lives a comfortingly long time ago. I was more aggressive then than I am today, some people were even said to be intimidated by me, but I was an easy target, all the same. We're easy targets at twenty-five, if only someone discovers the enormous bull's-eye.

*And where was it?*
Oh, where it can usually be found in self-confessed budding literary geniuses. My idealism. My romanticism. My passion to capitalize the L in life. I wanted something difficult and dangerous to happen to me. I wanted a hard time. Well, I got it. I'd come from a small, safe, relatively happy provincial background—my Newark neighborhood in the thirties and forties was just a Jewish Terre Haute—and I'd absorbed, along with the ambition and drive, the fears and phobias of my generation of American Jewish children. In my early twenties, I wanted to prove to myself that I wasn't afraid of all those things. It wasn't a mistake to want to prove that, even though, after the ball was over, I was virtually unable to write for three or four years. From 1962 to 1967 is the longest I've gone, since

becoming a writer, without publishing a book. Alimony and recurrent
court costs had bled me of every penny I could earn by teaching
and writing, and, hardly into my thirties, I was thousands of dollars in
debt to my friend and editor, Joe Fox. The loan was to help pay for
my analysis, which I needed primarily to prevent me from going out
and committing murder because of the alimony and court costs
incurred for having served two years in a childless marriage. The
image that teased me during those years was of a train that had been
shunted onto the wrong track. In my early twenties, I had been
zipping right along there, you know—on schedule, express stops
only, final destination clearly in mind; and then suddenly I was on the
wrong track, speeding off into the wilds. I'd ask myself, "How the
hell do you get this thing back on the right track?" Well, you can't.
I've continued to be surprised, over the years, whenever I discover
myself, late at night, pulling into the wrong station.

*But not getting back on the same track was a great thing for you,
presumably.*
John Berryman said that for a writer any ordeal that doesn't kill
him is terrific. The fact that his ordeal did finally kill him doesn't make
what he was saying wrong.

*What do you feel about feminism, particularly the feminist attack
on you?*
What is it?

*The force of the attack would be, in part, that the female charac-
ters are unsympathetically treated, for instance that Lucy Nelson in*
When She Was Good *is hostilely presented.*
Don't elevate that by calling it a "feminist" attack. That's just
stupid reading. Lucy Nelson is a furious adolescent who wants a
decent life. She is presented as better than her world and conscious
of being better. She is confronted and opposed by men who typify
deeply irritating types to many women. She is the protector of a
passive, defenseless mother whose vulnerability drives her crazy. She
happens to be raging against aspects of middle-class American life
that the new militant feminism was to identify as the enemy only a
few years after Lucy's appearance in print—hers might even be
thought of as a case of premature feminist rage. *When She Was*

*Good* deals with Lucy's struggle to free herself from the terrible
disappointment engendered in a daughter by an irresponsible father.
It deals with her hatred of the father he was and her yearning for the
father he couldn't be. It would be sheer idiocy, particularly if this
*were* a feminist attack, to contend that such powerful feelings of loss
and contempt and shame do not exist in the daughters of drunks,
cowards, and criminals. There is also the helpless Mama's boy Lucy
marries, and her hatred of his incompetence and professional innocence. Is there no such thing in the world as marital hatred? That will
come as news to all the rich divorce lawyers, not to mention Thomas
Hardy and Gustave Flaubert. By the way, is Lucy's father treated
"hostilely" because he's a drunk and a petty thief who ends up in
jail? Is Lucy's husband treated "hostilely" because he happens to be
a big baby? Is the uncle who tries to destroy Lucy "hostilely" treated
because he's a brute? This is a novel about a wounded daughter who
has more than sufficient cause to be enraged with the men in her life.
She is only "hostilely" presented if it's an act of hostility to recognize
that young women can be wounded and young women can be
enraged. I'd bet there are even some enraged and wounded women
who are feminists. You know, the dirty little secret is no longer sex;
the dirty little secret is hatred and rage. It's the tirade that's taboo.
Odd that this should be so a hundred years after Dostoyevsky (and
fifty after Freud), but nobody nice likes to be identified with the stuff.
It's the way folks used to feel about fellatio in the good old days.
"Me? Never heard of it. Disgusting." But is it "hostile," really, to take
a look at the ferocity of the emotion they call "hostility"? *When She
Was Good* is not serving the cause—that's true. The anger of this
young woman isn't presented to be endorsed with a hearty "Right
on!" that will move the populace to action. The nature of the anger is
examined, as is the depth of the wound. So are the consequences of
the anger, for Lucy as for everyone. I hate to have to be the one to
say it, but the portrait isn't without its poignancy. I don't mean by
poignancy what the compassionate book reviewers call "compassion." I mean you see the suffering that real rage is.

*But supposing I say to you that nearly all the women in the books
are there to obstruct, or to help, or to console the male characters.
There's the woman who cooks and consoles and is sane and calm-*

*ing, or the other kind of woman, the dangerous maniac, the obstruc-*
*tor. They occur as means of helping or obstructing Kepesh or Zucker-*
*man or Tarnopol. And that could be seen as a limited view of*
*women.*

Let's face it, some women who are sane also happen to know how
to cook. So do some of the dangerous maniacs. Let's leave out the
sin of cooking. A great book on the order of *Oblomov* could be
written about a man allying himself with woman after woman who
gorge him with marvelous meals, but I haven't written it. If your
description of the "sane," "calm," and "consoling" woman applies
to anyone, it's to Claire Ovington in *The Professor of Desire*, with
whom Kepesh establishes a tender liaison some years after the
breakup of his marriage. Now, I'd have no objection to your writing a
novel about this relationship from the point of view of Claire Ovington—I'd be intrigued to see how she saw it—so why do you take a
slightly critical tone about my writing the novel from the point of view
of David Kepesh?

*There's nothing wrong with the novel's being written from David*
*Kepesh's point of view. What might cause difficulties for some read-*
*ers is that Claire, and the other women in the novel, are there to help*
*or hinder him.*

I'm not pretending to give you anything other than his sense of his
life with this young woman. My book doesn't stand or fall on the
fact that Claire Ovington is calm and sane, but on whether I am able
to depict what calmness and sanity are like, and what it is to have a
mate—and why it is one would want a mate—who possesses those
and other virtues in abundance. She is also vulnerable to jealousy
when Kepesh's ex-wife turns up uninvited, and she carries with her a
certain sadness about her family background. She isn't there "as a
means" of helping Kepesh. She *helps* him—and he helps her. *They*
*are in love.* She is there because Kepesh has fallen in love with a
sane and calm and consoling woman after having been unhappily
married to a difficult and exciting woman he was unable to handle.
Don't people do that? Someone more doctrinaire than you might tell
me that the state of being in love, particularly of being passionately in
love, is no basis for establishing permanent relationships between
men and women. But, alas, people, even people of intelligence and

experience, *will* do it—have done it and seem intent on going on
doing it—and I am not interested in writing about what people
*should* do for the good of the human race and pretending that's what
they *do* do, but writing about what they do indeed do, lacking the
programmatic efficiency of the infallible theorists. The irony of Kepesh's situation is that having found the calm and consoling woman
he can live with, a woman of *numerous* qualities, he then finds his
desire for her perversely seeping away, and realizes that unless this
involuntary diminution of passion can be arrested, he'll become
alienated from the best thing in his life. Doesn't that happen either?
From what I hear this damn seeping away of desire happens all the
time and is extremely distressing to the people involved. Look, I
didn't invent the loss of desire, and I didn't invent the lure of passion,
and I didn't invent sane companions, and I didn't invent maniacs. I'm
sorry if my men don't have the correct feelings about women, or the
universal range of feelings about women, or the feelings about
women that it will be okay for men to have in 1995, but I do insist
that there is some morsel of truth in my depiction of what it might be
like for a man to be a Kepesh, or a Portnoy, or a breast.

*Why have you never reused the character of Portnoy in another
book, the way that you have used Kepesh and Zuckerman?*

But I did use Portnoy in another book. *Our Gang* and *The Great
American Novel* are Portnoy in another book. Portnoy wasn't a
character for me, he was an explosion, and I wasn't finished explod-
ing after *Portnoy's Complaint*. The first thing I wrote after *Portnoy's
Complaint* was a long story called "On the Air" that appeared in Ted
Solotaroff's *American Review*. John Updike was here a while ago
and while we were all having dinner one night, he said, "How come
you've never reprinted that story?" I said, "It's too disgusting." John
laughed. He said, "It is, it's a truly disgusting story." And I said, "I
didn't know what I was thinking about when I wrote it." And that is
true to some degree—I didn't want to know; the idea was *not* to
know. But I also did know. I looked in the arsenal and found another
dynamite stick, and I thought, "Light the fuse and see what happens." I was trying to blow up more of myself. This phenomenon is
known to students of literary survey courses as the writer changing
his style. I was blowing up a lot of old loyalties and inhibitions,

literary as well as personal. I think this may be why so many Jews
were incensed by *Portnoy's Complaint.* It wasn't that they'd never
heard about kids masturbating before, or about Jewish family fighting. It was, rather, that if they couldn't even control someone like me
anymore, with all my respectable affiliations and credentials, all my
Seriousness of Purpose, something had gone wrong. After all, I
wasn't Abbie Hoffman or Lenny Bruce, I was a university teacher
who had published in *Commentary.* But at the time it seemed to me
that the next thing to be serious about was not being so goddamn
serious. As Zuckerman reminds Appel, "Seriousness can be as stupid
as anything else."

*Weren't you also looking for a fight, writing* Portnoy's Complaint?
I'd found a fight without looking for it long before that. They never
really got off my ass for publishing *Goodbye, Columbus,* which was
considered in some circles to be my *Mein Kampf.* Unlike Alexander
Portnoy, my education in petit bourgeois morality didn't come at
home, but after I'd left home and begun to publish my first short
stories. My own household environment as a youngster was much
closer to Zuckerman's than to Portnoy's. It had its constraints, but
there was nothing resembling the censorious small-mindedness and
shame-ridden xenophobia that I ran into from the official Jews
who wanted me to shut up. The moral atmosphere of the Portnoy
household, in its repressive aspects, owes a lot to the response of
persistent voices within the official Jewish community to my debut.
They did much to help make it seem auspicious.

*You've been talking about the opposition to* Portnoy's Complaint.
*What about the recognition—how did its enormous success affect
you?*
It was too big, on a larger and much crazier scale than I could
begin to deal with, so I took off. A few weeks after publication,
I boarded a bus at the Port Authority terminal for Saratoga Springs,
and holed up at Yaddo, the writer's colony, for three months. Precisely what Zuckerman should have done after *Carnovsky*—but he
hung around, the fool, and look what happened to him. He would
have enjoyed Yaddo more than he enjoyed Alvin Pepler. But it made
*Zuckerman Unbound* funnier keeping him in Manhattan, and it made
my own life easier, not being there.

*Do you dislike New York?*

I lived there from 1962 until I moved to the country after *Portnoy's Complaint*, and I wouldn't trade those years for anything. New York *gave* me *Portnoy's Complaint* in a way. When I was living and teaching in Iowa City and Princeton, I didn't ever feel so free as I did in New York, in the sixties, to indulge myself in comic performance, on paper and with friends. There were raucous evenings with my New York friends, there was uncensored shamelessness in my psychoanalytic sessions, there was the dramatic, stagey atmosphere of the city itself in the years after Kennedy's assassination—all this inspired me to try out a new voice, a fourth voice, a less page-bound voice than the voice of *Goodbye, Columbus*, or of *Letting Go*, or of *When She Was Good*. So did the opposition to the war in Vietnam. There's always something behind a book to which it has no seeming connection, something invisible to the reader which has helped to release the writer's initial impulse. I'm thinking about the rage and rebelliousness that were in the air, the vivid examples I saw around me of angry defiance and hysterical opposition. This gave me a few ideas for my act.

*Did you feel you were part of what was going on in the sixties?*

I felt the power of the life around me. I believed myself to be feeling the full consciousness of a place—this time New York—for the first time really since childhood. I was also, like others, receiving a stunning education in moral, political, and cultural possibilities from the country's eventful public life and from what was happening in Vietnam.

*But you published a famous essay in* Commentary *in 1960 called "Writing American Fiction" about the way that intellectuals or thinking people in America felt that they were living in a foreign country, a country in whose communal life they were not involved.*

Well, that's the difference between 1960 and 1968. (Being published in *Commentary* is another difference.) Alienated in America, a stranger to its pleasures and preoccupations—that was how many young people like me saw their situation in the fifties. It was a perfectly honorable stance, I think, shaped by our literary aspirations and modernist enthusiasms, the high-minded of the second post-immigrant generation coming into conflict with the first great eruption of postwar media garbage. Little did we know that some twenty years later the philistine ignorance on which we would have liked to turn our backs would infect the country like Camus's plague. Any satirist writing a futuristic novel who had imagined a President Reagan during the Eisenhower years would have been accused of perpetrating a piece of crude, contemptible, adolescent, anti-American wickedness, when, in fact, he would have succeeded, as prophetic sentry, just where Orwell failed; he would have seen that the grotesquery to be visited upon the English-speaking world would not be an extension of the repressive Eastern totalitarian nightmare but a proliferation of the Western farce of media stupidity and cynical commercialism—American-style philistinism run amok. It wasn't Big Brother who'd be watching us from the screen, but we who'd be watching a terrifyingly powerful world leader with the soul of an amiable, soap opera grandmother, the values of a civic-minded Beverly Hills Cadillac dealer, and the historical background and intellectual equipment of a high school senior in a June Allyson musical.

*What happened to you later, in the seventies? Did what was happening in the country continue to mean much to someone like you?*

I have to remember what book I was writing and then I can remember what happened to me—though what was happening to me was largely the book I was writing. Nixon came and went in '73, and while Nixon was coming and going I was being driven quite crazy by *My Life as a Man*. In a way I had been writing that book on and off since 1964. I kept looking for a setting for the sordid scene in which Maureen buys a urine specimen from a poor pregnant black woman in order to get Tarnopol to think he's impregnated her. I thought of it first as a scene for *When She Was Good*, but it was all wrong for Lucy and Roy in Liberty Center. Then I thought it might go into *Portnoy's Complaint*, but it was too malevolent for that kind of comedy. Then I wrote cartons and cartons of drafts of what eventually turned out to be *My Life as a Man*—eventually, after I finally realized that my solution lay in the very problem I couldn't overcome: my inability to find the setting appropriate to the sordid event, rather than the sordid event itself, was really at the heart of the novel. Watergate made life interesting when I wasn't writing, but from nine to five every day I didn't think too much about Nixon or about Vietnam. I was trying to solve the problem of this book. When it seemed I never would, I stopped and wrote *Our Gang;* when I tried again and still couldn't write it, I stopped and wrote the baseball book; then while finishing the baseball book, I stopped to write *The Breast.* It was as though I were blasting my way through a tunnel to reach the novel that I couldn't write. Each of one's books *is* a blast, clearing the way for what's next. It's all one book you write anyway. At night you dream six dreams. But *are* they six dreams? One dream prefigures or anticipates the next, or somehow concludes what hasn't yet even been fully dreamed. Then comes the next dream, the corrective of the dream before—the alternative dream, the antidote dream—enlarging upon it, or laughing at it, or contradicting it, or trying just to get the dream *right.* You can go on trying all night long.

*After* Portnoy, *after leaving New York, you moved to the country. What about rural life? Obviously it was used as material in* The Ghost Writer.

I might never have become interested in writing about a reclusive writer if I hadn't first had my own small taste of E. I. Lonoff's thirty-five years of rural splendor. I need something solid under my feet to kick off my imagination. But aside from giving me a sense of the Lonoffs' lives, the country existence hasn't offered anything as yet in the way of subject. Probably it never will and I should get the hell out. Only I happen to love living there, and I can't make *every* choice conform to the needs of my work.

*What about England, where you spend part of each year? Is that a possible source of fiction?*

Ask me twenty years from now. That's about how long it took Isaac Singer to get enough of Poland out of his system—and to let enough of America in—to begin, little by little, as a writer, to see and depict his upper Broadway cafeterias. If you don't know the fantasy life of a country, it's hard to write fiction about it that isn't just description of the decor, human and otherwise. Little things trickle through when I see the country dreaming out loud—in the theater, at an election, during the Falklands crisis, but I know nothing really about what means what to people here. It's very hard for me to understand who people are, even when they tell me, and I don't even know if that's *because* of who they are or because of me. I don't know who is impersonating what, if I'm necessarily seeing the real thing or just a fabrication, nor can I easily see where the two overlap. My perceptions are clouded by the fact that I speak the language. I believe I know what's being said, you see, even if I don't. Worst of all, I don't hate anything here. What a relief it is to have no culture-grievances, not to have to hear the sound of one's voice taking positions and having opinions and recounting all that's wrong! What bliss—but for the writing that's no asset. Nothing drives me crazy here, and a writer *has* to be driven crazy to help him to *see*. A writer needs his poisons. The antidote to his poisons is often a book. Now if I *had* to live here, if for some reason I were forbidden ever to return to America, if my position and my personal well-being were suddenly to become permanently bound up with England, well, what was maddening and meaningful might begin to come into focus, and yes, in about the year 2005, maybe 2010, little by little I'd stop writing about Newark and I would dare to set a story at a table in a wine bar on Kensington Park Road. A story about an elderly exiled foreign writer, in this instance reading not the *Jewish Daily Forward* but the *Herald Tribune*.

*In these last three books, the Zuckerman novels, there has been a reiteration of the struggle with Jewishness and Jewish criticism. Why do you think these books go over the past so much as they do? Why is that happening now?*

In the early seventies, I began to be a regular visitor to Czechoslovakia. I went to Prague every spring and took a little crash course in political repression. I'd only known repression firsthand in somewhat more benign and covert forms—as psychosexual constraint or as social restriction. I knew less about anti-Semitic repression from personal experience than I did about the repressions Jews practiced upon themselves, and upon one another, as a consequence of the history of anti-Semitism. Portnoy, you remember, considers himself just such a practicing Jew. Anyway, I became highly attuned to the differences between the writer's life in totalitarian Prague and in free-wheeling New York, and I decided, after some initial uncertainty. to focus on the unreckoned consequences of a life in art in the world that I knew best. I realized that there were already many wonderful and famous stories and novels by Henry James and Thomas Mann and James Joyce about the life of the artist, but none I knew of about the comedy that an artistic vocation can turn out to be in the U.S.A. When Thomas Wolfe tackled the subject he was rather rhapsodic. Zuckerman's struggle with Jewishness and Jewish criticism is seen in the context of his comical career as an American writer, ousted by his family, alienated from his fans, and finally at odds with his own nerve endings. The Jewish quality of books like mine doesn't really reside in their subject matter. Talking about Jewishness hardly interests me at all. It's a kind of sensibility that makes, say, *The Anatomy Lesson* Jewish, if anything does: the nervousness, the excitability, the arguing, the dramatizing, the indignation, the obsessiveness, the touchiness, the play-acting—above all the *talking*. The talking and the shouting. Jews will go on, you know. It isn't what it's talking *about* that makes a book Jewish—it's that the book won't shut up. The book won't leave you alone. Won't let up. Gets too close. "Listen, listen—that's only the half of it!" I knew what I was doing when I broke Zuckerman's jaw. For a Jew a broken jaw is a terrible tragedy. It was to avoid this that so many of us went into teaching rather than prizefighting.

*Why is Milton Appel, the good, high-minded Jew who was a guru for Zuckerman in his early years, a punching-bag in* The Anatomy Lesson, *someone that Zuckerman wants to desanctify?*

If I were not myself, if someone else had been assigned the role of being Roth and writing his books, I might very well, in this other incarnation, have been his Milton Appel.

*Is Zuckerman's rage at Milton Appel the expression of a kind of guilt on your part?*

Guilt? Not at all. As a matter of fact, in an earlier draft of the book, Zuckerman and his young girlfriend Diana took exactly opposite positions in their argument about Appel. She, with all her feisty inexperience, said to Zuckerman, "Why do you let him push you around, why do you take this shit sitting down?" and Zuckerman, the older man, said to her, "Don't be ridiculous, Dear, calm down, he doesn't matter." There was the real autobiographical scene, and it had no life at all. I had to absorb the rage into the main character even if my own rage on this topic had long since subsided. By being true to life I was actually ducking the issue. So I reversed their positions, and had the twenty-year-old college girl telling Zuckerman to grow up, and gave Zuckerman the tantrum. Much more fun. I wasn't going to get anywhere with a Zuckerman as eminently reasonable as myself.

*So your hero always has to be enraged or in trouble or complaining.*
My hero has to be in a state of vivid transformation or radical displacement. "I am not what I am—I am, if anything, what I am not!" The litany begins something like that.

*How conscious are you as you are writing of whether you are moving from a third- to a first-person narrative?*
It's not conscious or unconscious—the movement is spontaneous.

*But how does it feel, to be writing in the third person as opposed to the first person?*
How does it feel looking through a microscope, when you adjust the focus? Everything depends upon how close you want to bring the naked object to the naked eye. And vice versa. Depends on what you want to magnify, and to what power.

*But do you free yourself in certain ways by putting Zuckerman in the third person?*
I free myself to say about Zuckerman what it would be inappropriate for him to say about himself in quite the same way. The irony would be lost in the first person, or the comedy; I can introduce a note of gravity that might be jarring coming from him. The shifting within a single narrative from the one voice to the other is how a reader's moral perspective is determined. It's something like this that we all want to do in ordinary conversation when we employ the indefinite pronoun "one" in speaking of ourselves. Using "one" places your observation in a looser relationship to the self that's uttering it. Look, sometimes it's more telling to let him speak for himself, sometimes it's more telling to speak about him; sometimes it's more telling to narrate obliquely, sometimes not. *The Ghost Writer* is narrated in the first person, probably because what's being described is largely a world Zuckerman's discovered outside of himself, the book of a young explorer. The older and more scarred

he gets, the more *inward*-looking he gets, the further out *I* have to get. The crisis of solipism he suffers in *The Anatomy Lesson* is better seen from a bit of a distance.

*Do you direct yourself as you are writing to make distinctions between what is spoken and what is narrative?*
I don't "direct" myself. I respond to what seem the liveliest possibilities. There's no necessary balance to be achieved between what is spoken and what is narrated and six lines of dialogue may be just the ticket for one writer, and two thousand pages of dialogue and six lines of narrative the solution for another.

*Do you ever take long chunks that have been dialogue and make them into narrative, or the other way around?*
Sure. I did that with the Anne Frank section of *The Ghost Writer*. I had trouble getting that right. When I began, in the third person, I was somehow *revering* the material. I was taking a high elegiac tone in telling the story of Anne Frank surviving and coming to America. I didn't know where I was going so I began by doing what you're supposed to do when writing the life of a saint. It was the tone appropriate to hagiography. Instead of Anne Frank gaining new meaning within the context of my story, I was trying to draw from the ready store of stock emotions that everybody is supposed to have about her. It's what even good actors sometimes will do during the first weeks of rehearsing a play—gravitate to the conventional form of presentation, cling to the cliché while anxiously waiting for something authentic to take hold. In retrospect, my difficulties look somewhat bizarre, because just what Zuckerman was fighting against, I was in fact succumbing to—the officially authorized and most consoling legend. I tell you, no one who later complained that in *The Ghost Writer* I had abused the memory of Anne Frank would have batted an eye had I let those banalities out into the world. That would have been just fine; I might even have got a citation. But I couldn't have given myself any prizes for it. The difficulties of telling a Jewish story—How should it be told? In what tone? To whom should it be told? To what end? Should it be told at all?—was finally to become *The Ghost Writer*'s theme. But before it became a theme, it apparently had to be an ordeal. It often happens, at least with me, that the struggles that generate a book's moral life are naively enacted upon

the body of the book during the early, uncertain stages of writing.
That *is* the ordeal, and it ended when I took that whole section and
recast it in the first person—Anne Frank's story told by Amy Bellette.
The victim wasn't herself going to talk about her plight in the voice of
"The March of Time." She hadn't in the *Diary,* so why should she
in life? I didn't want this section to *appear* as first-person narration,
but I knew that by passing it through the first-person sieve, I stood a
good chance of getting rid of this terrible tone, which wasn't hers, but
mine. I did get rid of it. The impassioned cadences, the straining
emotions, the somber, overdramatized, archaic diction—I cleared it
all out, thanks to Amy Bellette. Rather straightforwardly, I then
cast the section *back* into the third person, and then I was able to get
to work on it—to write rather than to rhapsodize or eulogize.

*How do you think you have influenced the environment, the
culture, as a writer?*
Not at all. If I had followed my early college plans to become an
attorney, I don't see where it would matter to the culture.

*Do you say that with bitterness or with glee?*
Neither. It's a fact of life. In an enormous commercial society that
demands complete freedom of expression, the culture is a maw.
Recently, the first American novelist to receive a special Congres-
sional Gold Medal for his "contribution to the nation" was Louis
L'Amour. It was presented to him at the White House by the President. The only other country in the world where such a writer would
receive his government's highest award is the Soviet Union. In a
totalitarian state, however, *all* culture is dictated by the regime;
fortunately we Americans live in Reagan's and not Plato's Republic,
and aside from their stupid medal, culture is almost entirely ignored.
And that is preferable by far. As long as those on top keep giving the
honors to Louis L'Amour and couldn't care less about anything
else, everything will be just fine. When I was first in Czechoslovakia, it
occurred to me that I work in a society where as a writer everything
goes and nothing matters, while for the Czech writers I met in
Prague, nothing goes and everything matters. This isn't to say I
wished to change places. I didn't envy them their persecution and the
way in which it heightens their social importance. I didn't even envy
them their seemingly more valuable and serious themes. The triviali-

zation, in the West, of much that's deadly serious in the East is itself a subject, one requiring considerable imaginative ingenuity to transform into compelling fiction. To write a serious book that doesn't signal its seriousness with the rhetorical cues or thematic gravity that's traditionally associated with seriousness is a worthy undertaking too. To do justice to a spiritual predicament that is *not* blatantly shocking and monstrously horrible, that does *not* elicit universal compassion, or occur on a large historical stage, or on the grandest scale of twentieth-century suffering—well, that's the lot that has fallen to those who write where everything goes and nothing matters. I recently heard the critic George Steiner, on English television, denouncing contemporary Western literature as utterly worthless and without quality, and claiming that the great documents of the human soul, the materpieces, could only arise from souls being crushed by regimes like those in Czechoslovakia. I wonder then why all the writers I know in Czechoslovakia loathe the regime and passionately wish that it would disappear from the face of the earth. Don't they understand, as Steiner does, that this is their chance to be great? Sometimes one or two writers with colossal brute strength do manage, miraculously, to survive and, taking the system as their subject, to make art of a very high order out of their persecution. But most of them who remain sealed up inside totalitarian states are, as writers, destroyed by the system. That system doesn't make masterpieces; it makes coronaries, ulcers, and asthma, it makes alcoholics, it makes depressives, it makes bitterness and desperation and insanity. The writers are intellectually disfigured, spiritually demoralized, physically sickened, and culturally bored. Frequently they are silenced completely. Nine-tenths of the best of them will never do their best work just because of the system. The writers nourished by this system are the party hacks. When such a system prevails for two or three generations, relentlessly grinding away at a community of writers for twenty, thirty, or forty years, the obsessions become fixed, the language grows stale, the readership slowly dies out from starvation, and the existence of a national literature of originality, variety, vibrancy (which is very different from the brute survival of a single powerful voice) is nearly impossible. A literature that has the misfortune of remaining isolated underground for too long will inevitably become provincial, backwards, even naive, despite the fund of dark experience that may inspire it. By contrast, our work here hasn't been deprived of authenticity because as writers we haven't been stomped on by a totalitarian government. I don't know of any Western writer, aside from George Steiner, who is so grandiosely and sentimentally deluded about human suffering—and "masterpieces" —that he's come back from behind the Iron Curtain thinking himself devalued because he hasn't had to contend with such a wretched intellectual and literary environment. If the choice is between Louis L'Amour and our literary freedom and our extensive, lively, national literature on the one hand, and Solzhenitsyn and that cultural desert and crushing suppression on the other, I'll take L'Amour.

*But don't you feel powerless as a writer in America?*
Writing novels is not the road to power. I don't believe that, in my society, novels effect serious changes in anyone other than the handful of people who are writers, whose own novels are of course seriously affected by other novelists' novels. I can't see anything like that happening to the ordinary reader, nor would I expect it to.

*What do novels do then?*
To the ordinary reader? Novels provide readers with something to read. At their best writers change the *way* readers read. That seems to me the only realistic expectation. It also seems to me quite enough. Reading novels is a deep and singular pleasure, a gripping and mysterious human activity that does not require any more moral or political justification than sex.

*But are there no other aftereffects?*
You asked me if I thought my fiction had changed anything in the culture and the answer is no. Sure there's been some scandal, but people are scandalized all the time; it's a way of life for them. It doesn't mean a thing. If you ask if I *want* my fiction to change anything in the culture, the answer is still no. What I want is to possess my readers while they are reading my book—if I can, to possess them in ways that other writers don't. Then let them return, just as they were, to a world where everybody else is working to change, persuade, tempt, and control them. The best readers come to fiction to be free of all that noise, to have set loose in them the consciousness that's otherwise conditioned and hemmed in by all

that *isn't* fiction. This is something that *every* child, smitten by books, understands immediately, though it's not at all a childish idea about the importance of reading.

*Last question. How would you describe yourself? What do you think you are like, compared with those vividly transforming heroes of yours?*

I am like somebody who is trying vividly to transform himself out of himself and into his vividly transforming heroes. I am very much like somebody who spends all day writing.

# Doctor or Pornographer? Clive Sinclair Talks to Philip Roth about His New Book

Clive Sinclair/1984

From *Jewish Chronicle*, 2 March 1984, 12 © 1984 by Jewish Chronicle. Reprinted by permission.

Bless Philip Roth, the Baruch Spinoza of the spermatozoa, likewise excommunicated by the self-appointed guardians of the Jewish heritage and the Yiddish tradition. For he has suffered the injustice of being misread. Why? Because he is not sentimental, because his eye is ironic. Nevertheless, it should be clear to any perceptive reader that Roth respects his elders, even Sophie Portnoy, but especially Jewish fathers, nearly as much as his independence.

So why can't Irving Howe, that quintessential Jewish intelligence, see it? Roth, who has undoubtedly been stung by his accusations of mockery and betrayal, calls it "one of the oddest misreadings that any contemporary writer has run into." At the same time the ill-founded semitic hostility has given him a subject, being behind the three Zuckerman books, of which *The Anatomy Lesson* is the latest.

"I couldn't have avoided it," added Roth, "it was just too big. I have no idea how my career would have gone if this stuff hadn't kicked it off. But it did. It began the day I took my first step—'You don't walk right! Why does he walk like that?' Hush. Just let him walk.

"Some Gentile critics can't understand why Zuckerman responds so to these swipes. They don't understand why comparisons to Goebbels and Streicher hurt so much, idiotic though they may be. Updike, in his view of *The Anatomy Lesson*—which is, by the way, first class—says that by the time a writer's forty, he should be over his home town gripes.

"Doesn't that strike you as peculiar? They don't understand the historical magnitude of this thing. Updike adds that by the time a writer's fifty, certain reviews shouldn't matter to him anymore. But this isn't a review, this is history. And Zuckerman is up to his knees in history."

Jewish history, of course. His mother dies in *The Anatomy Lesson*. Her last word, written on a scrap of paper, is "holocaust." In fact Roth based this incident upon an anecdote he once heard, but it fits beautifully into the novel, so cleverly that its significance is easy to miss.

"It isn't just a scrap of paper," said Roth. "It's history. Some people are in terrible trouble. Zuckerman's in terrible history. And because of that history nothing is casual, not even a little piece of paper." Zuckerman can't throw it away, of course, but he doesn't know what to do with it either. So he folds it up and puts it in his wallet. It is akin to Roth's own use of Judaism; it is not always apparent, but it is ever-present.

"Now, the fact that it was his mother's last word would always have significance," added Roth, "but she might have written any-thing and he would have kept it as a sentimental token, but that's not why he's keeping it. He's keeping it because his little mother wrote something so powerful. These little women whom others would dismiss as little more than Miami Beachniks can't be dismissed, because they can write the word 'holocaust'. And they have some-how earned it, too.

"Part of me wishes the misreading had never happened, but I also know that it's been my good luck; that the opposition has allowed me to become the strongest writer I could possibly have been. In fact my Jewish detractors insisted upon my being a Jewish writer by their opposition. I'm rather surprised that I've spent these past six years of my life, from 44 to 50, which is really the filet mignon, writing these three books. I'd much rather have had some fun."

That's what all writers say, myself included. Certainly poor Nathan Zuckerman would like some. Instead he is afflicted by an ineffable ache that affects his mind also, withering his inspiration. This pain becomes his obsession, as does his search for a cure. Associating his torment with the writing that has reputedly caused the death of his father he seeks salvation in the profession he sees as its opposite. He decides to become a doctor and applies to the appropriate depart-ment of his alma mater in Chicago. But Zuckerman can no more escape his writing than he can his pain. Thus the very drugs he uses to suppress the latter only succeed in releasing the former, and once in Chicago he assumes the persona of Milton Appel, pornographer, in place of nice Dr. Zuckerman.

"Look," said Roth, "the powerful thing for me in this book was the willed extremism at either end of the moral spectrum: that is, the doctor *and* the pornographer. And that's what gave the book point for me. If Zuckerman had just gone back to Chicago to be a doctor, it would have been a very sentimental book indeed. Had he just indulged himself in the pornographer impersonation, that would have been another kind of book, too: a lark.

"For me the inspiration came when the two things joined—held each other in check. He goes to Chicago because he wants to be a doctor, but actually behaves like a pornographer. The most telling lines for me, which no one has quoted yet, are when Zuckerman says this about the pornographer, 'The more he sits with me, the more I find to like . . . the moral stubbornness, the passionate otherness . . . maybe he is what makes one secretly proudest of being a Jew after all.' "

Irving Howe wouldn't agree, nor would the "real" Milton Appel. For Milton Appel, whose name Zuckerman is blackening, is a critic who looked unfavourably down upon him from the high-ground of Jewish morality, as Howe once looked upon Roth. Zuckerman, already defeated in single combat by this high priest, decides to fight dirty. And Appel the Porno King turns out to be his most successful literary creation in years. Nor can he stop the voice, once it has taken him over. "That's a cry against the Appels, isn't it?" asked Roth, referring to this disreputable dybbuk's loquacity. " 'Let him speak!' That's what you hear at a rally when someone starts to talk and everyone says, 'Shut up!' Except someone who says, 'No! Let him speak!'

"That's what I feel about writing. Zuckerman's 'Life of Appel' is vicious and nasty, most disrespectful, and yet it's the best thing he does. What's to be done about that? That the best thing you do is reprehensible."

Needless to say, Roth's intentions are anything but reprehensible. Despite all the humiliations heaped upon him, Zuckerman clings to his individuality; for better or worse he is stuck with the "burden of self." That phrase, small as it is, put me in mind of *Herzog,* wherein a similar battle is waged. Herzog has his Reality Instructors, Zuckerman his diagnosticians. As Roth puts it, "Bellow casts an enormous shadow," and it is difficult for any Jewish-American writer to move outside the penumbra. Roth, a dealer in different kinds of consciousness, stands on the far edge, illuminated by Zuckerman burning.

"I let them go," said Roth of the four women who are Zuckerman's comforters. "Because I didn't want to stop the fire that was burning down the middle of the book. I didn't want to break any of the obsession, the character's obsession." This obsession with "flesh degraded and transformed" puts Roth in the company of Kafka. "I don't want to make too much of the comparison," said Roth, "it's self-serving to bring in Kafka. In any comedy of humiliation there's an inevitable likeness to what Kafka wrote about. But I suppose if you do shake up Kafka and Bellow together, you get some kind of concoction that is inspiring. The one extreme is 'Metamorphosis' and the other is *Herzog*. They are different kinds of comedies of humiliation. As are my Zuckerman books."

After writing *The Anatomy Lesson* Roth deserves some fun, though I don't imagine he'll get any, being obsessed by the need to write, and being blessed (or cursed) by the ability to transmute life into art.

# A Confusion of Realms

## Ian Hamilton/1985

From *The Nation*, 1 June 1985, 679-81 © 1985 by The Nation Company, Inc. Reprinted by permission.

*I imagine you get annoyed when critics read this trilogy as straight confession. Zuckerman as Philip Roth. Yet sometimes it's hard not to read it this way.*

It's very easy to read it this way. This is the easiest possible way to read. It makes it just like reading the evening paper. I only get annoyed because it isn't the evening paper that I've written. Shaw wrote to Henry James, "People don't want works of art from you, they want help." They also want confirmation of their beliefs, including their beliefs about you.

*But surely the journalistic approach is inescapable—unless the reader forgets everything he knows or has read about you, Philip Roth.*

If my books are so persuasive that they are utterly convinced, these readers, that I give them life red hot, untransformed, as it's lived, well, I suppose that's not the worst cross any novelist has had to bear. Better than their not believing me at all. The fashion now is to praise books you don't believe in. "This is really a great book—I don't believe in it at all." But I *want* belief, and I work to try to get it. If all these subtle readers can see in my work is my biography, then they are simply numb to fiction—numb to impersonation, to ventriloquism, to irony, numb to the thousand observations of human life on which a book is built, numb to all the delicate devices by which novels create the illusion of a reality more like the real than our own. End of lecture. Or shall we pursue this further?

*Since you're enjoying it so, why not a little further? In The Anatomy Lesson there is the character Milton Appel, a distinguished and powerful literary critic. Reviewers have confidently identified him as Irving Howe. I won't ask you to confirm or deny this. I do think,*

192

*though, that once the identification is made, it becomes hard for the reader not to pursue the biographical interest (i.e., Roth versus Howe) at the expense, sometimes, of the fictional clash between Zuckerman and Appel.*

I wouldn't write a book to win a fight. I'd rather go 15 rounds with Sonny Liston. At least it would be over in an hour and I could go to bed. But a book takes me two years, if I'm lucky. Eight hours a day, seven days a week, 365 days a year, that's the only way I know how to do it. You have to sit alone in a room with only a tree out the window to talk to. You have to sit there churning out draft after draft of crap, waiting like a neglected baby for just one drop of mother's milk.

Anybody who did this to win a fight would have to be even more obsessive than I am. And angrier too. Milton Appel is not in this book because I was once demolished in print by Irving Howe. Appel is in this book because half of being a writer is being indignant. And being *right.* If you only knew how *right* we are. Show me a writer who isn't furious about being misrepresented, misread, or unread, and who isn't sure he's right.

You can't. My trilogy is about the vocation of an American writer, who is a Jew, to boot. If I left out the feuds and the paranoia and the brooding indignation, if I left out the fact that *they are wrong and we are right,* I would not be telling the whole unpretty truth about what goes on inside the heads of even Nobel Prize winners. I happen to know a couple of Nobel Prize winners. Move in very lofty circles, I do, and let me assure you, despite Their Great Contribution to Humanity, they are not so sweet and forgiving as you might expect. They too might not object if their critics were pelted with offal while being drawn down Fifth Avenue in cages.

*Appel does come out of their argument rather well—better than Zuckerman, in fact. In their showdown telephone conversation one rather squirms for Zuckerman.*

Of course you give the other guy the best lines. Otherwise it's a mug's game.

*That old magnanimity.*

Yes, my strong suit. Known for it. But it happens also to be a structural necessity. Tilting at yourself is *interesting,* a lot more interesting than winning. Let the vituperation flow and the mouth froth, but underestimate the opposition and you weaken the book. For me the work, the writing work, is transforming the I-madness into he-madness. Last point about Appel. Zuckerman's rage against Appel has less to do with Appel than with Z.'s physical condition. As if the willed self-absorption of the writer isn't imprisoning enough, there is the forced self-absorption in his chronic pain.

If it weren't for Zuckerman's physical pain, there'd be no Appel in this book. Zuckerman wouldn't have his harem of Florence Nightingales. Wouldn't decide at forty to become a doctor and bolt for Chicago, oozing Percodan at every pore. Forget Appel. This book is about physical pain and the havoc it wreaks on one's human credentials. If Zuckerman were in good fighting shape, why would he fight with his literary enemies on the Jewish magazine he calls *Foreskin?* He wouldn't bother.

*But because the pain isn't diagnosed, because it's a mystery pain, we might tend to view it as symbolic pain, as pain visited upon him by the Appels, by the less than first-rate women, by the state of Zuckerman's career, and so on.*

Symbolic pain? Could be for all I know. But in a real shoulder. What hurts is a real neck and shoulder. The trouble with pains is they don't feel symbolic, except maybe to critics.

*What is your diagnosis?*

I'm a writer, not a doctor. My diagnosis is that these things happen. When I was writing this book, I said to myself, "I want someone who has known chronic pain to be able to read this book and say, ''That's it, that's what it's like." I wanted to be as realistic and *unsymbolic* as possible. Not knowing the source of one's pain doesn't make it symbolic: it just makes it hurt more. Not that it would be a comfort to Zuckerman if he knew, say, that he had cancer. Sometimes knowing is worse, sometimes not knowing is worse. My book is about not knowing. Look, diagnoses abound in this book. Everybody *else* knows. They've all got him pegged, just like Appel. All his women know what's wrong with him. Even the trichologist who treats his baldness knows why he's losing his hair: "undue pressure." This book is *crammed* with people who know what's wrong with Zuckerman. I leave the diagnosing to his comforters. I try to stay out of it.

*Of course Zuckerman ends the book in an advanced state of metaphor, with his mouth wired shut by surgery.*

He breaks his jaw falling on a tombstone in a Jewish cemetery, after overdosing on painkillers and booze. What's so metaphorical about that? Happens all the time.

*But he's silenced, completely. He can't write because of his agonising shoulder, and he can't speak because of his broken mouth.*

Let me tell you a story. Back in 1957 I published, in *The New Yorker,* a short story called "Defender of the Faith." I was twenty-four and I was pretty excited about it. Then the story came out and it enraged a lot of Jewish readers of *The New Yorker.* Among the enraged was an eminent New York rabbi who wrote a letter of protest to the Anti-Defamation League of the B'nai Brith—a very worthy organisation, by the way, that's fought anti-Semitic discrimination in the U.S. courts for decades, and keeps an eye on the anti-Semites so they don't get out of hand. They've been known to do that. Anyway, one line of the rabbi's letter I never forgot. "What is being done to silence this man?" Well, to their credit, they never tried it. Free country, the U.S.A., and nobody appreciates that better than the Jews. But I remembered that line. What is being done to silence this man? It came to me when I was writing this book, and that's why I broke Zuckerman's jaw. I did it for the rabbi.

*So the charge of defamation started early on?*

It started when I started. It has somewhat distinguished my career from most of my American colleagues. I was taken to be an inflammatory fellow when I was still in my swaddling clothes. In its own strange way, the furor coming right at the start probably has given my writing a direction and emphasis that it might not have had otherwise. It's difficult to ignore such an assault, particularly at twenty-four. Back then I did two things: began to explain myself and began to defend myself.

*How did you make your case?*

I was invited to speak at synagogues and temples and Jewish community centres, and I went out and spoke. People stood up and shouted at me during the question periods. It was a good thing. I owe a lot to the opposition. They dragged me screaming out of the

Department of English. There were real people out there who got
inflamed. They didn't write papers about what they read—they got
mad. What a surprise.

*So by the time you wrote* Portnoy's Complaint, *you already had
an inflamed Jewish readership, so to speak?*
I also had an appreciative Jewish readership. Even a few Gentiles
reading me, too. But as for my Jewish detractors, no, they wouldn't
stop. They wouldn't let up, no matter what I wrote. So I thought
finally, "Well, you want it, I'll give it to you." And out came Portnoy,
apertures spurting.

*What about your own family? How did they respond?*
To the attacks on me? They were stunned. They were hurt. They
heard a lot about my inadequacies from their hoity-toity neighbours.
They would go to a lecture about me at their temple, expecting a star
to be pinned on their boy just like back in grade school. Instead
they'd hear from the platform that sleeping in my bedroom all those
years, and eating with them at their table, was a self-hating anti-
Semitic Jew. My mother had to hold my father down in his seat, he'd
get so angry. No, they were all right. They recognised too many
folks they knew to think such people as I'd described had never
walked around New Jersey.

*Your own father then isn't like Zuckerman's father, who on his
deathbed curses his son for the books he writes?*
I never said he was. You're confusing me with all those astute book
reviewers who are sure that I am the only novelist in the history of
literature who has never made anything up.

*In each of these last two books, Zuckerman suffers a bereavement.
In the second book,* Zuckerman Unbound, *his father dies calling him
"Bastard." In* The Anatomy Lesson, *Zuckerman's mother dies, and
Zuckerman is left with a piece of paper on which his mother has
written the word "Holocaust."*
Yes. She's dying of a brain tumor. Her neurologist comes to her
hospital room to ascertain just how far gone she is and asks her
to write her name for him on a piece of paper. This is in Miami Beach
in 1970. She's a woman whose writings otherwise consist of recipes
on index cards, knitting instructions, and thank-you notes. When the

The novel is a striking departure for Mr. Roth, in many ways
different from anything he has written before. Things happen and
then seem not to have happened. Zuckerman dies, his eulogy is
delivered—and then it turns out that he may not have died at all.

"I thought if I had Zuckerman die it might enlighten, if only
momentarily, the sages who insist that I write only about what has
happened to me," Mr. Roth says. "Now I only hope I don't kick off
before the book comes out—otherwise the wisdom will be that I
based Zuckerman's funeral on my own." The question of whether
Zuckerman is really dead, he says, was intentionally left in doubt.
"It's really up to the reader," he says. "As you see in the book, I
myself play it both ways."

"This novel, to me, is a book of contradictory yet mutually entangling narratives," he says. "I think the reader has the sensation
from chapter to chapter of the rug being tugged from under him. I
think of *The Counterlife* as a laboratory in which I've run a series of
fictional experiments about what things would be like *if*. You see
the characters in various incarnations. Transformations are going on
at all levels. Zuckerman's English wife pretty much sums things up
when she says to him toward the end of the book, 'Radical change is
the law of life,' and then adds, 'But you overdo it.'

"In addition," he says, "I was interested in the impact of place on
people. Consequently you get the chapter titles—Basel, Judea,
Gloucestershire and finally Christendom, which is Zuckerman's name
for London, for his experience of the place. I wanted to see what the
intelligence I call Zuckerman could yield up unencumbered by the
ordeal of his own development. The trilogy *Zuckerman Bound* is
very much about the development of a man whose life consists of
fictionalizing life. In this book, that man exists fully. He and his
fictionalizing mind have *become*."

The chapters in the book set on the West Bank, or Judea, as the
militant Zionist calls it, and in England are likely to cause controversy—a controversy that Mr. Roth has long been familiar with. In
the "Judea" chapter, Shuki, Zuckerman's leftist Israeli friend, urges
him not to write about a right-wing militant Israeli Zionist named
Mordecai Lippman—who totes a gun in and around the West Bank
settlement he has founded and tells the Arabs that military might will
settle everything. Shuki remarks that such people are the last thing

Israel needs for American Congressmen to be reading about because
Israel depends on the billions of dollars it receives from the United
States. Mr. Roth, of course, *has* written about the fictional Mordecai
Lippman.

"Whether characters such as Mordecai Lippman exist is not even
an issue for debate," Mr. Roth says. "To me, the aggressive, hyper-
dramatic West Bank leader Lippman is the very embodiment of the
book's concern with the reversal and reshaping of existence. Changing history and one's apparent destiny is what his political program is
all about. In a novel about how the imagination constructs reality, the
imagination of Mordecai Lippman doesn't seem to me out of place."

In "Christendom," that is, in London, Zuckerman encounters a
good deal of anti-Semitism—from his gentile British wife's sister and
from her mother. Mr. Roth, of course, spends part of each year in
London with Claire Bloom, his longtime companion, and the question arises as to how much, if any, of this chapter is based on what he
has observed there. "I think, to begin with, that the kind of English
anti-Semitism that Zuckerman runs into exists, period," he says.
"How extensive it is, I have no idea. But neither does Zuckerman. He
wonders, have I just fallen into a little pocket here with the family I've
married into, or have I stumbled into something that's endemic
throughout the establishment. He doesn't know. The book is not
sociology and it's not a statistical study. The evidence Zuckerman has
to go on is ambiguous. It isn't as though he's in Freud's Vienna or
Heine's Berlin, where you got pretty good signs. England's a rather
more self-concealing society."

A major concern of many of the characters in the book, the friends
and relatives of Zuckerman, is a lack of privacy, a fear that he will
write about them. Does Mr. Roth have this problem with his friends
and relatives?

"I would if I were in their position," he says. "I certainly wouldn't
want to be living with a loudmouthed novelist, and I sympathize with
those who do. But it's a struggle, isn't it? Privacy is the domain of the
novelist. The invasion of their privacy accounts for much of our
interest in Emma Bovary, in Anna Karenina, in Raskolnikov and
Lord Jim. The serious, merciless invasion of privacy is at the heart of
the fiction we value most highly."

Twenty-seven years ago, Mr. Roth broke into public consciousness with *Goodbye, Columbus* and won a National Book Award. He has changed greatly since then, he says. "Twenty-seven years ago I was 26, and now I'm 53. Twenty-seven years ago, I was just starting out, with all that implies about energy, confidence, innocence and ambition. I think I've put on plenty of pounds as a writer since then. And I would hope that most of those pounds are muscle. On the other hand, each book seems to me more of an ordeal than the one before. Up against those first books, you're a different kind of fighter from the kind of fighter you are later on. Certainly you lose your naïve expectations. If the goal is to be innocent of all innocence, I'm getting there."

# The Varnished Truths
# of Philip Roth

## Paul Gray/1987

From *Time,* 19 January 1987, 78–80. © 1987 Time Warner Inc. Reprinted by permission.

Some 30 pages into Philip Roth's new novel, a character named Henry Zuckerman comes up with a decidedly odd idea. The setting is Henry's dental office in northern New Jersey; the atmosphere shimmers with the sexual tension generated for weeks now by the presence of Wendy, Dr. Zuckerman's new employee. " 'Look,' he said, 'let's pretend. You're the assistant and I'm the dentist.' 'But I *am* the assistant,' Wendy said. 'I know,' he replied, 'and I'm the dentist—but pretend anyway.' " This fiction seems indistinguishable from the facts of the matter. But once the artifice begins, so does the fun.

Others can play make-believe, of course; Roth has argued for years that everyone does so all the time. So let's pretend. Philip, the younger son of Herman and Bess Roth, was born in Newark in 1933. He . . . he *was* born in Newark . . . grew up loving baseball and enjoying summer outings to the Jersey shore. He was a bright student, and after graduating from Weequahic High School in 1950, he spent a year at the Newark extension of Rutgers University. Then, wanting to see something of the world outside his hometown, he transferred to Bucknell in central Pennsylvania, where he acted in college drama productions; founded, wrote for and edited a literary magazine; and graduated magna cum laude with a B.A. in English.

Where next? Well, say he took an M.A. at the University of Chicago and decided to go on for the Ph.D. He met and married Margaret Martinson, the mother of two children by a previous marriage. When his first attempts at short stores were routinely rejected, Roth gave up his literary aspirations and buckled down to his academic career. He earned his doctorate and went on to teaching positions at the University of Iowa and Princeton. The Roths live in suburban Philadelphia, where he is a professor of English at the

University of Pennsylvania. His critical books include *The Jewish American Novel: Is Enough Enough?* and *Franz Kafka: The Sit-Down Comic.*

It could have happened that way. In fact, a lot of it did. But this refraction of reality is not nearly as interesting as it might be. To punch it up a bit, suppose that Roth's fiction was clamorously acclaimed; that his first published volume, *Goodbye, Columbus* (1959), won the National Book Award and made the author a name to be reckoned with at 27. Implausible, true, but more dramatic than the other version. And what about that happily-ever-after marriage? Maybe it lasted only a few years before plummeting into an acrimonious separation in 1963 that left Roth deep in debt, thanks to legal expenses, and sent him reeling into five years of psychoanalysis. Awful, but for the sake of the narrative not bad. Right about here a reversal of fortune would do nicely. So our hero wrote *Portnoy's Complaint* (1969), the novel that made him rich, famous and controversial. *Goodbye, Columbus* and *Portnoy* were snapped up by Hollywood. And then . . . and then Roth fell in love with a movie star.

That last touch may strike some as overdoing it. But going too far has been a hallmark of Roth's fiction from the beginning. His early stories provoked some Jewish readers to condemn him for anti-Semitisim; *Portnoy* gave him a reputation as a sex maniac. His three books about Nathan Zuckerman, *The Ghost Writer* (1979), *Zuckerman Unbound* (1981) and *The Anatomy Lesson* (1983), have led to charges that Roth is trapped in narcissistic reverie, writing about a writer who resembles himself. As if thumbing his nose at such comments, the author now offers *The Counterlife* (Farrar, Straus & Giroux; 324 pages; $18.95). It features, naturally, Nathan Zuckerman.

There are other things in this novel that Roth's detractors will probably dislike. Nathan, a self-conscious fellow, does not allow the reader to forget that the words on the page are made up, inventions: "Being Zuckerman is one long performance and the very opposite of what is thought of as *being oneself.*" So much for sincere, straight-from-the-shoulder storytelling. People who want to know what *really* happens in a work of fiction, a peculiar but widespread desire, are

going to find themselves bewildered. Only one incontestable fact can
be gleaned from the book: *The Counterlife* got written.

And written, it should be added, with Roth's customary verve, wit
and intelligence. It hardly matters that the plot does not flow forward
but rather screeches to a number of halts, that each new beginning is
a refutation of what has gone before. The individual scenes inspire
absolute belief; Roth's art is such that he can make events seem not
only plausible but inescapable even while announcing over and over
again that none of them occurred.

The complications of *The Counterlife* ripple out from a central
conceit. A man with a heart condition finds that the medication he
must take renders him impotent. Hence Henry Zuckerman, 39, faces
the bleak prospect of life without any more after-work office trysts
with his alluring assistant. Similarly, Henry's famous older brother
Nathan, 45, cannot marry an Englishwoman named Maria and create
both the child and the settled life that, after three failed marriages, he
now desperately wants. The only solution in both cases is bypass
surgery. The Zuckerman brothers face the same difficult choice, but
for diametrically opposed reasons. Henry, the responsible family
man, has to decide whether to put his life on the line for a fling;
Nathan, the notorious womanizer and hedonist with money to burn
and an immaculate Manhattan apartment, must risk all for father-
hood.

Both brothers go under the knife and never emerge. Life is unfair,
and fiction can be even worse. But what transpires in a novel need
not be irreversible. So Henry may survive instead and go to Israel,
where he joins a settlement on the West Bank and tries to find, or
lose, himself in Jewish history. Nathan may come out of the operating room a new man, get married and move to England with his
lovely and reassuringly pregnant wife. Other variations surface.
Perhaps Nathan alone dies, and Henry, going through his late brother's effects, comes upon the manuscript of a book that has chapters
with the same titles, in the same order, as *The Counterlife*. Henry
reads about his alleged affair with Wendy and becomes enraged: "Of
all the classics of irresponsible exaggeration, this was the filthiest,
most recklessly irresponsible of all."

It is also possible that Nathan has dreamed up this scene, further
slandering Henry by portraying his imaginary outrage at being lied

about and exploited in the first place. If Nathan is indeed guilty of
such cold, despotic manipulation, then Maria's sense of uneasiness in
his presence makes perfect sense. Near the end, she informs Nathan,
"I'm leaving you and I'm leaving the book."

Much will be made of the technical virtuosity of *The Counterlife,*
with the result that readers who might love the novel may be driven
away. No one but members of creative-writing programs or departments of literature should sit still for another recitative of postmodern-
ism's bag of tricks. The text, you see, is the generator of life, not its
transcript; the only real plot that stories convey is the process of their
telling. Or, as Nathan writes in a letter to Henry, "We are all the
invention of each other, everybody a conjuration conjuring up
everyone else. We are all each other's authors." Or, as Maria observes, "I know characters rebelling against their author has been
done before."

Indeed it has. But Roth manages to draw blood from stony pre-
cepts. His novel is an elaborate verbal gesture; it is also an impassioned portrayal of the moral choices open to living, breathing men
and women, a mirror of a familiar world rendered mysterious and
magical. *The Counterlife* is a metaphysical thriller; the quarry is
nothing less than the elusive nature of truth.

The three years Roth spent writing *The Counterlife* have left him
satisfied ("I gave it my all") and resigned to the prospect of being
misunderstood once again. He expresses hope that Nathan's putative
death in the novel will discourage people from reading his fiction as
autobiography, but he is not optimistic. "I write about what *could*
have happened," he says, "not what *did* happen. Why that's so hard
to grasp I don't understand. I have once in a while started off just
setting down some incident I'd actually gone through and I can
hardly get past the first paragraph without veering off into something
that *didn't* happen, which is always more interesting. I'm highly
sensitive to boredom. I think it's an occupational requirement."

To the unpracticed eye, Roth's ordinary routine might seem the
epitome of boredom. His favorite place to write is a gray colonial
1790 farmhouse set on roughly 40 acres of land in Connecticut's
Litchfield County. He bought the place in 1972, in part to get away
from the demands and notoriety that had hounded him after *Portnoy.* He got plenty of solitude for his money, sometimes, he acknowl-

edges, a bit too much: "Night up here can come down like a heavy
thing." Before that happens, Roth has usually put in a reclusive day.
By 9:30 each morning he has walked some 50 yards from his house
to a two-room cottage that serves as his study. He emerges around 1
for lunch and then disappears until 4:30 in the afternoon, when it is
time for a swim in his pool or, if the weather has turned chilly, for a
six-mile walk. He spends evenings listening to classical music and
reading.

Roth's monastic schedule varies only a little when Actress Claire
Bloom, 55, is in residence. The two have lived together since 1976
and occasionally worked together as well. His co-adaptation of *The
Ghost Writer* appeared on PBS's American Playhouse in 1984, with
Bloom playing a woman trapped in her writer-husband's hermetic life
somewhere in New England. Roth and Bloom are hardly trapped;
they now divide each year between Connecticut and her house
in London. "We try not to be apart for more than a month at a
time," says Roth. The author and the actress are, in some ways, an
odd match; she needs people, other actors, crews, audiences for her
work just as much as he requires isolation for his. So when Bloom is
in rural Connecticut, her enforced idleness leads to a good deal of
teasing banter. He: "There *is* no social life around here." She (to a
visitor): "That's what he keeps telling me." He: "*Nobody* goes to
parties. Hey, I got you a telephone, didn't I?"
   Actually, he is not as curmudgeonly as this byplay suggests. In
Connecticut, Roth and Bloom regularly see such neighboring friends
as Arthur Miller, Richard Widmark and William Styron; London, her
turf, involves plenty of evenings with theater and literary people,
including Harold Pinter and Lady Antonia Fraser.
   Another form of recreation for Roth is travel. In the early '70s, he
left for Prague. An impression later arose that he went to Czechoslovakia out of guilt, a rich American attempting to atone for his success
by visiting oppressed Soviet-bloc writers. "Guilt?" Roth asks. "I was
out to have a good time." But he found Prague "overwhelming
within an hour. I felt, as I did when I went to Jerusalem later, that this
was a place I had to see again."
   He made visits each spring and friends among Czech artists. This
experience had literary consequences: *The Prague Orgy,* a novella

recounting Nathan Zuckerman's misadventures in that city, included
as the coda for the trilogy published as *Zuckerman Bound* (1985);
and Roth's editorship of a series, "Writers from the Other Europe,"
which has given Eastern European writers exposure in the West.
Roth's access to Prague ended in the mid-'70s, when his visa was not
renewed. He had been tailed and questioned there, as had those
who associated with him. "After I left one time," he recalls, "the
authorities went to one of my Czech friends and demanded to know
what Roth was up to, what does he want here. My friend answered,
'Haven't you read his books? He comes for the girls.' "

The distraction from his work Roth most willingly tolerates is baseball.
"My fandom," he says, without a trace of irony, "is the most interesting fact of my life." He talks eagerly about going to games as a boy
and watching the old Newark Bears of the International League
along with his older brother Sanford and his father, now a retired
insurance-company executive. His boyhood passion was the Brooklyn Dodgers. "I went off to college, and then the Dodgers went off to
L.A.," he says, shaking his head. Eventually, he transferred his
allegiance to the New York Mets. Last summer he had a dish antenna
installed atop an outbuilding on the Connecticut property so he
could follow the fortunes of the Mets on the road.

He also had lunch with Keith Hernandez, the Mets' All Star first
baseman. Describing this event, Roth seems star struck. "I asked him
whether he read stories in the papers the next day about the game
he'd played in the night before. You know what he said? 'Why
should I? I know what happened.' I realized then why I don't have to
read reviews of my books. I know what happened."

"If I ever wrote an autobiography," he says, "I'd call it *The
Counterbook*." The prospect seems unlikely. Bare facts alone do not
particularly interest Roth, nor does the unfettered imagination. His
specialty is the varnished truth. Life offers problems for the writer to
rephrase: "The radical restructuring of questions is what gives me my
books. My gift is to pretend." The closest he has come to displaying
himself directly in fiction is probably in a 1973 essay/story, *"I Always
Wanted You to Admire My Fasting"; or, Looking at Kafka.* Prospec-
tive biographers may imagine this piece to be a trove of information,
a crucial key to the Roth enigma. The narrator is called Roth by his

friends, he has an older brother, the year is 1942, and the setting is Newark. The only jarring note among these corresponding details is that young Roth's Hebrew teacher happens to be Franz Kafka, somehow risen from his grave in Prague and an immigrant in America. When asked if this narrative is not autobiographical, save for that one outrageous detail, the author confesses at last. "I'll tell you the truth. Kafka *was* my Hebrew teacher. Only my name is not Roth."

# Writers Have a Third Eye

## Alvin P. Sanoff/1987

From *U.S. News & World Report*, 2 February 1987, 61–62.
Copyright, 2 February 1987, *U.S. News & World Report*.
Reprinted by permission.

I wouldn't want to live with a novelist: Writers are highly voyeuristic
and indiscreet. But the writer should be no more ruthless with others
than with himself. If he's indiscreet about others and discreet about
himself, then it's a mug's game. The same intensity of focus should
be turned inward as outward.

Needless to say, people get angry if they feel they've been misrepresented even if it's in fiction. As one of the characters in my new
book says: It isn't that his brother the novelist used the facts; it's that
he distorted them. What galls him most is where the line is thin
between the invented and the real and everything has the most
distorted meaning. I can understand how the relatives and friends of
a novelist must feel.

My colleague John Updike said very aptly in a memoir he wrote
recently, "Shame is not for writers." He's right. It's not that one
doesn't feel shame or that one is shameless, but it's to be struggled
against.

Fiction has an obligation to be about those things that we're too
ashamed to talk about with those we trust the most. It isn't a matter
of what we're ashamed to say in public; why shouldn't we be
ashamed to say things in public? Why should we make revelations to
people who have nothing to do with us? But it's the things you don't
even want to say to the people you trust that constitute a big portion
of your real life. And I think fiction—at least my kind of fiction—is
about that.

Writers always have a third eye that's watching, a third ear that's
listening, a judge who seems to be working for the writer in you and
isn't working for the husband, the lover, the son, the father that
you happen to be. There is an act of self-removal writers are capable
of that may look inhumane.

My new book is very much a work by a middle-aged writer. It is
about "counterliving" in all its aspects. By that I mean the desire for
renewal. In one way or another all the major characters are involved
in the drama of self-renewal and transformation. The ideas of renewal and the possibility of change are a kind of leitmotif of middle
age.

For me personally, the act of renewal does not come from changing my life in a dramatic way, as some of the main characters do. My
renewal comes through abandoning the last book to go on to write
a different kind of book. As I go through each of my books in my
mind, I see a lot of abandonment of narrative positions—using up
and discarding the way I tell a story, the way I seize hold of the
material, dramatize it and use language. I salvage what I can from
each book, and the rest is discarded.

*The Counterlife* feels like the most complex narrative position I've
taken. I keep changing my angle of vision from book to book
because I'm trying to sink my claws deeper into the material. In this
book I decided to keep changing the angle within the book. The
novel wanted to go every which way, and I let it, not knowing quite
what was going to turn up. For a long time, I was in a deep state of
confusion, uncertainty and frustration. That's par for the course in
the first year of a book. But this was even more confusing than in the
past.

After about a year I had this pile of what I could best call contradictory narratives, by no means really resembling the finished book. I
thought: "Well, the confusion is the issue. Don't worry that the
narratives contradict each other. The story seems better this way."

The form was both the most troubling and the most exhilarating
element. The material you have; it sits there. Everybody in the
subway has a subject they can write about. But what you do with the
subject—how you treat the material—is what writing fiction is all
about.

I'm very bad at guessing what the reaction to this book—or any
book—will be. To begin with, when I'm writing, I studiously try not to
think about that. In fact, it's very easy not to; I have my hands full
just writing. When the book comes out I'm generally surprised by
virtually every reaction—not because I'm innocent. I'm not. It is
simply an astonishing phenomenon. The reactions are never quite

what you think they will be. But you can assume that somebody is going to be scandalized by some element.

Writing every book has been difficult since I did the first—*Goodbye, Columbus*. Frustration has mostly been the problem. The writing all happens so slowly, and there's no way of forcing it. I've no desire to produce books any more quickly. It's just that you're carrying this thing with you all the time and you're not quite sure what it is you're carrying. You're sort of like a busboy in a restaurant, loaded up with dirty dishes—and blindfolded. The guy says, "Find the kitchen." Well, you may or may not have an accident on the way. If you get to the kitchen and get to the dishwasher, it's an enormous feat.

There is a typical process I follow in writing. I sit down and stick with it and put in regular hours and regular days. But each book throws up its own problems, and the previous book is not much help in solving the problems of the new one. In that way, writing is a singular profession. Other professionals who have been doing their jobs diligently for 25 or 30 years aren't faced with that dilemma. When the dermatologist opens the door to his waiting room where there are 10 people, I imagine he feels that he can handle everything that's there. If he can't, then it probably can't be done, especially after 25 years or so of practice.

But, in writing, when you begin a new project you really get very little help from all you've done in the past. You're accustomed to the discipline. You know what your process is, and if you follow it you're probably going to get through. Aside from that, there's very little to go on, because in a way you're trying to throw off the way you did it before. You can't treat the new patient like the old one.

There are writers like Trollope who more or less did it the same way from book to book. I wouldn't disparage that. He was so confident in his perception; he had so much authority in his manner. But I, from book to book, have different motives that seem to require drastically different narrative positions.

My motive in each book is something I discover as I go along. It doesn't have to do with something I want to say; it has to do with the way I want to present things.

For instance, it only dawned on me along the way in this book that

I was discussing at much greater length than ever before the relationship between two brothers. In fact, I never really had done that
previously, touching upon it only glancingly in *Zuckerman Bound.* I
said: "Well, then, this is a subject here. Go after it. Sink your teeth
into it."

In real life I do have a brother: He's five years older and a retired
advertising man, who is now an artist in Chicago. But my relationship
with him is nothing like the one between the brothers in the book.

It's interesting that when I was writing I suddenly discovered which
of my friends had brothers. Normally, people tell you about their
families and, by and large, you don't listen. But when I'm writing and
have two brothers as characters, I listen when someone mentions his
brother. Writing makes you a very good listener. Similarly, when you
think you're going to write about Israel, then everything in the
newspaper that's about Israel is alive to you, every Israeli you meet is
of interest to you. You're voracious. You want everything to feed the
book. Much does, and then you move on. It's amazing how little you
care about who has a brother or who is an Israeli when the book is
finished.

I like solid ground under my feet when I write. Once I have that,
then I can leap. Sometimes I invent something, and then luckily I
meet somebody to whom it has happened. But generally I first have
to read about it in a newspaper or in the *New England Journal of
Medicine,* and then I think, "There's something there."

When I did *The Anatomy Lesson,* I went down and spent a day—
from about 6 in the morning until the evening—with a surgeon. I just
wanted to hang around and be sure I was getting things right. It isn't
that I do research; mine is really after the fact. I spin the story out,
not constrained by facts, and then frantically run around to find out if
I made a terrible error. It lets me be freer. By and large, you can use
your head and figure out if you've got it right or wrong because what
you're involved with mostly is the sense of the event. The details
you can take care of later.

When I finished this book I gave it to two English friends to read to
see if I got the language of Britain right. I don't know in how many
places the language was wrong. It can be something important, or it
can be something small—such as the word "smart," which we use in
America to mean clever or intelligent and they use to mean elegant.

I had a British charcter say somebody was smart, meaning clever, and that wouldn't do.

When I was a student, virtually every writer I read influenced me. As an undergraudate, I suppose the most telling book was *Catcher in the Rye*. I think in a way I discovered narrative voice by reading it and *Huckleberry Finn*—not that I wanted to copy either writer, but I discovered what the power of a voice was. Then in 1954, my last undergraduate year, I read *The Adventures of Augie March,* Saul Bellow's book, and that dazzled me. It seemed to me that Bellow had thrown off all the constraints. He wasn't bound by the academic sense of literature that I, for one, had begun to get into my head as an undergraduate. I suppose a few years later I thought Bernard Malamud's first short stories and his book *The Magic Barrel* were very special. He came at material that I vaguely had some sense of and brought it to life in a completely original way.

The arguments, personalities and language of Bellow and Malamud are very vivid to me. But how was I going to handle it? What approach to take? I saw in Bellow a very big approach, and I saw in Malamud another approach—not bigness but a very singular and extraordinary voice. I didn't care to imitate either man, but they certainly were powerful stimulants.

Then, as the years went by, others came to mean a great deal to me. I only came to read Kafka seriously in my late 20s. At about the same time, I began to read Céline. I could also mention James, Flaubert and Chekhov, all of whom have meant as much to me as a reader as they have as a writer. There is no separation between the two. One is always reading for the writer, and one is always reading as a writer.

# Life, Counterlife

## Katharine Weber/1987

From *Connecticut*, February 1987, 45–47, 49 © 1987 by
Katharine Weber. Reprinted by permission.

To get to the 1790 farmhouse in northwestern Connecticut where
Philip Roth has lived since 1972, one drives on a series of winding
back-country roads, the last two of which are unpaved.

The writer greets me at the car with a polite but unnecessary,
"Hello, I'm Philip Roth." The interview, he says, is to take place in
his studio, which lies beyond an old barn (which sports a dish
antenna) in sight of the house. As we cross the lawn toward the
studio, which still resembles the guest cottage it once was, Roth
points out a little old man in an overcoat by a tree. "The elderly
gentleman standing as if rooted by that big tree is my father," he
says, as though he were one more feature in the landscape of 200-
year-old trees, tumbledown stone walls, rolling fields and winter-
purple hills.

An 18th-century house with its back to the road is a rare thing,
Roth explains. "In the 1920s, the owner of the house had the money
and was able to persuade the town to move the road from the front
to the back, past the old apple orchard. When I first saw the house,
one of the things I liked about it was that it faces nowhere."

Roth's desk sits in front of large windows that provide an uninter-
rupted view of some 40 acres of that nowhere: It is here that the
author of *Goodbye Columbus* (1959) and the notorious *Portnoy's
Complaint* (1969) produced *The Great American Novel* (1973), *My
Life as a Man* (1974), which he had begun in 1969, *Reading Myself
and Others* (1975), *The Professor of Desire* (1977), and his most
recent work, the Zuckerman trilogy—*The Ghost Writer* (1979),
*Zuckerman Unbound* (1981) and *The Anatomy Lesson* (1983). A
novella called *The Prague Orgy* was added to the trilogy and published in one volume called *Zuckerman Bound* in 1985.

In *The Ghost Writer,* a young Nathan Zuckerman pays a call on a

214

famous writer who has "married the scion of an old New England
family and lived all these years 'in the country'—that is to say, in the
*goyish* wilderness of birds and trees where America began and long
ago had ended."

When the young writer arrives at E. I. Lonoff's "clapboard farmhouse . . . at the end of an unpaved road," he writes, "I could begin
to understand why hiding out . . . with just the birds and the trees
might not be a bad idea for a writer, Jewish or not." Looking out of
Lonoff's windows, Zuckerman sees "the bare limbs of big dark
maple trees and fields of driven snow. Purity. Serenity. Simplicity.
Seclusion. All one's concentration and flamboyance and originality
reserved for the grueling, exalted transcendent calling. I looked
around and I thought, 'This is how I will live.' "

The wood-panelled studio is furnished plainly—a desk, an IBM
typewriter, a posturepedic office chair and two drafting lamps. Roth
spends most of his days here, starting first thing in the morning after
breakfast and exercise. He stops for a very brief lunch, either alone
or with Claire Bloom, the British actress who has been his companion for 10 years, and continues working into the late afternoon, with
breaks for occasional walks outside. After supper, there is reading
or television. The couple lives quietly, seeing friends occasionally,
going to New York once every month or so.

Roth, the man the *Washington Post* once described as "a tall
skinny man wearing a cheap watch," sprawls in the leather depths of
his chair and awaits questioning with an edgy patience. He warns of
interviews in print that contain inaccuracies. Corrections are in order.
Is this to be an interview or a counter-interview?

By way of mocking the notion that his personal life could have the
least relevance to any discussion of his books, Roth offers himself
for scrutiny from top to bottom, beginning with his shoes (which
come from Brooks Brothers, although the replacement laces he
favors are purchased locally) to his socks (from Gimbels), to his
corduroy pants, which are "quite old," to his belt, which is "very
wide, the kind people wore in the '60s." From there he moves on to
his underwear "which is, I assure you, quite modest," to his blue
cotton shirt, purchased within the year at a nearby general store, and
to an offer to disclose the nature of his dental fillings.

The black digital watch really is cheap; it cost $21 at an airport counter. Roth wears it on his right wrist (because he is left-handed) and one of the watch's many superfluous features is a Fahrenheit temperature reading at the push of a button. Because of poor design, the temperature measured is actually that of Roth's wrist. "Tell your readers that my wrist temperature was 82.2," he says, with mock seriousness followed by a bark of laughter.

All of this is only one way of saying that to know everything isn't necessarily to know anything. Roth makes this point over and over in his new novel, *The Counterlife*, published this month by Farrar, Straus & Giroux. It is the 53-year-old writer's 12th novel and 16th published book. *The Counterlife* is dedicated to the man beside the tree—"To my father at 85"—and again features the character Nathan Zuckerman.

Written in five segments, the book is a virtuoso performance, with Roth offering relentless challenges to the reader. Nothing is as it seems, the rules are continually broken, and because Roth plays games with the conventions of fiction and narrative—at one point a character decides to leave the book, and at another, the pages we have just been reading are destroyed—we are left with very few certainties. The book is about possibilities and counter-possibilities. Ironies abound: An impotent man risks surgery in order to regain his sex life and ends up losing his life altogether; a writer's eulogy turns out to have been written by the dead man; a Jew who feels no connections while in Israel finds himself embracing religion after a few weeks in London.

Roth on *The Counterlife:*

"There are really five discrete versions of the book. The rug is pulled out from under you once, then again, but you don't know it at the time, and then it happens a third time, and then you get to the end, and you see that there *is* no rug, there's no floor, you just keep dropping through the fiction. . . .

"What you're left with are five mutually entangled, somewhat contradictory narratives that sometimes appear to be joined and then are not, and then there's outright contradiction. In chapter one the brother is dead, and in chapter two he isn't. In chapter three the story appears to follow but doesn't: The hijacking never took place. Then chapter four is a complete reversal, and it's Zuckerman who is ill and not his brother, and Zuckerman dies, and there is his funeral, at which his brother Henry can't give the eulogy, but then goes to Zuckerman's apartment in search of his brother's journals, where he recorded Henry's love affair with a Swiss woman. . . . He finds the manuscript of this book and destroys part of it, but he leaves a section called 'Christendom,' about marriage and Maria, and then you get that at the end of the book, but not until Maria has a long conversation with Zuckerman's ghost. So you see, it's not a consecutive narrative. It has a lot of beginnings, a lot of middles, and a lot of endings."

*The Counterlife* is likely to be controversial and popular. Roth has only a passing interest in its debut.

"What has always struck me as bizarre about publication is that the book was finished seven months ago. I've been thinking of other things, I've been back and forth, fumbling with a new project. . . . My book comes out. I haven't forgotten it by any means, but it's not the live issue it was in my life when I was writing it. It's what I lived with, it was central to my life, it had my total concentration. It had me, it owned me, but that's over. Now it has a fate which is separate from mine. I'm not indifferent to its fate; obviously, I'd like it to be recognized for what it is. I wouldn't have published it if I didn't think it was good. But I feel that its reception is an event over which I have no control. I'd be mad to get tied up in it, so I try somewhat to look at its publication as an anthropological event."

This book, like the rest of Roth's fiction, contains some details that many readers will be tempted to see as autobiographical. How does Roth react to this perception of his writing?

"The relationship between my life and my work doesn't interest me the way it interests some readers, and frankly it's a pain in the ass. Suppose Roth did every single thing in every single book that he's written? So then what? And in this book, Zuckerman dies. And I died. And then I came back to life. And then my brother died. And what if my father had died? Suppose it was all true, every detail. So then what? That's what I always ask. Suppose I tell you that I did every single thing in all these books—say I had heart surgery—do you want to see my chest?—say I did everything even if it's contradictory. I hate to sound so weary, but even if all that were true, then so what?"

Actually, Roth does sound a bit weary, but he also sounds like a man who is deeply committed to his work. Roth on being a writer:

"Writing isn't hard work, it's a nightmare. Coal mining is hard work. This is a nightmare. . . . I'm not saying I'm uncomfortable—the nightmare doesn't have to do with money or health or a vast unhappiness. If I were a 53-year-old gynecologist, I would have everything worked out. I could look out into a waiting room full of patients and know that I have the competence, because it would be proven. I would know that I could do it.

"I'm not at all sure that I can do it when I'm working. There's a tremendous uncertainty that's built into the profession, a sustained level of doubt that supports you in some way. A good doctor isn't in a battle with his work; a good writer is locked in a battle with his work. In most professions there's a beginning, a middle, and an end. With writing, it's always beginning again. Temperamentally, we need that newness. There is a lot of repetition in the work. In fact, one skill that every writer needs is the ability to sit still in this deeply uneventful business."

After living and working in New York for several years, Roth decided in 1969 that he needed a change. He had come to find city life distracting and noisy, and *Portnoy's Complaint* had just been published, attracting attention and making Roth feel "rather visible." Having spent extended periods of time at Yaddo, the writers' colony in Saratoga Springs, Roth had developed a love of the countryside, which he had first experienced while at Bucknell University in the Susquehanna Valley. Roth spent a happy year in Woodstock, N.Y., and was looking for a permanent house there when he happened to hear about the farmhouse in Connecticut.

Roth spends a few months of each year in London, where Claire Bloom maintains a house—her work schedule somewhat dictates their movements—but he thinks of Connecticut as home.

"I didn't move to Connecticut so much as I moved to the country—I moved 100 miles away from New York City. The best way to get the job done is to block the turbulence out so you can make your own turbulence. So I live this uneventful life when I'm in Connecticut. This part of the state particularly is like the Switzerland of America. It's also beautiful, and one mustn't forget that. In about half

an hour"—Roth gestures in the direction of the approaching sun-
set—"it will be so beautiful you'll hardly be able to look at it. And
that's terrific, I like that. I have lots of affection for these acres.

"When I used to live here all the year round I was stirred by the
winters. They were so white—and that incredible cold. It's very
stirring . . . and it fits in with sitting by yourself and doing this
calculated brooding. On the other hand, I think if I lived here all the
time and never went anywhere, it wouldn't be a good idea. I imagined that in *The Ghost Writer*. I tried to project forward—suppose this
is the way I always lived—what would I feel like in 20 years? So I
choose not to stay here all the time. But it's a wonderful anchor, a
base, a haven. It's as good as any I've ever known."

The sun is setting. It *is* almost too beautiful to look at. We walk
around the house. Roth troubled by the universal worries of a home-
owner. Where is the man with the new gutters? He promised last
week. The lawn has been damaged by the fellow who comes to clear
away snow.

Bloom has gone off in the Saab on an errand. We speak of the
virtues of Saabs. Roth's father is nowhere in sight, but music—a
Beethoven symphony—pours from the house. Towels hang on a
clothesline by the back door; they must be frozen into boards.
Chilled but unfailingly polite, Roth walks me to my car and advises
me on his favorite route to New York City. He heads toward the
house, rubbing his hands, shoulders hunched against the cold. It's
nearly dark, but the bare oaks that follow the line of the ghost road in
front of the house are silhouetted against the sky.

# PW Interviews: Philip Roth

## Katharine Weber/1988

Reprinted from the August 26, 1988 issue of *Publishers Weekly*, published by the Cahners Publishing Company, a division of Reed Publishing USA. Copyright © 1988 by Reed Publishing USA.

When *The Counterlife* won the National Book Critics Circle Award earlier this year, Philip Roth, traveling in Israel, sent a taped acceptance speech to the NBCC awards ceremony. The book he had just completed was on his mind as he spoke of the relationship between fact and fiction:

"You begin with the raw material, the facts. . . . This can take days, it can take years. The mind conducts the examination at its own pace . . . and one day turns the facts over to the imagination. . . . The butcher, imagination, wastes no time with niceties: it clubs the facts over the head . . . slits its throat, and with its bare hands, it pulls forth the guts. . . . By the time the imagination is finished with a fact, believe me, it bears no resemblance to a fact. . . . Eventually, there's a novel. . . ."

With Farrar, Straus & Giroux's publication next month of his 17th book, *The Facts: A Novelist's Autobiography,* Roth returns to the raw material, the facts of his own life from which he has drawn many elements of his novels and stories. *The Facts* is an astonishing and original autobiographical narrative that can be read as a counterpunch to *The Counterlife*—a counterlife to the fictions.

Meeting with *PW* in a book-lined conference room at FSG, Roth appears to be brimming with energy and vitality. He is a young 55, and has grown only a little more bald and gray than in his most recent bookjacket photos. There is no hint of his breakdown in spring 1987 when, following minor surgery, he suffered "a prolonged physical ordeal that led to an extreme depression," which carried him "right to the edge of emotional and mental dissolution," as he writes in *The Facts.*

Getting "bluer and bluer," unable to work at all, Roth says he finally began to write "three- or four-page bits" about his childhood and early memories. Those first sketches later evolved into the first section of *The Facts,* called "Safe at Home."

"I didn't conceive of it as a book at the time," says Roth. "I didn't *conceive* of it. I just began to *do* it, the way you do occupational therapy. It never entered my mind to write an autobiography."

When pressed further about his momentary turning away from fiction, Roth refers to the opening pages of *The Facts,* which begin with a letter from Roth to Nathan Zuckerman, his fictional counterpart. In the letter, Roth explains his reason for writing the books, saying that he appears "to have gone about writing . . . absolutely backward, taking what I had already imagined, and, as it were, dessicating it, so as to restore my experience to the original, pre-fictionalized factuality."

Roth describes his need to find himself after his illness as an "effort to repossess my life." In order to "transform myself into *myself,* I began rendering experience untransformed."

If Roth didn't know what he was about while he was writing the autobiographical narrative, he certainly knew what he had when he was finished. His letter to Zuckerman goes on to say, "This manuscript embodies my counterlife, the antidote and answer to all those fictions that culminated in the fiction of you. If in one way *The Counterlife* can be read as fiction about structure, then this is the bare bones, the structure of a life without fiction."

The letter ends with a question: "Is the book any good? Be candid." Awaiting readers at the other end of Roth's narrative is Zuckerman's letter back to Roth: "Don't publish," he says, and points out many flaws in the manuscript. He quotes his wife Maria at length (Roth comments to *PW,* "I like it when Maria says, 'Uh-oh, still on that Jewish stuff, isn't he?' "), and ends in a plea to Roth "to alter the imaginative course so long ago laid down for you."

Roth says he began to write the letter to Zuckerman somewhere at midpoint, when "I began writing about why I was writing the book." At one stage he considered having Zuckerman comment in the margins of the manuscript. At another point he considered an appearance from Alexander Portnoy, "but he doesn't exist today. I would have no access to such a character. It's been a hell of a long time. Zuckerman is very fresh. I'm close to the character. In some ways, you could say this is a sequel to *The Counterlife.*"

Divided into five segments, the memoir takes the reader from the security of Roth's early childhood on through his college years, romances, marriage, and the publication of his first three books. *The Facts* leaves off with Roth on the eve of publication of *Portnoy's Complaint,* the novel that was to transform his public image and provoke even more accusations of "Jewish self-hatred" than had *Goodbye, Columbus, Letting Go* or *When She Was Good.* Zuckerman's circumstances in the closing pages of the book mirror Roth's: he and Maria are about to give birth, not metaphorically to a work of fiction, but fictionally, to a perhaps metaphoric baby.

While Roth is free to invent the facts for Zuckerman, can we trust him to have given us the straight goods about himself, as he says he does?

"These are the facts, your honor, as I remember them," replies Roth solemnly, and then he laughs, as he does frequently during the interview, a real "ha-ha-ha" laugh. "There is nowhere that I deliberately mislead anybody. There are omissions, yes. It's a very short book. It only takes us to age 36. It's about what it's about. It's not about what it's not about.

"There were other parts to the book that aren't there now. It went farther along in time. But that wasn't as interesting, I suppose, because a calm and orderly life is not as interesting as pressure and crisis. This is very much about finding a voice, isn't it? What happened after didn't matter to me in the same way."

Central to Roth's story is his marriage to a woman he calls Josie. Now dead, she was an alcoholic, an unstable shrew—as Roth portrays her—who lied and manipulated in incredible ways. She once went so far as to fake a pregnancy, purchasing urine for the test from a pregnant black woman in a park. This event found its way into *My Life As A Man,* only one of many episodes in Roth's life that he reveals as the basis for specific incidents in his fictions.

In his letter, Zuckerman carps at Roth for changing the names of most of the women in his life. Above all, Zuckerman says, "Josie is the real antagonist, the true counterself, and shouldn't be relegated like the other women to an allegorical role." Though he allowed Zuckerman to suggest that he give Josie her own name, Roth did not do so. "I didn't want to read those names in the reviews," he says, "and I wanted to protect the privacy of those people. I wrote the first draft with everybody's names, because that was helpful to me. David Rieff [Roth's editor at Farrar, Straus] read the manuscript with the real names."

Roth calls Rieff "a terrific reader, an excellent editor," one of several fine editors with whom he has worked. From his first book with George Starbuck at Houghton Mifflin to Joe Fox, Jason Epstein and Aaron Asher, Roth says, "I've had the best editors anyone could have at every publishing house I've been with."

Revealing that he works without a contract, he explains, "I don't want a contract or money until I'm done. *All* done. I want to be able to abandon a project at any point. I don't want the pressure to finish something because I have a check. The only book I ever took money in advance for was *Letting Go.*"

Represented by Candida Donadio until 1970, Roth has felt no need for an agent since then. "I don't mind doing business myself," he says. "I don't need someone to stand between me and my publisher and say the dirty word 'money.' I can say it."

Time and again, when *PW* raises points about the autobiography, instead of responding directly, Roth quotes criticism from Zuckerman or Maria in *The Facts*. Roth has lived with the actress Claire Bloom for more than a dozen years, for example, but she is never mentioned. "Yes, Zuckerman makes that point," agrees Roth. When the subject of psychoanalysis is raised—Roth was in analysis from 1962 to 1969, but omits mention of it—he responds, "Yes, Zuckerman calls me on that." He really has all the bases covered, then, doesn't he? Roth explodes with laughter, but points out, "Except the business of covering the bases isn't covered."

More seriously, he adds, "The Zuckerman letters have another function as well, as part of the novelist's autobiography. This is autobiography too—this is to give you some sense of what it is to be a writer. The letters are also what they appear to be: a genuine challenge to the book. Yet that challenge comes from me. We know, therefore, that this self-challenging aspect is a very strong ingredient in my life as a novelist. That's what I thought the inspiration was in the last section. So it really didn't have to do with covering the bases, but rather with establishing, as dramatically as I could, the whole notion of self-challenge."

Is Maria right when she observes that Roth is "not interested in happiness?"

"That's what she concludes," says Roth. "I'm not taking sides with Maria, or Zuckerman, or me. This is an interpretation, and it's there to allow the reader to enlarge his perception of the book."

Roth says he enjoyed writing Maria's part the most "because with the Zuckerman and Maria letters, I was working my way back into writing fiction."

*The Facts* leaves Zuckerman expressing fear that, like Roth, he'll have a breakdown. Psychoanalysis, while omitted from *The Facts*, has clearly been a significant factor for Roth. When asked to characterize his analysis, Roth is playfully evasive. Was this a traditional five-days-a-week analysis? "I think there were eight days a week." Asked to compare his writing of *The Facts* to the process of analysis, he responds, "In analysis you organize your life according to the perspective of psychoanalysis. You are a willing patient. This is not the work of a patient. The analysis isn't interested in the facts so much as the associations to the facts. . . .

"Writing leads to controlled investigation. The object of analysis is uncontrolled investigation. The goal was to write about things that strike me as tedious without being tedious."

Isn't that what a great writer does?

"There wasn't a great writer around. There was only me."

In *The Facts* Roth says he is "worn out and tired of further fictionalizing." Is he still?

"For the time I was writing *The Facts*, I wasn't engaged in that laborious job, I was engaged in this laborious job. Like most writers my age, I'm tired of a lot of things, and this was a vacation, although not a pleasant vacation. I'm tired of sitting alone in a room. It's a nice prison."

Roth sits alone in rooms in northwestern Connecticut, where he has a studio next to his 18th-century house, and in London, where he has spent parts of most winters for the past several years. He plans now to spend less time in London and more time here, probably in New York.

He is currently at work again, but won't characterize it in any way.

"I don't know what I'm writing," he says. "It's too amorphous to say." He concedes that it *might* be about Nathan Zuckerman. Perhaps he has taken Zuckerman's advice to heart. "The distortion called fidelity is *not* your metier—you are simply too real to outface full disclosures," writes Zuckerman in his letter at the end of *The Facts*. "It's through *dissimulation* that you find your freedom from the falsifying requisites of 'candor.' . . . Your medium for genuine self-confrontation is me."

# From Philip Roth, "The Facts" as He Remembers Them

## Mervyn Rothstein/1988

From *The New York Times*, 6 September 1988, sec. C, 17, 20. © 1988 by The New York Times Company. Reprinted by permission.

**Q.** Now vee may perhaps to begin. You were born in Newark, on March 19, 1933. Your parents, Herman and Bess Roth, named you Philip. You are a writer, primarily a novelist. But now, seated in your publisher's office at Farrar, Straus & Giroux, you say that you have written an autobiography, entitled *The Facts*. Why an autobiography?

**A.** It happened, you know. It emerged. This is where my inclinations took me.

**Q.** You write in *The Facts* that in the spring of 1987, after having minor surgery, you suffered "a prolonged physical ordeal that led to extreme depression," and that you wound up on the brink of emotional and mental dissolution. You don't say any more—but did this have anything to do with your decision to write an autobiography?

**A.** It's very private, and what I say in the book is really all I intend to say. But I began to write these memoirs as a way of facing something other than my difficulties. Strangely, it was a major disruption in my life that triggered this book; ordinarily, I'd say that most of my books begin in a period of calm and order and certain peacefulness. But a real disruption to concentration, focus and health initiated the writing here. And I wrote my way out of a serious depression.

**Q.** What parts of your life does the book cover?

**A.** It's about the apprenticeship of a writer. It's about the facts of my life as a writer, and how the writer came to be made. I tell about my family and my father, and his impact on my life. There's my neighborhood, and its impact on my life. There's a rather extended portrait of college, and its effect on my life. There's a portrait of a very lurid and tragic marriage, and its impact on my life. There's a portrait of another relationship with a woman, and its effect on me. There's a picture of a key scene in my struggle with my Jewish critics, and its effect on my life. And I write about how I discovered the voice that led me to write *Portnoy's Complaint*. Pretty intimate revelations. It answered my curiosity about how it all had come to pass.

**Q.** And yet at the same time the book is very different from an autobiography. The central portion is autobiographical, but the first part is a letter from you to Nathan Zuckerman, your major fictional character in recent years, asking him to read the manuscript and give you his opinion. And the final chapter is Zuckerman's response—in which he strongly questions your ability as an autobiographer. He says that you are "the least completely rendered of all your protagonists."

"In this book you are not permitted to tell what it is you tell best," he writes (or you write). ". . . In the fiction you can be so much more truthful without worrying all the time about causing direct pain. You try to pass off here as frankness what looks to me like the dance of the seven veils—what's on the page is like a code for something missing."

"Is this really 'you,' " Zuckerman asks, "or is it what you want to look like to your readers at the age of 55?"

**A.** This is a set of facts. I called the book *The Facts*, not *The Dirt*. I didn't wirte *The Dirt*. That's another book. I think this one tells a considerable amount about how somebody, in this case me, becomes a writer. In the end, there is someone who comes along, another voice, that questions, not the truthfulness, but the ability of the writer to be revealing in this form. It's the muse speaking, isn't it? The muse says, "You can't do this, you're better at the other thing." The muse, in effect, says: "You're too discreet. This isn't sufficiently savage. Candor's a kind of cover."

Now one shouldn't accept what Zuckerman says at face value. He has self-interest operating there—he wants to exist, he wants me to write about him, not about myself. And he also makes a good case as to why he's a better vehicle. The autobiography consists in part in the clash of those points of view, of being torn between the facts and the fiction, torn between the autobiographical impulse to understand something and the fictionalizing impulse to understand something. Which is the way to understand it—not for the world, not for any other writer, but for me?

Zuckerman casts doubt on the project, and this doubt, this uncertainty about my perception, is a powerful part of this writer's makeup. You're not sure you have a purchase on things. My impulse is to problematize material. I don't like when it sits flat on the page. I like when it's opposed by something else, by another point of view. At the end, the book seems to me to dramatize the doubt. In a sense Zuckerman's been all too convincing. But I meant the challenge to be strong. There's no sense mounting a weak challenge. There should be a tension between the body of the book and Zuckerman's reaction, just as the chapters of *The Counterlife* exist in a state of tension with each other. It's similar to what I did in *The Counterlife*—doubt is cast on what came before. This is a counterbook—it's my counterlife.

**Q.** Why Zuckerman?

**A.** I was halfway through the writing when I felt the need for a countervoice to oppose me. So I began to summon up my countervoices. At first I thought that since Portnoy, Alexander Portnoy, was a lawyer, he might well cross-examine me.

A couple of years ago in an interview with you, I said that I would never bring Portnoy back, unless I saw signs in the street saying "Bring Back Portnoy." Some weeks later I was taking my daily walk in the Connecticut woods, and some wag had hung a sign on a tree in the middle of nowhere. It said, "Bring Back Portnoy."

But Portnoy was too remote. Zuckerman wasn't.

**Q.** An excerpt from *The Facts* that deals with your marriage appeared recently in *Vanity Fair*. Some people who read that have said that such a bizarre portrait of a disturbed, vengeful woman—your wife, "my worst enemy ever," you call her—could only have been written by a misogynist. How would you respond?

**A.** My response to these people is that they've led very sheltered lives. They should consider themselves very fortunate. If I had had another marriage, I would have been delighted to write about it. But I happened to have had that one. People have experienced much worse.

But to get back to Zuckerman's comments. Autobiographies do give us information. They do give us a sense of the life and the progress of the writer. They don't necessarily mislead us. I vouch for these facts. This is more or less how it came to pass.

I think that my experience in college, for instance, at Bucknell, was as I wrote it—from a distance, of course, of many years. Sure, that may be a distorting factor. But I checked it out with various people. I talked to lots of people in my past. I didn't just rely on my memory. I sent that chapter to my old Bucknell English teacher. Not for a grade, though she gave me one. I said, "Mildred, how did I do?" and she said, "An A for content, a B for style."

When I wrote the Chicago stuff, I talked to friends who were there when I was there. I went out and walked around, because it quickens your memory. I spoke to my brother, I spoke to my father. I treated the job a bit as a journalist. I was my own fact checker.

In response to an excerpt about my childhood in New Jersey that was published in the *Times Book Review*, I got about 20 letters, almost all of them from people I'd been to high school with, which was rather wonderful. I heard from Seymour Feldman, who's a philosophy professor at Rutgers and who used to be the third baseman on our neighborhood team. We had lunch, and we had a terrific time together. I hadn't seen that guy since I went off to college. He wasn't a dear friend, he was a baseball friend. I was never in his house, and he was never in mine. But we had a lot to talk about. Not just the past, but what had happened since, and what the impact of that particular past had been on our lives.

Almost all my friends' fathers were butchers, or bakers, or tailors, and all these boys grew up to be professors and psychoanalysts. The feeling I got was the richness of the place. I got enormous pleasure from seeing how these people had worked out, knowing they had come from backgrounds no more intellectually or culturally privileged than my own.

**Q.** One final question. As Zuckerman asks, what is it that led someone with such an idyllic, pastoral childhood into such a lurid, pathological marriage? As Zuckerman says in *The Facts,* "What's left out is the motive."

**A.** (He smiles.) I made a mistake.

# What Facts? A Talk with Roth

## Jonathan Brent/1988

From *The New York Times Book Review*, 25 September 1988, 1, 46–47. © 1988 by The New York Times Company. Reprinted by permission.

*Philip Roth has often been accused of relying too heavily on the facts of his life in his fiction. Almost as though in answer to his critics, he writes in his autobiography that "every genuine imaginative event begins down there, with the facts." In an interview last month in Chicago, we talked about the problems he faced in telling the story of his life, and how that story relates to his fiction. I asked him first about the extent to which we've got—and he's got to—the facts, or what the facts, finally, are.*

Well, there are all sorts of facts, aren't there? This is a particular set of facts whose accuracy I will vouch for. I could undoubtedly come up with a different set of facts that would give my biography a very different slant. These facts delineate the sociology of my apprenticeship as a writer. What's emerged is a portrait of the artist as a young American.

*How do you account for that portrait, as opposed to some other, dominating here?*

Most likely it's the result of my having lived abroad, in London, for very long stretches of time during the last 11 years. At the conclusion of *The Counterlife,* Nathan Zuckerman says, "England made a Jew of me in only eight weeks, which, on reflection, might be the least painful method." It took me longer but eventually I came to understand the dimensions of my Americanness better than I ever had before.

*What happened to you living in England—what exactly did you see?*

I saw how much more in tune I am with a forceful society like our own, fueled by immigration, where the ambition is naked and the animus is undisguised and the energy is relentless and expended openly, without embarrassment or apology. Obviously there are any number of energetic, unapologetic people in London brimming with foul animus and cutthroat ambition; nonetheless, what's driving the society isn't dramatized with anything like the turbulent intensity that animates America. I'm speaking of intellectual and literary intensity no less than the intensity behind all the American trash, the intensity that's generated by the American historical drama of movement and massive displacement, of class overspreading class, region overtaking region, minority encroaching on minority, and the media cannibalizing the works.

Try to imagine England inviting, on the scale that the U.S. does, the cultural and political clashes—and, above all, the linguistic and racial "impurities"—that are the inevitable consequence of permitting millions and millions of foreigners alien to the mainstream society, language and political heritage to settle into one's developed country year in and year out. The wholesale colonization of England's major cities by third world immigrants—and only little more than half a century after those cities had been colonized by tens of millions from the impoverished classes of eastern and southern Europe—is unthinkable.

*Are you suggesting, somewhat like Zuckerman, that over 11 years you eventually came to feel as alienated there as a Jew as you did as an American?*

No—or at least not so long as Israel wasn't the subject of conversation. As I indicate in *The Facts,* for me being a Jew and being an American are indistinguishable, the one identity bound up and given shape by the other.

Of course, the lack of intellectual and literary intensity that I found in England might possibly have to do with the relative unimportance, in London, of Jews as critics and propagandists for modernism during the decades when, on the Continent, the modernist temperament was being formed in no small part by Jews. We know that it's impossible to account for the revolutionary transformation of art and ideas—from the turn of the century until the rise of Hitler—in Prague, Warsaw, Berlin and Vienna without understanding the reinvigorating force supplied by emancipated Jews as artists, critics, publishers, editors, columnists, satirists and psychoanalysts, and also as the eager consumers of what was new, strange and difficult in the arts. In Warsaw the phenomenon was called—not necessarily approvingly—the "Jewification" of the Polish intelligentsia. The coterie audience that used to turn out in Vienna to hear the gentile Robert Musil read in public from his unpublished masterwork is said, by Musil's biographer, to have been 90 percent Jewish. And in New York, in the 30's and 40's, it was Philip Rahv and his circle of enemies and friends at the *Partisan Review* whose vigorous exchanges on European modernism helped eventually to gain attention in America for artists and thinkers not at all in the American grain.

But unlike in Prague, Warsaw, Berlin, Vienna and New York, in London there was never the sort of Jewish presence to help engender, in the arts, a sustained subversion of the conventional and the traditional or to consume its byproducts—not in an intimidatingly class-bound, monolithic culture whose idea of civility, especially during these decades of artistic renewal in Europe, was so ruthlessly genteel and whose principle of social organization was exclusion. English cultural pressures managed to produce a generally tame and unremarkable society of Jews—and that is a unique cultural achievement.

*In* The Facts *you say what instigated an autobiographical work like this one was a severe depression and breakdown you suffered after some minor surgery had gone awry in the spring of 1987 and laid you low for a prolonged period. Are you suggesting now that it may have been your long English residence that actually induced you to write this book, perhaps in order to redefine yourself as an American to yourself?*

No, the form, at least, was dictated by an emotional ordeal growing out of a physical mishap that, to my astonishment, carried me a very long way from the author that I was accustomed to thinking of as myself. To recover this person who'd all but abandoned me required some conscientious remembering. I mounted my memories like a ladder until I found this lost being, myself, at the moment when he'd emerged from his first big battles to regroup his forces and go on. This doesn't mean that, when I looked back, my voluntary, part-time exile didn't provide a perspective that clarified the American factors that had determined my choice of a wife no less than they did my upbringing and education. The contrasts between the two English-speaking societies did indeed outline this Americanness for me, but that discovery was one that I could have taken up in fiction just as well. However, this was a period when, to put it mildly, I was not feeling psychologically robust or physically independent enough to imagine anything *because all I was doing was imagining things.* There is a vast world of intelligent consciousness between the illusions of a man who feels himself going mad and the illusions made by a man who is writing a novel, even a novel that may be driving him mad. A menaced self can't successfully entertain any more illusion than what's already hounding it into despair. The job was to suppress illusion, all illusion, and to haul myself in by my lifeline.

*You've referred to the difficulty of doing nothing but "imagining things," and in much of your recent work there is a quarrel between the "imagination" and the "facts." I'm thinking of the disagreement, for instance, between Zuckerman and his father in* The Ghost Writer *when his father says, "People don't read art—they read about people." And in* Zuckerman Bound *Zuckerman reflects, "That writing is an act of the imagination seems to perplex and infuriate everyone." In writing* The Facts *did you feel you were taking this quarrel in a new direction?*

I'm not, in the body of the book, quarreling with the imagination but suppressing it. While I was writing I thought how much more interesting an event or a character—including the central character—might become were I to veer from the facts and push things in a different direction. Alternatives more colorful or explosive or provocative or enigmatic often flickered at the edge of my attention. But ignoring the temptation to develop them was exactly the discipline that was new to me. The task wasn't to transform meager facts into compelling fiction but to try to find ways to make of interest things that looked to me too ordinary—or tedious or trivial—*without* turning for invigoration to the imagination, as I've instinctively done in the past.

When Zuckerman appears at the end of *The Facts* to argue that the book reeks of self-censorship, that it's an evasive collection of half-truths and half-portraits and shouldn't be published, then this quarrel you speak of between the imagination and the facts is reignited. And perhaps not necessarily to my advantage. With this last pair of books, instead of taking the quarrel in a new direction, I may have temporarily blinded myself as to which direction to take. *The Counterlife* owes a good deal to the doubt thrown on the credibility of whatever is imagined there, and now along comes Zuckerman in *The Facts* to make a very good case against the credibility of what I *don't* imagine here. So where does that leave me other than knee-deep in skepticism?

*You speak in* The Facts *of your intention of making yourself "visible" to yourself. I think that in the critique of your autobiography written purportedly by your character, Nathan Zuckerman, he is quite apt about all the silences, the blank spaces in the portrait. Is this blankness also part of who you are to yourself? Doesn't all the white space in the picture somewhat change the notion of the facts, as well?*

Sure, blank space is part of who one is to oneself. You know and also you don't know. But there's a difference, on the one hand, between not knowing and not knowing that you don't know and, on the other, not knowing and knowing *why* you don't know—and even, paradoxically, knowing what it is you don't know. Inasmuch as it's Zuckerman who claims to know a lot that I don't know, it may be that I'm not myself completely in the dark—providing that what he claims to know is *worth* knowing. To put it simply, I didn't think the book complete without a Zuckerman casting serious doubt on autobiographical objectivity as an attainable goal. One reader of mine, Paul Fussell, who agrees with Zuckerman, tells me that instead of being subtitled *A Novelist's Autobiography*, *The Facts* should have been called *An Autobiographer's Novel*.

*Do you agree with Zuckerman?*

I agree with Zuckerman. I also agree with myself. This book wouldn't be my autobiography without Zuckerman there as a challenge, putting a torch to the whole thing, nor, of course, would it be autobiography if he were there by himself. Either without the other is a fiction.

*The critical issue in writing is always not what story you tell but how you tell it. Your way of telling stories has changed quite a bit from* Portnoy's Complaint *to* The Counterlife *to* The Facts. *Has this been something you've consciously concerned yourself with?*

It's an instinctive concern. There are writers who have a lifelong set stance with which they stand at the plate to take their swings. I'd say that Isaac Singer is such a writer, particularly in his short stories. He is a natural, spontaneous storyteller who never seems confined by the conventions that he's established for himself. These conventions are the source of his confidence and bring out the best in him. Over and over again Isaac Singer will write a story about somebody coming up to Isaac Singer and telling him a story and over and over again the fiction is alive and interesting and informed by that wisdom Singer makes out of plain-spoken directness.

My writing temperament is more mercurial. I turn quickly on my own methods and am most suspicious of my work when it's coming easily and is, as it were, underproblematized. With each new project I feel like, and I am, a clumsy beginner. The swing from *When She Was Good* to *The Great American Novel* was just as marked as the swing from *Portnoy's Complaint* to *The Counterlife* or the swing from *The Breast* to *The Facts.* There is no more virtue in this sort of movement than there is in taking more or less the same approach in book after book the way Anthony Trollope did; looked at in a certain way it may even reveal a fundamental failure of vision. But for good or bad, what activates my talent is remaining responsive to my own inclinations and trying to find for them, each time out, the congruent mode of expression.

*The writers of Eastern Europe, who have been a longstanding interest of yours, engage in a kind of internal argument with themselves as Czechs or Poles or Hungarians or Soviets, and in doing so oppose the kitsch surrounding them. You argue against your experience, too, but as someone in whom a certain kind of kitsch has been internalized. In other words, it's not political kitsch or social kitsch, it's the nonmeaning and clichés of the inner self that I see Zuckerman opposing. But in* The Facts *you seem to be writing with the grain, not against it. Is this an instance of you letting down your guard against yourself? And doesn't this open you up to a whole new form of misunderstanding: not Philip Roth the anti-Semite, self-hater, etc.; but Philip Roth the regular guy, the well-meaning victim of a vicious*

*woman, etc.? What is the image you want the reader to take away
from* The Facts?

I can't say that I've thought much about this book *having* readers,
even though Zuckerman's critique holds that its faults almost all
derive from my inability to un-self-consciously—to *unmanipula-
tively*—address readers about my own life while speaking in my own
name. It's true that I've altered names of real people and a few
identifying details along the way in order, as best I can, to protect a
portion of the privacy of some of those I've been intimately involved
with. That would seem to involve a consciousness of readers. But,
frankly, to repeat what I said earlier, all the while this book was being
written it was the image that the *writer* was to take away from *The
Facts* that mattered most.

Does this book open me up to a whole new form of misunderstanding? Look, we are all of us opened up to a new form of
misunderstanding when we say hello to our neighbor in the morning,
let alone to a husband, a wife or a child. Zuckerman would contend
that I *invite* misunderstanding by labeling what is a fiction an autobiography—that misunderstanding is what I'm after. But he could be
wrong, you know.

# Philip Roth Faces "The Facts"
## Linda Matchan/1988

From *The Boston Globe*, 4 October 1988, 65–66. © 1988 by
*The Boston Globe*. Reprinted by permission.

LITCHFIELD COUNTY, Conn.—"Make yourself at home," says novelist
Philip Roth. "You came here to snoop."

Roth is not fond of being interviewed: this he makes clear from the
outset. He has twice canceled this appointment before eventually
relenting, allowing the reporter to "worm" her way in, as he good-
naturedly puts it once she gets there. He has warily insisted on
certain ground rules, one being that questions be restricted to material in his new book.

But, after all, it's hard to blame the guy. There aren't many
novelists who take quite the beating that Philip Roth does.

The recipient of the 1987 National Book Critics Circle Award, the
author of *Goodbye, Columbus* and *Portnoy's Complaint,* Roth has
been the target of more venom than even Norman Mailer. He has
been described as a self-hating Jewish pornographer. A malicious
destroyer of women. An obsessive anti-Semite whose greatest obsession is himself.

Yet, Roth is regarded by many critics as one of the finest contemporary writers in the country. In a recent review of his new autobiography, for instance, the *New York Times Book Review* hails him as a
"comic and satiric genius."

Still, they are always in evidence—the Irate Readers, the Deeply
Offended—the instant a Roth book hits the stands. Rhoda Koenig,
for example, who recently reviewed Roth's new autobiographical
work, *The Facts,* for *New York* magazine, pronounces him a "high-
minded" narcissist who is "egotistical, manipulative, self-protective,
and cold."

All these nasty words for a man born in Newark who makes his
living making up sentences. The inventor of the unforgettable Alexander Portnoy, a Jewish, sex-obsessed, shiksa-chasing claustrophobic

who rages—300 pages of rage!—on his psychoanalyst's couch
against his overprotective mother and constipated father. The creator
also of Nathan Zuckerman, the libidinous writer with a savage wit
who gives his own father a fatal coronary because he writes such
dirty books.

"Roth is like the New York Yankees," says David Reiff, Roth's
editor at Farrar, Straus & Giroux. "People hate the New York Yankees. It's the sort of writer he is. I can't think of anyone given less the
benefit of the doubt. He gets more bad press than anyone else
around."

All this, of course, leads one to wonder whether Philip Roth, face
to face, will turn out to be the sort Mrs. Portnoy would have called
"an independent big shot." A "Mr. Smart Guy."

But no. As Sophie Portnoy might also have said, "So? What's the
big deal?"

In person, Roth, 55, seems just a nice fellow. Cynical, yes. Biting,
yes. Affected, maybe a little. But certainly benign enough, funny, and
exceedingly obliging in an interview. Lanky, with a receding hairline
and sagging chin, wearing very white running shoes and well-worn
beige cords, Roth resembles an accountant on his day off more than
the globe-trotting neurotic you'd expect from the books.

He lives in a warmly decorated 1792 farmhouse in the woods of
northwest Connecticut, which he shares with the English actress
Claire Bloom. He divides his time between Connecticut and London,
where Bloom has a house and a daughter, opera singer Anna
Steiger, and he describes his existence as one marked, mostly unen-
tertainingly, by "an awful lot of solitude. A bit more than I like."

Roth, who has published 17 books, is being interviewed at a time
he says he doesn't especially relish, "a moment I'm not nuts about in
publishing." It is the post-publication period, the interval following
the completion of a book, when he feels the writing is behind him but
is just getting the attention of the public.

"I've always thought of the reception of a book as a kind of wall a
book has to go through to have its life, before it gets into libraries and
people's houses," he says.

"In book publishing, you finish a work about eight months earlier
than it comes out. There is a large gap between when you rid
yourself of it and its appearance in the world. Eight months is a long

time; it's hard to clear the deck. You begin something else, but the other damn thing is half with you. One is interviewed, which is beside the fact of writing. There are reactions to the book, some of which are hostile, which is never pleasant.

"You don't want to be hurt. A fellow novelist once described to me the reaction of a colleague to criticism. In the old days, he said, he was thin-skinned. Now, he has no skin."

Actually, the last couple of years have been rather troubling for Roth, as he explains in an unusual prologue to his book. (It takes the form of a letter to his alter ego Nathan Zuckerman, the hero of three of Roth's novels and a novella).

In the spring of 1987, Roth explains to Zuckerman, "what was to have been minor surgery turned into a prolonged physical ordeal that led to an extreme depression that carried me right to the edge of emotional and mental dissolution."

To restabilize himself, "in the effort to repossess life," he undertook what he calls a process of "self-investigation." He began, methodically and at the typewriter, to un-fictionalize himself, to tap out what had happened as opposed to what he'd imagined. He was worn out, he says, with 30 years of "coaxing into existence a being whose experience was comparable to my own and yet registered a more powerful valence." He hoped to recover his passion for writing, to "get back to that high-spirited moment when the manic side of my imagination took off and I became my own writer."

The Facts is the result. It is an unconventional autobiography, a sort of five-act drama—childhood in Newark, college at Bucknell, disastrous early marriage, object of Jewish wrath, literary fame and death of hated wife—in which the curtain falls at age 35.

It also includes a guest appearance by the indomitable Nathan Zuckerman, who writes a long, snide letter back to Roth and suggests that he trash The Facts. "You make a fictional world that is far more exciting than the world it comes out of," is Zuckerman's ultimate judgment.

These days, Roth finds himself—as usual—being called on to defend his writing methods. Why, for instance, Zuckerman?

"Let me put it this way," explains Roth, whose speaking manner bears traces of the college professor he once was. "Imagine the book without him. Without Zuckerman, you have a very different kind of book, a conventional autobiography. But I don't want to write it. Let the other guy write it. It's not a matter of being unconventional just to be unconventional. That would be silly. But it would be an incomplete autobiography, at least to me. My life includes *this*. The life I spend with Zuckerman is much more interesting than the life I spend without him. Zuckerman is part of my autobiography."

Zuckerman's abiding function is to be—in Zuckerman's words—Philip Roth's "front man." In Roth's words, "he's my Charlie McCarthy. The tradition in ventriloquism is that the dummy is always smarter than the ventriloquist; the joke is to have the dummy always being critical of the ventriloquist. Zuckerman is my dummy. He shows off for me, he challenges me. He's my creature, but that makes him all the more audacious."

He adds: "In clinical terms, it's called schizophrenia. But it's not called schizophrenia if you're in charge."

Whether Zuckerman will surface again in a novel is something Roth doesn't know. "I am writing *something*," Roth says, glancing towards his desk with a look that is almost pained. "But it bears no resemblance to prose, let alone a book. I'm filling the time."

Writing does not come easily to him, he says, as opposed to someone like John Updike, who has an innate fluency—or so Roth surmises from Updike's productivity.

"I am pretty clumsy," Roth acknowledges. "I have to knock my head against the wall quite a bit. It takes me roughly two years to write a book, and the first 18 months are misery—false starts, confusion, desperation. It's in the last six months that the whole damn thing gets written."

Yet he found writing an autobiography was an "exhilarating" experience in some ways. "I found it enjoyable in ways that fiction isn't," Roth says, in part because he treated the job as a journalist, calling up old acquaintances and teachers, some of whom he hadn't seen since boyhood, to verify information. "It was a nice change from the isolation."

Has writing *The Facts* accomplished one of its desired purposes—to restore Roth's zeal for writing fiction?

"It remains to be seen," responds Roth. "My brain is a little tired. I suspect other writers who have been at it 30 years would say the same thing. You *pump* this out of yourself."

Meanwhile, it is life as usual. Morning "ablutions." Familia for breakfast. Work from 10 a.m. till 6 in his studio behind the house, with an hour off for exercise. Then, it's back to the house, a drink, a newspaper, dinner, a quiet evening and sleep, except for an occasional Mets game and, once or twice a week, a visit with friends. Same thing, roughly, for life in England, except factor in homesickness for American extroversion.

"I find England a very opaque society," said Roth. "It's one of those countries where, if you're not born there, it is hard to grasp the intellectual life. Here, people tend to be exhibitionist and outgoing. You go out to dinner here with three or four friends, and the first thing you talk about is what's in the paper. The English people I know are witty and charming. But they don't talk about the dailiness of politics and culture."

Despite the apparent exoticism of his bicontinental existence, despite the high-profile neighbors—among them Arthur Miller and William Styron—Roth claims his life is not as enchanting, as high-flying, as it would appear.

"I make what a gynecologist in Hartford makes," he says. "And *he* gets it *every* year. Yes, I own a house. Everybody in America owns one! I own a car. Most people own two!"

He looks around, surveying the furnishings in his studio. "I seem to have a lot of desk lamps," Roth said. *"That's* where I splurge."

Roth seems in some ways mystified by the uproar he still triggers, by the way readers still assume his characters are precisely him.

"I'm not going to pretend that I'm Portnoy. Why should I? Writing is a performance. I imbue the characters with aspects of my personality. I'm the writer. I'm not the actor."

Why, even Zuckerman misunderstands him, grumbling in his letter to Roth that *The Facts* is too selective: those aren't all the facts.

"Zuckerman is wrong," says his embattled creator. "I think the book is pretty candid. I've come as close to the truth as I can." Roth sounds indignant. "Zuckerman can say whatever he wants. That's *his* business."

# An Interview with Philip Roth

## Asher Z. Milbauer and Donald G. Watson/1988

From *Reading Philip Roth* (New York: St. Martin's, 1988), 1–12. © 1988 by St. Martin's Press. Reprinted by permission.

*Many critics and reviewers persist in writing about Roth rather than his fiction. Why this persistence after all these years?*

If that's so, it may have to do with the intensity with which my fiction has focused upon the self-revealing dilemmas of a single, central character whose biography, in certain obvious details, over-laps with mine, and who is then assumed "to be" me.

*The Ghost Writer* was automatically described in the press as "autobiographical"—which means about Roth's personal history—because the narrator, Nathan Zuckerman, is an American-Jewish writer, my age, born in Newark, whose earliest writing elicits a protest from some Jewish readers. But as a matter of fact, that about constitutes the similarity between my history and Zuckerman's in that book. The unsettling opposition from his father that young Zucker-man confronts and that propels the moral plot of *The Ghost Writer,* I happen to have been spared; the intelligent, fatherly interest taken in his work by a renowned, older writer whose New England house-guest he's lucky enough to be at twenty-three, resembles no experi-ence of mine starting out in the fifties; nor have I ever met a woman to whom I have been romantically drawn because she resembled Anne Frank, or whom I mentally transformed into Anne Frank and endowed with her status in order to try to clear myself of Jewish charges of self-hatred and anti-Semitism.

Though some readers may have trouble disentangling my life from Zuckerman's, *The Ghost Writer*—along with the rest of *Zuckerman Bound* and *The Counterlife*—is an imaginary biography, an inven-tion stimulated by themes in my experience to which I've given considerable thought, but the result of a writing process a long way from the methods, let alone the purposes of autobiography. If an avowed autobiographer transformed *his* personal themes into a detailed narrative embodying a reality distinct and independent from his own day-to-day history, peopled with imaginary characters conversing in words he'd never heard spoken, given meaning by a sequence of events that had never taken place, we wouldn't be surprised if he was charged with representing as his real life what was an outright lie.

May I quote John Updike? Asked about my Zuckerman books, he said to an interviewer "Roth's inventing what looks like a *roman-à-clef* but is not."

*But if your books are misread, other than by John Updike, isn't that more or less the fate of most good writing? Don't you expect to be misread?*

That novelists serve readers in ways that they can't anticipate or take into account while writing doesn't come as news to someone who spent eight years with *Zuckerman Bound.* That's the story told on nearly every one of its 800 pages, from the opening scene, when Nathan the budding writer enters Lonoff's living-room seeking absolution from sins committed in his juvenilia against his family's self-esteem, to its conclusion on the day that, as an established writer in his forties, he is forced to surrender to the Prague police the wholly harmless Yiddish stories that they've decided to impound as subversive.

The only reading resembling the ideal reading that a writer sometimes yearns for is the writer's reading of himself. Every other reading is something of a surprise—to use your word, a "misreading," if what's meant isn't reading that's shallow and stupid but that's fixed in its course by the reader's background, ideology, sensibility, etc.

To be misread in any way that bears thinking about, however, a writer has to be *read* as well. But *those* misreadings, conferred by skillful, cultivated, highly imaginative, widely read misreaders, can be instructive, even when quite bizarre—witness Lawrence's misreadings of American literature; or Freud's, the all-time influential misreader of imaginative literature. So are those misreaders, the censors, influential, though for other reasons. And *are* the Soviet censors necessarily misreading, in Solzhenitsyn's fiction, his political aims? Though censors may appear to be the most narrow-minded and perverse of

all misreaders, at times they may be more discerning about the
socially injurious implications of a book than the most tolerantly
open-minded audience.

Serious misreading has little to do with a text's impenetrability—
geniuses misread nursery rhymes; all that's required is for the genius
to have his own fish to fry.

*In the light of this, what about an audience? Do you think you
have one, and, if so, what does it mean to you?*

I've had two audiences, a general audience and a Jewish audience.
I have virtually no sense of my impact upon the general audience,
nor do I really know who these people are. By a general audience I
don't refer, by the way, to anything vast. Despite the popularity of
*Portnoy's Complaint,* the number of Americans who had read, with
any real attention, half of my books—as opposed to those who may
have read one or two—can't number more than 50,000, if that. I
don't think any more about them when I'm at work than they think
about me when they're at work. They're as remote as the onlookers
are to a chess player concentrating on the board and his opponent's
game—I feel no more deprived or lonely than he does because
people aren't lined up around the block to discuss his every move.
Yet an unknowable audience of 50,000 judicious readers (or inventive misreaders) whose serious, silent attention I freely command is a
great satisfaction. The enigmatic interchange between a silent book
and a silent reader has struck me, ever since childhood, as a unique
transaction, and, as far as I'm concerned, it's what the public side
of the novelist's vocation has to come down to.

Counterbalancing the general audience has been a Jewish audience affording me, really, the best of both worlds. With my Jewish
audience I feel intensely their expectations, disdain, delight, criticism,
their wounded self-love, their healthy curiosity—what I imagine the
writer's awareness of an audience is in the capital of a small country
where culture is thought to mean as much as politics, where culture *is*
politics: some little nation perpetually engaged in evaluating its
purpose, contemplating its meaning, joking away its shame, and
sensing itself imperiled, one way or another.

*Why do you irritate Jews so much?*

Do I any longer? Certainly "so much" must be an exaggeration by now, though one that I've helped unintentionally to perpetuate because of the writer's predicament in *Zuckerman Bound*. After fifteen books I myself have become much less irritating than the Zuckerman I've depicted, largely because the Jewish generation that didn't go for me is by now less influential and the rest are no longer ashamed, if they ever were, of how Jews behave in my fiction.

Because it *was* shame—theirs—that had a lot to do with that conflict. But now that everybody's more confident about the right of Jews to have sexual thoughts and to be known to engage in authorised and unauthorised erotic practices, I think that stuff is over. On the whole Jewish readers aren't quite so responsive to other people's ideas (real or imaginary) of what constitutes socially acceptable Jewish behaviour, and don't appear to be obsessively worried that damaging perceptions of them can be indelibly imprinted on the public mind through a work of fiction, and that these will set off an anti-Semitic reaction. American Jews are less intimidated by Gentiles than they were when I began publishing in the 1950s, they are more sophisticated about anti-Semitism and its causes, and altogether less hedged-in by suffocating concepts of normalcy.

This isn't because they have been socially blinded by the illusory gains of assimilation, but because they are not so preoccupied as they once were with the problematical nature of assimilation, and are justifiably less troubled by ethnic disparities in the new American society of the last fifteen years—a society created by a massive influx of over twenty million people far less assimilable than themselves, about eighty-five per cent of them non-Europeans, whose visible presence has re-established polygenesis as a glaring and unalterable fact of our national life. When the cream of Miami is the Cuban bourgeoisie, and the best students at M.I.T. are Chinese, and not a candidate can stand before a Democratic presidential convention without flashing his racial or ethnic credentials—when *everybody* sticks out and doesn't seem to mind, perhaps Jews are less likely to worry too much about *their* sticking out; less likely, in fact, *to* stick out.

In addition to the shame I fomented there was the menace I was said to pose by confirming the beliefs of the committed Jew-hater and mobilising the anti-Semitism latent in the Gentile population generally. Years ago, the eminent scholar of Jewish mysticism,

Gershom Sholem, published an attack upon *Portnoy's Complaint* in an Israeli newspaper, predicting that not I but the Jews would pay the price for that book's imprudence. I learned about Sholem's article only recently in Israel—a university professor from Tel Aviv summarised Sholem's argument for me and asked what I thought of it. I said that history had obviously proved Sholem wrong: more than fifteen years had passed since the publication of *Portnoy's Complaint* and not a single Jew had paid anything for the book, other than the few dollars it cost in the bookstore. His reply? "Not yet," he said; "but the Gentiles will make use of it when the time is right."

The Jews I still irritate, who angrily disapprove of me and my work, are for the most part like the Israeli professor: for them the danger of abetting anti-Semitism overrides nearly every other consideration.

Of course there must be many Jews as well as many Gentiles who don't care for my books because they don't think that I know how to write fiction. Nothing wrong with that. I'm pointing rather to a psychological or ideological orientation, a view of politics and history that *had* to make *Portnoy's Complaint* anathema to a certain group of Jewish readers. Though the example of the Israeli professor might seem to suggest otherwise, this particular Jewish orientation seems to me to be disappearing just *because* of the existence of Israel and its effect upon Jewish self-consciousness and self-confidence in America.

I'm not referring to the pride that may be inspired in American Jews by Israeli military victories or military might—it's not images of Israel triumphant or naive notions of Israeli moral infallibility that have signalled to American Jews that they needn't any longer be too tightly constrained by protective self-censorship, but just the opposite, their awareness of Israel as an openly discordant, divisive society with conflicting political goals and a self-questioning conscience, a Jewish society that makes no effort to conceal its imperfections from itself and that couldn't conceal them from the world even if it wanted to. The tremendous publicity to which Israeli Jews are exposed— and to which they're not unaddicted—has many causes, not all of them always benign, but certainly one effect of unashamed, aggressive Israeli self-divulging has been to lead American Jews to associate a whole spectrum of behaviour with which they themselves may have preferred not to be publicly identified, with people perceived as nothing if *not* Jews.

*To move to a more general subject, do you think of fiction as a way of knowing the world or of changing the world?*

As a way of knowing the world as it's not otherwise known. Clearly a lot can be known about the world without the help of fiction, but nothing else engenders fiction's kind of knowing because nothing else makes the world *into* fiction. What you know from Flaubert or Beckett or Dostoyevsky is never a great deal more than you knew before about adultery or loneliness or murder—what you know is *Madame Bovary, Molloy,* and *Crime and Punishment.* Fiction derives from the unique mode of scrutiny called imagination, and its wisdom is inseparable from the imagination itself. The intelligence of even the most intelligent novelist is often debased, and at the least distorted, when it's isolated from the novel that embodies it; without ever intending to, it addresses the mind alone rather than suffusing a wider consciousness, and however much prestige it may be accorded as "thought," ceases to be a way of knowing the world as it's not otherwise known. Detached from the fiction a novelist's wisdom is often just mere talk.

Novels *do* influence action, shape opinion, alter conduct—a book can, of course, change somebody's life—but that's because of a choice made by the reader to use the fiction for purposes of his own (purposes that might appall the novelist) and not because the novel is incomplete without the reader taking action. The 1967 conference near Prague, organised by Czech intellectuals around themes in Kafka, turned out to be a political stepping-stone to Dubček's reform government and the Prague Spring of 1968; nonetheless it was not something that Kafka invited, could have foreseen, or would necessarily have enjoyed. Ways of knowing the world that he entitled *The Trial* and *The Castle*—which to most people still look like no way of knowing anything—were exploited by these Czech intellectuals as a means of organising a perception of *their* world persuasive enough to augment a political movement already underway to loosen the bonds of Soviet totalitarianism.

*You sound as though you really prefer that fiction should change nothing.*

Everything changes everything—nobody argues with that. My point is that whatever changes fiction may appear to inspire have usually to do with the agenda of the reader and not the writer.

There is something that writers do have the power to change and that they work to change every day, and that's writing. A writer's first responsibility is to the integrity of his own kind of discourse.

*Do you feel that the importance, if not even the integrity, of fictional discourse, is threatened by rivals like film and television and the headlines, which propose entirely different ways of knowing the world? Haven't the popular media all but usurped the scrutinising function that you attribute to the literary imagination?*

Fiction which has a scrutinising function isn't merely threatened, it's been swept away in America as a serious way of knowing the world, almost as much within the country's small cultural élite as among the tens of millions for whom television is the only source of knowing anything. Had I been away twenty years on a desert island perhaps the change in intelligent society that would have astonished me most upon my return is the animated talk about second-rate movies by first-rate people which has almost displaced discussion of any comparable length or intensity about a book, second-rate, first-rate, or tenth-rate. Talking about movies in the relaxed, impressionistic way that movies invite being talked about is not only the unliterate man's literary life, it's become the literary life of the literate as well. It appears to be easier for even the best-educated people to articulate how they know the world from a pictured story than for them to confidently tell you what they make of a narrative encoded in words—which goes some way to explaining why what the verbal narrative knows has itself become less knowable. It requires a kind of concentrated thought that has become either too difficult or too boring or both.

The popular media have indeed usurped literature's scrutinising function—usurped it and trivialised it. The momentum of the American mass media is towards the trivialisation of everything, a process presided over and munificently abetted during the last six years by the Great Trivialiser himself. The trivialisation of everything is of no less importance for Americans than their repression is for the Eastern Europeans, and if the problem does not seem to have achieved the same notoriety at the PEN Club as political repression, it's because it flows out of political *freedom*. The threat to a civilised America isn't the censorship of this or that book in some atypical school district somewhere; it's not the government's attempt to suppress or falsify this or that piece of information; it's the *superabundance* of information, the circuits *burgeoning* with information—it's the censorship of *nothing*. The trivialisation of everything results from exactly what they do *not* have in Eastern Europe or the Soviet Union—the freedom to say anything and to sell anything however one chooses.

There are now writers in the West tempted to think that it might really be better for their work if they were oppressed in Moscow or Warsaw rather than twittering away free as the birds in London, New York or Paris. There's a perverse undercurrent of persecution-envy around, an envy of oppression and the compression of freedom. It's as though without an authoritarian environment imaginative possibilities are curtailed and one's literary seriousness is open to question. Well, unfortunately for writers who may be afflicted with such longings, the intellectual situation for thinking Americans in no telling way mirrors, parallels, or resembles what is horrifying for thoughtful people in the Soviet orbit. There is, however, a looming American menace that evokes its own forms of deprivation and suffering, and that's the creeping trivialisation of everything in a society where freedom of expression is anything but compressed.

The Czech writer Josef Skvorecky, who now lives in Toronto, has said, "To be a bad writer in Eastern Europe, you *really* have to be bad." He means that in those countries the political origins of their suffering are plainly visible in everyday life and the predicament is constantly staring them in the face; personal misfortune is inevitably coloured by politics and history, and no individual drama is seemingly without social implications. What Skvorecky wryly suggests is that there is almost a chemical affinity between the consequences of oppression and the genre of the novel; what I'm saying is that in the unlikely, less graspable consequences of our unprecedented Western freedom, there may well be a subject for imaginative scrutiny of no less gravity, even if it doesn't light up and flash "Serious! Significant!" and "Suffering! Suffering!" in everybody's face. Our society doesn't lack for imaginative possibilities just because it isn't plagued by the secret police. That it isn't always as easy to be interesting in our part of the world as it is in Skvorecky's occupied country, may only mean that to be a good writer in the West and of the West, you have to be very, very good.

*Was it not a problem for your generation of writers to establish the seriousness of your fiction without resorting to or falling back upon the established conventions of seriousness, be they the realism of James or the modernism of Joyce?*

That's a problem for every generation. Ambitious young writers are always tempted to imitate those verified by authority; the influence of an established writer upon a beginning writer has almost entirely to do with the search for credentials. However, finding a voice and a subject of one's own entails making fiction that may well prompt the writer's first readers to think, "But he can't be serious," as opposed to, "Ah, this is very serious indeed." The lesson of modernism isn't encapsulated in a technique that's "Joycean" or a vision that's "Kafkaesque"—it originates in the revolutionary sense of seriousness that's exemplified in the fiction of Joyce, Kafka, Beckett, Céline—even of Proust—fiction which to an unknowing reader probably bears the earmark less of seriousness than of high eccentricity and antic obsession. By now the methods of these outlandish writers have themselves become the conventions of seriousness, but that in no way dilutes their message, which isn't "Make it new," but "Make it serious in the least likely way."

*Has the "least likely way" for you been your kind of comedy?*

Comedy for me has been the most likely way. I could do it no other way, though it did require time to work up confidence to take my instinct for comedy seriously, to let it contend with my earnest sobriety and finally take charge. It's not that I don't trust my uncomic side or that I don't have one; it's that the uncomic side more or less resembles everyone else's, and a novelist's qualities have to have their own distinctive force. Through the expressive gradations of comedy I can best imagine what I know.

*Yet isn't Zuckerman, in* The Anatomy Lesson, *afraid that he is not "serious" enough, afraid that for all his physical ailments he is not "suffering" sufficiently? Isn't that why he wants to enroll in medical school, and, in* The Prague Orgy, *travels to Eastern Europe?*

Yes. His comic predicament results from the repeated attempts to escape his comic predicament. Comedy is what Zuckerman is bound by—what's laughable in *Zuckerman Bound* is his insatiable desire to be a serious man taken seriously by all the other serious men like his

father and his brother and Milton Appel. A stage direction that
appears in *The Prague Orgy* could easily have been the trilogy's title:
*Enter Zuckerman, a serious person.* Coming to terms with the profane realities of what he had assumed to be one of the world's
leading sacred professions is for him a terrific ordeal—his super-
seriousness is what the comedy's *about.*

Zuckerman Bound opens with a pilgrimage to the patron saint of
seriousness, E. I. Lonoff; it ends, as you point out, at the shrine of
suffering, Kafka's occupied Prague. Imagining himself married to
Anne Frank is the earliest escape that he attempts to contrive from
the seriousness that first challenges his youthful illusions about a
dignified role in the world. Judge Leopold Wapter, Alvin Pepler, the
Czech secret police, a crippling and unexplained pain in the neck—all
are representatives of impious life irreverentially encroaching upon
that seriousness he had once believed inherent to his high calling.
But what most successfully subverts the high calling's esteem is his
sizeable talent for depicting impious life: it's Zuckerman who gives his
dignity the most trouble.

The denouement of the trilogy begins midway through the third
volume, when, on the way to Chicago to become a doctor—for those
American Jews who most disapprove of him, the supreme embodiment of professional seriousness—Zuckerman adopts the disguise of
a pornographer and, abandoning whatever claim he believes he still
has to be taken seriously, transforms himself into a vessel of the
profane (in *every* sense of the word). Well, it's a long way from
pretending to be the husband of Anne Frank in E. I. Lonoff's
sanctum sanctorum, to proclaiming himself a vice king, at one with
the polluted, as publisher of *Lickety Split.* Like a good modernist
writer, Zuckerman the pornographer imagines at last the least likely
way to dramatise the serious lesson taught him by the chastening
ordeal of unhallowed existence.

I realize that this sort of ordeal, especially as suffered by the high-
minded, looks a little like an old, obsessional theme if you think of
Gabe Wallach in *Letting Go* or of David Kepesh in *The Breast* and
*The Professor of Desire.* The ordeal of an unhallowed existence is
really what Portnoy's complaining about, too.

*Are you complaining about it—is that why it's an old, obsessional
theme?*

Obsessional themes evolve from astonishment as much as from enduring grievance—a writer is not so much beset by the theme as by his underlying *naïveté* in the face of it. The novelist suffers from serious ignorance of his obsessional theme. He lays siege to it time and again because the obsessional theme is the one he least understands—he knows it so well that he knows how little he knows.

My answer to the question is no: no complaint from me about unhallowed existence—it's all you get and I'm not so refined as to feel defiled by it. Of course you come here to be insulted. It's what they put on the tombstones—*He Came Here To Be Insulted,* carved in letters three inches deep. Lowly life, however, so long as it doesn't tumble over into misery and horror, can still be entertaining, and, for all its grittiness, strangely uplifting. As young Zuckerman discovers in *The Ghost Writer,* what makes ours a species of moving creatures isn't the high purposes but the humble needs and cravings. Yet there *are* those high purposes, and inappropriate as they may be to an unhallowed existence, they have been provided for some odd reason and just won't seem to go away. My obsessional theme is calculating what it costs a creature of humble needs and cravings to be saddled with a high purpose as well.

*We realize that you are reluctant to appear to be explicating a book prior to its publication. However, without "explaining" it away, can you comment generally on the unusual form for* The Counterlife, *which is certainly unlike anything you've done before?*

Normally there is a contract between the author and the reader that only gets torn up at the end of the book. In this book the contract gets torn up at the end of each chapter: a character who is dead and buried is suddenly alive, a character who is assumed to be alive is, in fact, dead, and so on. This is not the ordinary Aristotelian narrative that readers are accustomed to reading or that I am accustomed to writing. It isn't that it lacks a beginning, middle, and ending; there are too *many* beginnings, middles, and endings. It is a book where you never get to the bottom of things—rather than concluding with all the questions answered, at the end everything is suddenly open to question. Because one's original reading is always being challenged and the book progressively undermines its own fictional assumptions, the reader is constantly cannibalising his own reactions.

In many ways it's everything that people don't want in a novel. Primarily what they want is a story in which they can be made to believe; otherwise they don't want to be bothered. They agree, in accordance with the standard author-reader contract, to believe in the story they are being told—and then in *The Counterlife* they are being told a contradictory story. "I'm interested in what's going on," says the reader, "—only now, suddenly, there are two things going on, three things going on. Which is real and which is false? Which are you asking me to believe in? Why do you bother me like this!"

Which is real and which is false? All are equally real or equally false.

Which are you asking me to believe in? All/none.

Why do you bother me like this? In part because there really is nothing unusual about somebody changing his story. People constantly change their story—one runs into that every day. "But last time you told me—." "Well, that was last time—this is this time. What happened was. . . ." There is nothing "modernist," "postmodernist" or the least bit avant-garde about the technique. We are all writing fictitious versions of our lives all the time, contradictory but mutually entangling stories that, however subtly or grossly falsified, constitute our hold on reality and are the closest thing we have to the truth.

Why do I bother you like this? Because life doesn't necessarily have a course, a simple sequence, a predictable pattern. The bothersome form is intended to dramatise that very obvious fact. The narratives are all awry but they have a unity; it is expressed in the title—the idea of a counterlife, counterlives, counterliving. Life, like the novelist, has a powerful transforming urge.

# Intimate Affairs
## Brian D. Johnson/1990

From *Maclean's*, 30 April 1990, 66–67. © 1990 by *Maclean's*.
Reprinted by permission.

Sex sells. That would explain the dust jacket of Philip Roth's new novel, *Deception,* which features a picture of a man's hand curled around the naked flank of a woman in bed. It would also explain the blurb, which describes the book as "Roth's most provocative novel about the erotic life since *Portnoy's Complaint.*" That work was published two decades ago, and Roth, now 57, has written another 13 novels since. But, for many readers, his name is still synonymous with *Portnoy,* the book with all those indelible images of the boy who could not stop masturbating.

Roth's characters are grown-up now. They no longer lock themselves in the bathroom. But, with their love affairs and lies, they are still playing games of sexual hide-and-seek. Roth's new novel is about adultery, in a manner of speaking. True to its title, *Deception* is deceiving. Despite the erotic hard sell of the dust jacket, there are no graphic descriptions of sex—or of anything else. The novel is pure dialogue, without a phrase of exposition or attribution, without a single "he said" or "she said"—just bare-naked talk.

*Deception* distills a number of Roth's favorite obsessions. It ponders the dilemmas of being male, being Jewish and being a writer. And, like his previous novel, *The Counterlife* (1986), the narrative hinges on a riddle about autobiography and fiction. With the possible exception of John Updike, Roth has plumbed the male psyche more thoroughly than any American novelist of his generation. It can become tedious—he sometimes writes as if he is stuck in a bad marriage with his own legacy. But, in *Deception,* he breaks fresh ground, at least stylistically. "You see Roth as a musician in this book," Updike, a friend of Roth's, told *Maclean's* last week. "It's tempting to see his work as variations on what seem to some people not enough themes. But you have to admire the way he sticks to his themes and, like Bach, does one more turn through his obsessions."

Roth's new book marks a departure in several ways. With *Deception,* he made a controversial move to a new publisher and received the largest contract of his career: $2.1 million for a three-book deal. Abandoning the literary house of Farrar, Straus & Giroux, Roth moved to the more commercial firm of Simon and Schuster. Recently, the chief executives of the two companies have been sniping at each other like combatants in a custody battle. His former publisher, Roger Straus, predicted that Simon and Schuster will lose more than $1 million on Roth. It printed 100,000 copies of *Deception,* although none of Roth's recent novels has sold even half that number. Simon and Schuster's Richard Snyde called Straus "a bad loser."

During a recent interview with *Maclean's,* Roth seemed merely amused by the issue of his commercial potential. He said that his new publisher "tried to put as much distance as he could between my old dust jackets and the new one. I said, 'Go ahead, do what you want to do and see what happens.' " Sitting in a lavish corner office high above midtown Manhattan, a Simon and Schuster executive roost borrowed for the interview, the novelist wore a tweed jacket and grey flannels, with a blue button-down shirt and a dark paisley tie. He talked about his life, his writing and the blurred boundary between them. "You get tired of your own voice, tired of your own sentences," he said. "This book is a momentary escape from all kinds of narrative building blocks that I have been playing with for a long time. It is primarily about two people in hiding. They have a sexual life, but the rest of their life is only talk—talking and listening are almost erotic activities."

Most of *Deception* consists of precoital and postcoital conversations between adulterous lovers: an unnamed literary Englishwoman and a Jewish-American novelist named Philip, who is living in London. Roth, too, is a Jewish-American novelist who has lived in London, but he insists that *Deception* is fiction, not autobiography. The novel's protagonist offers the same argument to his shocked wife after she discovers a notebook recording his conversations with his mistress. He tells her that he made the whole thing up, that she has been taken in by a trick of literary ventriloquism. "I write fiction and I'm told it's autobiography," says the fictional Philip. "I write autobiography and I'm told it's fiction."

*Deception* offers teasing glimpses through the keyhole that connects the two, but Roth is impatient when critics start fumbling for a skeleton key. It has been suggested that novelist Janet Hobhouse may be a model for Philip's mistress in *Deception*. Like the character, Hobhouse is a British writer who fell victim to cancer. And she once lived in an apartment upstairs from him, just as the narrator's lover lived upstairs from him in Roth's previous novel *The Counterlife*. Asked if Hobhouse was indeed a model, Roth grabbed a copy of *The New York Times,* scanned the front page and picked a woman's name at random: "Sarah Lyall. Suppose I say to you it's Sarah Lyall. Once you know that, what do you know? All you know is gossip, which is to know nothing. It's a silly game."

But Roth's peekaboo narrative provokes curiosity. And he admits that he is "ruthless" in exploiting personal intimacy and betraying confidences for the sake of a good story. "Anybody who enters a writer's life intimately knows that we play for keeps," he said. "It's a kind of gangsterism. I don't know why anybody has anything to do with me—I wouldn't." Laughing, Roth added, "Really, I should have a big sign that says 'Beware—vicious writer.' "

Willing to take her chances, British actress Claire Bloom, 59, has lived with Roth for the past 15 years. They share a farmhouse in Connecticut. Their relationship has had its rocky moments, he admits, but not because of any indiscretions that he has committed on the page. "Claire's in the same business," he said. "Writing is my acting—it's very much a kind of performance. You go into a room apart from other people and concentrate. You release inhibitions—and relinquish a sense of consequence." Added Roth: "You are both the performer and the audience, rather like a child playing by himself."

The son of a life insurance salesman and his wife, Roth was raised in Newark, N.J. As he later wrote in his 1988 memoir, *Facts: A Novelist's Autobiography,* he tried to fulfil "the mythological role of a Jewish boy growing up in a family like mine—to become the hero one's father failed to be." After starting a career as a university teacher, he won the National Book Award for his first book of stories, which featured a novella titled *Goodbye, Columbus* (1959). After *Letting Go* (1962), a belabored first novel about Jewish intellectuals, and *My Life as a Man* (1974), the thinly veiled story of his disastrous

marriage to Margaret Martinson, which ended with her death in
1968, the profane candor and wit of *Portnoy's Complaint* made Roth
famous in 1969.

In the 1970s, Roth attempted more fanciful works, including *The
Breast* (1972), the comic tale of a man who turns into a giant
mammary gland. But, during the past decade, Roth has devoted
himself to an increasingly self-absorbed style of personal realism. A
trilogy of novels, collected as *Zuckerman Bound* in 1985, features a
character named Nathan Zuckerman, a novelist famous for writing a
profane best-seller. Zuckerman resurfaced in *The Counterlife* and
underwent a quintuple bypass operation—eerily foreshadowing
Roth's own quintuple bypass last summer. "This was rather un-
canny," recalled Roth. "I thought, 'Not bad, what do you do next?'
Claire said, 'Just don't become a breast.' "

Roth's fiction is more typically fixated on the male organ—from the
candid confessions of masturbation in *Portnoy* to the passionate
defence of circumcision that concludes *The Counterlife*. Indeed, his
work contains some of the most introspective discourse about male
sexuality that American literature has to offer.

With *Deception,* Roth's duet in adultery, he finally gives equal time
to a female character—making her at least as authentic and sympathetic as the man. But the novel's viewpoint remains stubbornly
male. In one amusing stretch of playacting, the mistress interrogates
Philip in a mock trial, asking him, "Can you explain to the court why
you hate women?" Roth said that the scene grew out of *The Hand-
maid's Tale,* Margaret Atwood's 1985 novel about a future state that
enslaves women. Roth simply reversed the premise. "It was a tiny
inspiration," he added, "but I enjoyed it enormously—imagining a
feminist dystopia, a hard-nosed feminist state."

Roth clearly has a keen sense of politics that goes beyond gender
and Jewishness. Taking a number of trips to Prague in the early
1970s, he played an active role in helping to publish Eastern Europe's dissident writers. But the world's political landscape remains
largely absent from his own fiction. And when *The Bonfire of the
Vanities* author Tom Wolfe attacked American novelists for abandoning social realism in his now-notorious *Harper's* magazine essay last
November, he singled out Roth. Citing an early essay by Roth, Wolfe
wrote that it taught "a generation of serious young writers . . . that it

was time to avert their eyes." Roth says that he was misquoted. "Tom is not a good reader," he said. "I ran into him on the street about a month ago and took him for a cup of coffee to straighten him out." Referring to Wolfe's affection for impeccable white suits, Roth added, "We were both amused by each other's clothes—we were worlds apart."

Roth's writing agenda seems increasingly personal. He has just completed *Patrimony,* an autobiographical memoir about his father that is scheduled for publication next year. Meanwhile, he says that he is grappling with the beginnings of a new novel. "Whenever I finish a book, I'm absolutely empty," he said. "I don't know what the hell to write about. But, after a while, something starts to cook. And it's often an argument with your previous book—you try to undo it."

Constantly quarrelling with his characters—and himself—Roth appears to thrive on ambivalence. In *Deception,* he writes about "the terrible ambiguity of the 'I,' the way a writer makes a myth of himself." Tearing down the myth and building it up, Roth keeps improvising new variations. And as he redraws the line between truth and fiction, the object of the game, like an imaginary mistress, remains elusive.

# "Life *Is* and": Philip Roth in 1990
## Hermione Lee/1990

From *The Independent on Sunday*, 2 September 1990, 12–13. © 1990 by Hermione Lee. Reprinted by permission.

To the visitor, it looks like a perfect place to wrestle with a new book. The beautiful 1790s farmhouse is hidden away among the hills and immaculate colonial villages of the privileged New England Berkshires. Chipmunks cross the road in front of you as you take your walk, and deer come up from the surrounding woods to browse near the swimming-pool. In a splendid old barn by the house, wood is stacked for winter; inside, light rooms, a summer fire in the big hearth, good wine, good (vegetarian) food, good jokes and interesting talk.

The Philip Roth-Claire Bloom marriage certificate, dated 29 April 1990, is stuck on the fridge door and there are lots of running gags about despotic husbands and obedient wives. Roth and Bloom are renowned among their friends for sustained improvisations. For now, the world-famous actress and novelist are being good country folk. But in a smaller house a short walk away at the edge of a field, there's a study identical to the ones Philip Roth uses in London and New York, complete with IBM golfball typewriter, fax machine, exercise bike and a walking machine called a "Treadmill," where Roth is in business again.

On the whole, it is not rural seclusion that you look for in his books. You go to them for dazzling verbal pyrotechnics, startling analyses of cultural dislocation, energy, despair, and good Jewish jokes. Roth's *alter ego,* the Jewish American novelist Nathan Zuckerman, makes his fictionalised way through Roth's own journeys. He goes from Newark to Manhattan to the remote, snowbound Berkshires of the reclusive "maestro" of *The Ghost Writer*. He goes from America to England. He goes from the Prague of bitter jokes and comical desperation to the Jerusalem of competing fanaticisms. And it's the voices and conflicts, the painful stories that you most remember.

In *Deception,* Roth's new novel of secret adultery, the arena has been reduced to a writer's small London study. "Let's see how much attention you've been paying," the lovers say to each other, itemising the contents of the room. But the room might as well be the inside of a mind. And it's not the kind of love story in which we admire their bodies and find out about what they're wearing when they get dressed again. We just hear their voices.

A novel all in dialogue isn't a new departure for Roth, it's a concentrated version of what he's done before. *The Counterlife,* his great 1986 tale of conflicting cultural identities, has a lot to say about the erotics of speech. Nathan has a heart problem (illness and cure are persistent metaphors for Roth, from Portnoy's "complaint" to Zuckerman's "anatomy lesson"), so can't make love to Maria, the woman he loves. Instead, "they never stop talking . . . I expose myself to her voice as though it were her body." She calls it "the purest form of eros . . . that endless, issueless, intimate talk."

But the sound of stories isn't only erotic, it's also dramatic, political, disturbing; it's this novelist's raw matter. Lives into stories, stories into lives; that's the name of Roth's double game.

He deals succinctly with his characters' appearances. Nathan Zuckerman goes through five books without telling us much about what he looks like. Maria's genteel Gloucestershire mother expresses her deeper feelings by remarking that he is rather Mediterranean-looking. It might be safe to assume that when Nathan reaches 55 he will look not unlike Philip Roth, who makes a Hitchcockian appearance at his own character's funeral in *The Counterlife,* as a "bearded man of about fifty, a tall, thin man wearing gold-rimmed bifocals and a grey hat, looking from the conservative cut of his clothes as though he might be a broker—or perhaps even a rabbi."

Philip Roth is living in America now, after almost a decade of transatlantic commuting, and his rabbinical beard has been eradicated. Otherwise he looks much as he describes the anonymous gentleman at the funeral—though that discreet account leaves out the very intent, dark eyes and fierce black bushy eyebrows, the engaging smile, the chortle of laughter when he's amused, the low, usually quiet, engaging voice, and a physical demeanor marked—apart from some affable and expansive gestures and some eruptions of manic, brilliantly funny impersonations and anecdotes at the dinner table—

by a held-in, careful, self-contained manner, polite, attentive and deceptively mild. This self-controlled person is packed full with energy, likes to be amused and challenged, and is devastatingly quick to pick up on soft thinking or weak arguments. He listens well, he reacts to everything, for good or ill, and his talk is a fast-moving mixture of the reflective and the exuberantly dramatic. He can be relentless, but he's never a bore.

I met Roth first in 1982, because I'd written a short book about his work, and, after he read it, he invited me to have lunch with him to thank me for it. Roth's friends, when asked about him, will always have examples to give of this sort of generosity. He was then living partly in London, in Claire Bloom's house in Chelsea, and partly in his house in Connecticut. His second shell, in both places, was his study—austere, functional, undecorated, something of a monastic cell (the cell which he turns in his imagination into the love-setting for *Deception*). Over the next few years we would meet occasionally, sometimes socially but more often to talk about his work-in-progress.

Taking his cue (surprisingly, perhaps) from an essay on "Reviewing" by Virginia Woolf, Roth has developed the habit of giving late drafts of his work to a few interested readers for early criticism—a job which puts the critic on his/her mettle like no other. In the early Eighties he was in the middle of the Zuckerman "trilogy" that became *Zuckerman Bound*. And during its evolution his states of mind seemed to keep pace with the novels. In the limbo before starting each book he would be subdued and despondent; as the work took shape he would seem much more ebullient and outward-looking.

The Zuckerman phase culminated in *The Counterlife*. I read the draft at the end of 1985; it was revised in 1986 and published at the end of that year. It proved to be a watershed, not only in his "Zuckerman" period—the book's reviewers almost unanimously treated it as one of the major American novels of the decade, and as a great development in the Rothian themes of alternative selves for the Jewish-American novelist—but in his life. After that, a series of unlooked-for events changed things for him dramatically.

In the spring of 1987, Roth underwent a knee operation which went wrong, and in the aftermath of that disastrous and depressing episode he began to take a certain type of sleeping pill which—unknown to him—could create symptoms remarkably and horrifying

like a suicidal nervous breakdown. All through the summer of 1987,
back in rural Connecticut, he thought he was going mad. A friend put
him onto an expert who diagnosed the cause and got him off the
drugs.

Coming out of that trauma, he wrote *The Facts: A Novelist's
Autobiography*—non-fiction as therapy. The book is addressed by
Roth to Zuckerman, asking him if he should publish it or not. Zuckerman replies: take my advice, don't publish. You need *me*: where's
the anger? where's the energy? *The Facts* goes back to the "real-life"
basis of the novel *My Life as a Man,* and tells the story of Roth's
childhood, his college days, and his first marriage. It is a vivid,
absorbing, and unforgiving document, but it does not have the
rhetorical energy of the Zuckerman trilogy. As Nathan points out,
without him it *is* a subdued narrative. Given the personal circumstances at the time, the book's melancholy tone is not surprising.

Meanwhile, Roth was feeling an increasing sense of cultural isolation in England. What frustrated him, Roth says, was that he couldn't
*hear* the country. Nobody screamed at each other, nobody let rip,
nobody went on about things. Nobody came into a room for dinner—as they do every night in New York—saying, "You know what
gets me about this place?" Nobody—for instance—talked to him
about Northern Ireland. They talked to him reprovingly, to his
growing exasperation and bafflement, about American foreign policy
in Nicaragua, the outrageousness of bombing Libya, and the evils of
Israeli expansionism and militarism. He developed a distaste for what
he saw as fashionable anti-American leftism; it felt to him un-self-
critical and biased. And there also seemed to him, in public and in
everyday social life, to be a considerable amount of anti-Semitism.
Nathan and Maria have a terminal row about this at the end of *The
Counterlife.* Nathan takes exception to Maria's qualms about the
Jewish insistence on identity: "Talk about *Jewish* tribalism. What is
this insistence on homogeneity but a not very subtle form of *English*
tribalism? What's so intolerable about tolerating a few differences?"

Roth always tells you not to quote Nathan Zuckerman as if he were
Philip Roth. Still, there is no little similarity between the way Roth has
talked about complacent English liberal gentility, and what he gives
his character to say here.

By 1988 he was clearly falling in love with America again: its

energy, its staggering cultural diversity, its eloquence, its space for
outspoken argument. While he was moving back, he had several
books on the boil: *Deception,* a rewriting of the love-story with *The
Counterlife*'s "Maria," *Patrimony,* a moving account of his father's
last years, and a third shadowy book behind them. In the summer of
'89 a move was under way to go with the formidable New York agent
Andrew Wylie from his old publisher Farrar, Straus and Giroux (his
editor, David Rieff, was leaving publishing at the time) to Simon &
Schuster. The move was the source of more gossip, in the small
world of New York and London publishing, than there's been about
Roth since *Portnoy* days. The deal culminated in his signing a three-
book contract. He took $1.2m on delivery of the first two (he never
gets paid in advance for any book).

That same summer, Roth was preoccupied with his father's ill
health; and then he himself nearly died. Rushed into hospital, following an attack of breathlessness after his daily swim, he had the same
operation—quintuple heart bypass surgery—that he'd given to
Nathan Zuckerman in *The Counterlife.* "No good to me at all," he
said on the phone, "I've already used it."

Since then he's felt terrific: back in England earlier this year for
Claire Bloom's performance in *When We Dead Awaken* at the
Almeida, he celebrated his 57th birthday with enthusiasm. But his
own complete recovery had to be set against the death of his re-
doubtable father, the hero of *Patrimony.* All year, too, Roth has
watched with passionate interest the changes in Eastern Europe. He
went to Prague and did a long interview with Ivan Klima. He started
a new book, about which he will say nothing yet. And he and Claire
Bloom got married.

Roth's new relationship with America has changed even in the last
year. When I visited him in the spring of '89, and he and Claire
Bloom had settled into a light, cool, orderly apartment on the West
Side, near the Park, he showed me round his patch of New York as if
he'd just invented it. Everything delighted him: the glamorous city
skyline from the apartment window, the all-night Puerto Rican food
and flower shops, the hundred-and-one television channels, the New
York news stories that everyone was always discussing, the badinage
in every shop you went into, the busy vociferous *Jewishness* of New

York. Even the beggars at every street corner seemed part of the city's monstrous, excessive, absorbing life.

On Sunday morning he promised me the best bagels in New York for breakfast, but the shop was closed: Philip Roth had forgotten it was Passover. ("You'll dine out on *that*," he said ruefully.) The Mets were playing the Cubs at Shea Stadium, and we went out with the crowd. Roth explained the rules of the game to me extremely thoroughly and sang along with the baseball anthem. In *The Facts,* he describes "the intense adolescent camaraderie" of his Newark baseball-playing schooldays as "the primary means by which we were deepening our *Americanness.* Our parents were the first-generation of offspring of poor turn-of-the-century immigrants from Galicia and Polish Russia, raised in predominantly Yiddish-speaking Newark households where religious orthodoxy was only just beginning to be seriously eroded by American life." It was the first of the cultural encounters which would be central to the writing. Now, Ulysses back from his travels, he seemed to be re-enacting that excitement.

An important part of the pleasure of that return to America was in his teaching: two courses at Hunter College in New York, to students whom he describes as "excellent, garrulous, demanding." The courses are on Kafka, post-war European literature, and "the literature of extreme situations." The writers who interest Roth—Milan Kundera, Ivan Klima, Primo Levi, with whom he formed a close friendship in the Eighties—are, as he puts it, "writers in trouble," writing about suffering. From his editing of the series "Writers from the Other Europe" to his support of Salman Rushdie, he has always been a friend to, and a chronicler of, obstructed imaginations.

This year he is still teaching, but he has retreated to Connecticut to start another book. What happened to the intoxication with New York? "Starting a book is a depressing misery for me. I try to stay out of everybody's way while I'm doing it. That's what I'm doing now." Still, when I visited the rural retreat this summer, he did a hospitable job of not showing the depression.

I ask him if he feels he has changed in these last few years, and he tells me to read the books: "If there's any change in me it would register there." Claire Bloom says he has become a gentler person since the operation. In my view he seems to have become less

ferocious about England and more distanced from his earlier reputation for taboo-breaking and outrageousness; he would rather be
described, now, as ruminative than as shocking.

The seriousness and quietness in this "later" Roth—which comes
through when he talks about going to visit his hero Saul Bellow for
his 75th birthday party or writes about his feeling for his father—
doesn't mean there are going to be no more jokes, but it does mean
that he is increasingly depressed by readings of him which assume
that nothing is going on but narcissistic self-exposure. Because he
names himself as "Philip" in *Deception,* a good deal of the response
to the book has been along the lines of "If he is 'Philip,' then who is
*she?*" Roth doesn't much like gossip (he admires Pavese's suicide
note, "Not too much gossip, please."). The gossip over *Deception*
seems to him a typical narrowing of the subject of his work. And what
is that, I ask him. "What it has always been: a *large* effort of realism,
over 30 years, about consciousness and self-consciousness."

All the books are about performance. "You must change your
life," he quotes Rilke, in *The Breast.* Lives are changed through
some projection or impersonation. Roth makes Nathan say in *The
Counterlife:* "I, for one, have no self. What I have instead is a variety
of impersonations I can do . . . a troupe of players that I have
internalised. I am a theatre and nothing more than a theatre." Isn't
this of some interest, Nathan asks Maria pleadingly when she's had
enough of being in his book and is about to leave him and the book:
"It is *interesting* trying to get a handle on one's own subjectivity."
Interesting for *him,* she might reply. Feminist readers often have
a difficult time with Roth's books.

In *Deception,* a more enclosed and narrowly focused book than
*The Counterlife,* the game is to show how the writer impersonates a
lover, *in his writing.* But it's also about obstacles to freedom, which is
why the novel has other voices cutting across the lovers,' voices of
Roth's obstructed Eastern European characters—used here, perhaps,
for the last time?

The high-minded account of *Deception* is all very well, readers
might reply. But if Philip Roth is so averse to being gossiped about
and misread as a narcissist, why call his main character "Philip"?
Because, the writer tells the wife at the end of the novel, his writing is
about breaking taboos—and for the novelist to name himself in order

to show how his imagination works is to break one kind of fictional taboo.

"I cannot and do not live in the world of discretion, not as a writer, anyway. I would prefer to, I assure you—it would make life easier. But discretion is, unfortunately, not for novelists."

In his "life as a man," Roth is discreet. He doesn't like to go public with interviews, he doesn't hang about literary parties or go on television or appear on platforms. He leads a quietish life and his book of essays is not, like Norman Mailer's, called *Advertisements for Myself,* but, deliberately, *Reading Myself and Others.* He despairs of the label that is continually stamped on his work: ego-projection. He recently quoted to me, with delight, something he's just found in Borges: "The advantage of having imitators is that at last they cure you of yourself." That's surely not a line for an egomaniac's commonplace book.

And yet, nothing is simple. As Nathan points out memorably in *The Counterlife:*

> The burden isn't either/or, consciously choosing from possibilities equally difficult and regrettable—it's and/and/and/and/and as well. Life is and . . . This times this times this . . . Is an intelligent human being likely to be much more than a large-scale manufacturer of misunderstanding?

That's a fine account of the problem of being human, as well as the problem of describing or criticising someone's work. To set the life entirely against the writing is as obtuse as to collapse the writing into the life. It's the dilemma raised by all writers, but Roth raises it more acutely than most. There is, after all, something mischievous and teasing—yes, even self-engrossed—about the authorial presence in *Deception.* And for him to write, in *The Facts,* about the marriage he turned into the novel *My Life as a Man,* or about his father in *Patrimony,* is to invite an *ad hominem* reading.

Ask him about all this, and he refers you back to his writing. I think of him, walking down to the house at the edge of the woods, closing the door, and getting back on his Treadmill. He won't be reading this, or any of the reviews he gets here for *Deception.* He'll be on to the next impersonation.

# Facing a Father's Death
## Alvin P. Sanoff/1991

From *U.S. News & World Report*, 11 February 1991, 57.
Copyright, 11 February 1991, *U.S. News & World Report*.
Reprinted by permission.

*Is it possible to anticipate the impact that a parent's illness and death
will have on a child, even if that child is an adult?*

There may be people temperamentally and professionally better
prepared than I was for what happened. I knew that my father
couldn't live forever. Yet did I really know that? When he became
seriously ill with a brain tumor, it was a terrific shock. But paying
attention to the worst of it somehow mitigated the shock of events.

The very business of being there to pay attention was the method
by which I lived through it. Not being there to pay attention when my
mother died was—and remains—a loss. She died when I was in
London, where I lived for a long time. I spoke to her one Sunday—it
was my custom to call on Sunday morning. She was going out to
take a walk, and we were joking. That evening I went to bed, and at
about midnight the phone rang. My father told me that my mother
had died of a heart attack in a restaurant. I took a plane home the
next morning, but I didn't immediately get what had happened. I
kept wondering where she was. I had no such experience with my
father because I had been there to pay attention. It made a big
difference.

*As you look back on the experience, what surprised you the most
about it?*

What surprised me the most? I'm not being clever: that he died. All
the words that we spoke to each other and to the doctors, and the
words that I wrote down, all of them are, finally, just that, words. The
experience itself is another thing entirely. His death didn't happen in
the universe of words.

Perhaps those of us who live with and by words are a bit astonished by the real thing because we are always looking for the right

word to describe the thing. We assume that if we find the right word, we've captured the thing. The words become a substitute for the thing. But the thing is something different.

Since his death, my father's life before my birth has become much more vivid to me. I see the wholeness of his history in a way I never did before, for which I'm quite grateful. I've been looking at photographs of him when he was in his office, pictures of an office party or some occasion when he received an award. I found myself mesmerized by these pictures, even though I knew a lot about his work in the insurance business and was never excluded from it as a kid. Looking at these pictures has been educational, though what all this education is for is a question that I can't answer. Everything you learn just opens up six more questions. You discover that what you know is so partial, so small. You also discover just how deep the bond is between father and son, the totality of it—cultural, personal, biological, historical.

*In doing the book, did you learn a lot about yourself?*

No. But I learned a lot about him, again because I had to focus on him; I was a spectator at the event. Strange as it sounds for a 57-year-old man to be saying this, I never saw him more detached from his role as my father than I did during his illness. I saw him as a human being living out the end of his life. What I saw wasn't clouded, as it can be, by the habits of the relationship between father and son. I also saw him clearly because he was so vividly visible. He was a big personality. He was the energizing force wherever he went in his world.

He was joined to Newark by his job, and he was like a city reporter in his knowledge of the place. He started out as an insurance agent and his district covered, perhaps, one fifth of the city. Eventually, he became an assistant manager and then a manager. He knew *every* agent's district. He knew the politicians, the policemen, the firemen, not in their official roles but as householders, as people who bought insurance.

*What characteristics did you inherit from your father?*

There's no doubt of what one learns from such a father. Typical of the boys I grew up with in our neighborhood in Newark, I learned from my father how to work. I learned from him that work is life and life is work, and work is hard. I also learned how to focus. Whether it was school, girls, a job or success, the focusing skill was ingrained. I still see some of the fellows I grew up with, and that trait is in all of them. It's not what our fathers said that shaped us—it's what they did.

*Do you still feel your father's absence?*

In a strange way, the absence is greater than the presence was. Because when he was present in his 70s and 80s, he wasn't especially present in my life. We spoke on the phone. He was in Florida; I was in England. We saw each other from time to time, but when I went about my daily business I felt neither his presence nor his absence. That's what I mean when I say the absence is now greater than the presence.

I once asked the writer Isaac Singer about his brother, who died when Singer was a young man. And Singer said, "My brother's presence becomes greater and greater with each passing year. I talk to him more rather than less."

# A Moving Family Memoir on Life and Death in *Patrimony*

Lynn Darling/1991

From *Newsday*, 13 February 1991, sec. II, 49. © 1991 by *Newsday*. Reprinted by permission.

When Philip Roth was in college, he used to imagine that he carried his father about with him, that all he was learning in his freshman courses at Bucknell University, his father was learning, too. He was driven, he writes in his new book, *Patrimony,* by the "impassioned if crazy conviction that I was somehow inhabited by him and quickening his intellect right along with mine."

But Roth couldn't narrow the chasm Herman Roth had worked so hard to carve in the first place—the one that separated a father's eighth-grade education from the formidable intellectual accomplishments of his second son.

Nearly 40 years later, Philip Roth again sensed a collaboration with the man who over the years had been the preeminent tyrant, idol, nag and nemesis in his life. This time, it came as he was writing the story of his father's life and the slow ordeal of his dying. Herman Roth was 88 when his struggle with a massive brain tumor ended in October, 1989.

"I think my father set the tone," he says. "I think that's true. I think he's present in the telling in a strange way. To be sentimental, I've come to think of this as a piece of work we did together. Which we never did, of course."

But the image of the two of them lingers nonetheless, earthly son and ghostly father, if only because it highlights the slightly astringent solitude in which the writer is at the moment surrounding himself. He has submitted to this irksome ritual, the author interview, because it necessarily surrounds the publication of a book.

So Roth submits, but with the elaborate formality of a participant in a tea ceremony, a kabuki in which both players calibrate their responses to the part the other is playing. He is all politeness, but still

270

capable of the acerbic touché. "What a strategically clever thing to say," he murmers when a compliment on his writing is proffered.

He is 57, tall, thin, tweedy, softspoken and watchful, his decorous restraint a bit startling, tempting as it is to confuse his manner with the manic angst of Alexander Portnoy, the neurotic obsessions of Nathan Zuckerman. His answers to questions are gently elusive, nearly opaque. Roth, after all, has always been his own best literary subject, a resource too valuable to squander on the mayfly ephemera of journalism. From *Goodbye, Columbus* to *Portnoy's Complaint,* from *The Ghostwriter* to *Zuckerman Unbound* to *The Counterlife,* Roth has explored his tribe, his sexuality, his nightmares and his own ego in gorgeous, flamboyant prose.

Almost from the beginning, his fiction has been flecked with controversy: attacked as a self-hating Jew for *Goodbye, Columbus,* attacked once again for the exuberant sexual explorations and blithely lyric vulgarity of *Portnoy's Complaint,* the show stopper that made his name, his fame, and his fortune. Throughout a 30-year career that has seen the publication of 19 books, he has been hated by Jews, feminists, and non-aligned carpers of all persuasions, though even his critics are quieted by a writing style and an ear for dialogue matched by few American writers.

But the controversy never invaded Roth's own family circle. Herman and Bessie Roth were always proud of their son, from his first publication in obscure little magazines "that nobody read," right up through the firestorms that greeted *Portnoy's Complaint.*

"My father couldn't extract very much information from a sentence in a work of fiction. He could extract plenty of information from a newspaper, and he was devoted to the newspaper and read it every day. But a book he didn't know what its purpose was precisely. He was amused by the stories and delighted that there was my name. *Goodbye, Columbus* they read and they were amused . . . and of course they said, 'Is this so and so?' 'Is this so and so?' and I said whatever I said, whatever foolish literary thing I said in response to their good honest question."

*The Breast* is Roth's novel about a college professor who finds himself transformed into that particular piece of female anatomy. "My dear mother, I mean she didn't have to do this, I mean, it was enough to change my diaper, wasn't it, let alone reading *The Breast?*

But she read it, and she just gave it back to me, and I said, 'Ma, you don't have to say anything,' and she said, 'Well.' "

This time Roth has stepped away from fiction to write a straightforward account of his father—his attitudes and his obstinacies. It is also a moving meditation on fathers and sons, on parents and children, on the great debts incurred and paid, the great hungers, the great unfathomable love.

Not that Herman Roth would have approved of everything that Roth has included in his latest book. One of the most moving moments in *Patrimony* is Roth's account of one of his father's most humiliating moments. Recovering from a painful biopsy, Herman Roth loses control of his bowels while staying with his son at his Connecticut home; because he is almost blind at the time, his attempts to clean up the mess only make matters worse.

It is his son who cleans things up: "I thought I couldn't have asked anything more for myself before he died—this, too, was right and as it should be. You clean up after your father because it has to be cleaned up, but in the aftermath of cleaning it up, everything that's there to feel is felt as it never was before. It wasn't the first time that I'd understood this either; Once you sidestep disgust and ignore nausea and plunge past those phobias that are fortified like taboos, there's an awful lot of life to cherish.

The lesson, he decided, is his legacy: "So that was the patrimony. And not because cleaning it up was symbolic, but because it wasn't, because it was nothing less or more than the lived reality that it was."

It was also an episode that Herman Roth begged his son never to disclose. What would his father have thought of the book?

"I think about [that question] too," he says. "One doesn't want to be sentimental answering it. Well, I don't know what things he might not have liked so much. I don't know, he might not have liked some things. Who could?" he asks. "Who could? But he's dead. So we needn't speculate."

He talks rather nostalgically about the world in which he grew up in Newark in the '30s and '40s, a world of "rings within rings," of "multiple allegiances," to his family, to his Jewishness, to his street and neighborhood and city, state and country. He was imbedded in a culture and a generation and a time, so imbedded that it took all of his energy to escape that world as a young man, all of his anger to rage against it and all of his art to understand it.

Now he is famous and honored and rich; now the ideas come less frequently. He is not working on a novel at the moment; he is writing "something," though he doesn't yet know what form it will take.

There have been no children in this life, none of his own, that is. Was a longing to know a father's thoughts kindled or rekindled, by his meditation on his own father?

That, he says, requires a book to answer.

Well then.

In what ways does Roth resemble his father?

"I think the differences are the first thing I would notice," he begins. "I don't know, I guess I can't say again that it would require a book to answer that? I suppose *Patrimony* would have been that book. But you see, so much of my response, my primary response, is to transform experience into language, and his primary response was to do. That pretty much changes the orientation to life. But there is a similarity I see through reading the book, and that is a kind of dumb interest we shared in the things around us. We were constantly bringing things to each other. It was very primitive tribal stuff; it isn't so much that we were gift givers, but that they were real tokens or fetishes, that embodied something, a kind of dumb way we both had of making statements by exchanging things. It was all very Cro-Magnon."

There was another similarity, he says. "He had an unrelenting quality, and I know what that feels like; it primarily has to do with work. The idea that you don't have to work all the time, that's news to me."

# To Newark, with Love.
# Philip Roth.
## Mervyn Rothstein/1991

From *The New York Times,* 29 March 1991, sec. C, 1, 22. ©
1991 by The New York Times Company. Reprinted by permission.

"In my childhood imagination, Newark was always the East Coast of
the American mainland," says Philip Roth. "Beyond that was the
Hudson River, which was not that easy to cross in the old days. New
York was to us as Europe was to New York. So when people say to
me, 'You came from New York,' and I say, 'No, Newark,' and they
reply, 'Well, it's the same,' I say, 'No, it wasn't.' "

Mr. Roth, tall and trim and 58 years old, is standing in the rain
outside the main branch of the Newark Public Library and remembering the years he spent growing up in this city that he has written
about so often in so many of his most popular books.

From *Goodbye, Columbus,* to *Portnoy's Complaint* to Zuckerman
bound and unbound to *Patrimony,* his current best-selling memoir
about his father's battle to the death with a brain tumor, Mr. Roth has
created a Newark, in both its downtown section and the Weequahic
neighborhood of his childhood, that reflects and refracts the positives
and negatives of the American ethic of progress and assimilation that
was so much a part of his early existence.

He has returned to that Newark because of thoughts occasioned
by *Patrimony,* by memories of Herman Roth, his American-born
father, who was the child of Jewish immigrants, and by memories of
his father's courage, both in his final fight and in an earlier one: his
striving to make his children's lives better than his own.

The Newark Mr. Roth is visiting is, of course, very different from
the one in which he grew up. The city has for many years been in
decline, and there is great deterioration, though there is now hope for
the future, as exemplified by the recently announced plans to build a
performing arts center in the heart of the city.

But much of Mr. Roth's Newark is still there. In Washington Park, across from where he is standing, George Washington trained his troops. Down the street is the Newark Museum, with its recent $21 million reconstruction by the architect Michael Graves. And across from the museum is an old bank building that was part of the tiny Newark campus of Rutgers University. It is the building in which Mr. Roth spent much of his first year of college. And the library itself, where he went that year to study and do research, became a setting for his first book, *Goodbye, Columbus;* Neil Klugman, Mr. Roth's protagonist, worked there, thinking, among the boundless volumes, about Brenda Patimkin, the rich suburban princess of his dreams.

Sitting in the park, Neil Klugman also thought of his deep knowledge of Newark. That knowledge, Mr. Roth wrote, was "an attachment so rooted that it could not help but branch out into affection." As this rainy morning's visit makes clear, that attachment and that affection are as much Mr. Roth's as they are his character's.

"In 1880, Newark was a city of approximately 100,000 people, most of them of British stock," Mr. Roth says. "And then, between 1880 and World War I, 250,000 immigrants came, two and a half times the population." They came, Mr. Roth says, at a moment when Newark was "undergoing a powerful and dynamic transformation," and they helped it to boom.

And as the city grew, Mr. Roth says, the next generation, the children of these immigrants, took on another task, fought another struggle: the Americanization of *their* children.

"They had a particular task, an American task, and a particular cultural burden," he says. "Newark is the battleground, one of many cities in this country, on which the struggle took place. The job they had was to stand between the European family of their immigrant parents and the American realities of their young children. They were a generation of negotiators, of constructors, with the tenacious, stubborn will of the constructor."

And, Mr. Roth says, they succeeded, but not without a lot of pain. "They took blows from both sides," he says, "from the parents who clung to the rigorous orthodoxy and from the children who wanted to be rid of all that because they sensed immediately that it was useless in this society. The cultural struggle was bruising. The homes were full of conflict and tension; when you negotiate, there's always tension. And it created a lot of neurosis, too."

It is a neurosis that Mr. Roth has creatively mined for more than 30 years, a neurosis without which much of his art would not exist. But that neurosis is not what he has come to Newark to talk about. He is more interested in the other side of what the struggle created: a sense of community, a comradeship, a love of learning, a milieu of American success. Take, for instance, the library in front of which he is standing.

"It's a honey of a building," he says. "It was built at the end of the 19th century. I doubt my father was in here more than once; it was the children who used it. It was all very powerful and all very loaded. It was a place of grandeur; there was something overwhelming about it—it was a Renaissance palace, with its columns and its mural. Even just touching the marble banister on the marble staircase in the lobby was enough. The open stacks, all those books, the knowledge. What took place here was a robust engagement with all the new society had to offer."

That engagement, Mr. Roth says, was also an everyday resident of his Weequahic neighborhood, in the southwestern corner of the city. And a few minutes later, Mr. Roth is standing in that neighborhood, in front of his alma mater, Weequahic High School, right next door to his elementary school, Chancellor Avenue School. He is just a few blocks from Beth Israel Hospital, now Beth Israel Medical Center, where he was born. And he is just down the block from the house where he spent the first 10 years of his life.

"Chancellor Avenue was the big, unclogged coronary artery of my childhood," Mr. Roth says. "I went out the door of my house and in two minutes I was at school with my friends. I went home for lunch. I ran back out. I came home after school and played ball. Three days a week, I had to go to Hebrew school, for my grandparents' sake. Then we played until dinner. And after dinner, if it was still light I went out and played ball again."

And all the years he was at Chancellor Avenue School, the next goal in life was clear. When he was old and wise enough, he would go to the high school that was always in his view, a long, low, imposing building with the words "Weequahic High School, 1932" carved in gray stone above the doorway.

"The year to me was always significant," he says, "because it was the year before I was born. So for me, it had always been there."

Someone who was there when Mr. Roth graduated in 1950 was Max J. Herzberg, the principal, who set the school's commanding tone: serious scholarship.

"And it worked," Mr. Roth says. "There was a Jewish pantheon of Newark cultural figures. You wouldn't know them today unless you grew up in Newark, but we knew them all, and they were examples to us, at home and in school. And out of that school poured doctors and lawyers and psychoanalysts and investment brokers and successful businessmen. For my whole generation, it was always clear that through school, we would answer our parents' prayers."

Now Mr. Roth is crossing the road, and walking down the lower-middle-class street where he lived, still remembering. His eyes are in the past now, and it as if the heavyset man in a gray coat walking past him could become, reflected in his pupils, his father 50 years ago. It is a street of quiet houses, lined with trees that look as if they had stood there since his youth. If they had memories, they could no doubt recall a thin and smiling boy who played stoop ball on the steps of the houses, who collected the pods the trees shed and turned them into necklaces.

"We lived at the end of the street," Mr. Roth says. "It was practically the end of Newark. In about one more block, you're out of the city. And about three blocks in that direction, you're also out of the city. It was the absolute corner of Newark."

"The houses were all two-and-a-half-family houses," he says. "People from New York find this strange. There was a full apartment on the ground floor and a full apartment on the second floor. On the third floor, there was half an apartment, for a young couple or a bachelor or an elderly widow. So you lived in a house with another family and a half. There were probably about 40 houses on our street. A lot of people. The lawns were nice and there were no fences."

"In warm weather," he says, "people sat on the stoops and on beach chairs in the driveways. You were a kid, and you would go to sleep, and the windows would be open. You'd be sweating, trying to sleep, and you'd hear them, you'd hear their conversation all the time, and it would be very comforting."

He would also hear their radios: "They didn't have portable radios, but they could use an endless number of extension cords; World War II was on, and they wanted to hear the war news."

He approaches a house, newly painted a shade not quite yellow and not quite lime. "We lived here," he says. "On the second floor. The Levines lived upstairs and the Gombergs lived downstairs and we lived in the middle."

He looks at a spot on the sidewalk. "I remember standing right here the day, the hour, that World War II began," he says. "We were playing a game against the stoop on that Sunday afternoon. There was a football game on the radio. The Brooklyn Dodgers were playing the New York Giants. I was 8 years old, and they announced Pearl Harbor had been bombed."

He walks to the corner and glances down a hill, three blocks long. "In the winter, when it snowed, we would sled down this hill," he says.

"It was great," he says. "It was fun. That was the way it was. You had these circles of allegiance: the house, the street, the school, the neighborhood, the city, the state, the country. They were multiple allegiances, and they were all felt." And they helped create this new generation of Americans.

And yet—was all of that feeling positive? Was there no complaint? Certainly Portnoy had one. And so did Mr. Roth, in other books.

Well, of course there were complaints, he says: "The neighborhood was also constricting." Children always find their parents constricting, and the parents still had ties to the old ways that the children wanted nothing to do with. And there was all that neurotic tension he has spoken about. "I don't mean to idealize it," he says. "By the time we were adolescents, I and the others outgrew it. The reason I wanted to go away to college was to go away."

But of course, as any writer knows, you can never really get away. Newark is as much a part of Mr. Roth, in his books and in his writing, as it was a part of his father.

Mr. Roth's father began his career selling insurance in the 1930's, and his workday task was to go into many Newark homes to collect premiums and sell policies. "He brought Newark into our house every night," Mr. Roth says. "He brought it in on his clothes, on his shoes—literally on his shoes. He brought it in with his anecdotes, his stories. He was my messenger out into the city."

In *Patrimony*, Mr. Roth recalls his father's love of Newark, a love that lasted until Herman Roth's death: "He knows *every* street corner. Where buildings are destroyed, he remembers the buildings that were there. You mustn't forget anything—that's the inscription on his coat of arms. To be alive, to him, is to be made of memory— to him if a man's not made of memory, he's made of nothing. . . . *He's* the bard of Newark. That really rich Newark stuff isn't my story—it's his."

Well, yes it was Herman Roth's story. But as Philip Roth says, Newark is more than one person's story, and it is also his. Herman Roth may have been the bard of Newark, but when he died, that mantle, and that coat of arms, passed to his son. His all-American son, who must remember everything.

# Just a Lively Boy
## Molly McQuade/1991

I seem always to need to be emancipated from whatever has liberated me. College liberated me from home. I had to be emancipated from college by going to graduate school at the University of Chicago. I was liberated by Chicago from home and college. I had to be emancipated from the University of Chicago by moving to Manhattan and going on to live for a while in Europe.

Now when I look back on it all, I think, why didn't I go back to Chicago and be a writer there? Afterward I rather regretted that I hadn't stayed. I felt at home in Chicago. I've never felt at home in New York, and don't to this day.

The University and Hyde Park were good for me. Chicago, too. The high-powered intellectual center, the folksy, right-minded neighborhood, and the big city you could lose yourself in. I liked being the insider/outsider. All I ever feel like in New York is an outsider. I can't think of any other city in the world where I so quickly felt like an insider the way I did in Chicago.

I graduated from college in 1954, and went to graduate school because I thought I would be a professor and had to get a Ph.D.

I'd been to a cozy college in central Pennsylvania. I had some very good teachers there and all in all got a good education, but by and large anything resembling serious intellectual discord was buried alive, back during the '50s, under Bucknell's prevailing ethic of niceness. This enabled me to sharpen my satirical wit but I didn't enjoy much camaraderie or serious competition.

When I got to Chicago, I was thrilled by all the kindred souls. And there was a city—and I hadn't lived in a city since I was a kid in Newark. It was all exhilarating: the University, the new city, my new friends, manly independence. I felt that I was a man—and I began to write.

For the one year I was a student at Chicago, I took the standard

master's degree program in literature. Good courses with Elder
Olson, Morton Dauwen Zabel, and Napier Wilt, but also bibliography, historiography, Anglo-Saxon. Those classes were not for me.

I got to know the people who ran the *Chicago Review*. George
Starbuck was poetry editor (and later was my first editor, at a
publishing house—Houghton Mifflin). *Chicago Review* published one
of my first terrible short stories—my first publication outside of the
Bucknell College literary magazine. It's a story by somebody who's
twenty years old. That's all you can really say about it.

I got my master's degree in August of 1955. I was twenty-two.
Then I went into the army. If I had not gone into the army, I might
have proceeded right on for my Ph.D. It's strange for me to imagine
what my life would have been like had I succeeded at doing that. But
by the time I got out of the army, I'd become impatient with
schools—or, rather, with schooling. I came to New York to look for a
job. I was offered one at the *New Yorker* as a checker, and one at
Farrar, Straus & Giroux—which later became my publisher—as
a copy editor. But then I got a telegram from Napier Wilt, who was
Dean of Humanities, saying there was an opening in the freshman
composition program, and would I like to come back to Chicago to
teach? I jumped at the opportunity of returning. I taught at Chicago
for two years, from 1956 to 1958.

I was by then a little more willing to think of myself as a budding
writer. In the army, I had written some stories, and one that had been
published in *Epoch,* a magazine published at Cornell, was chosen for
Martha Foley's *Best American Short Stories of 1956.* That was a
boost. Also, I guess I was ripening. It was beginning to happen—
whatever happens. I was more confident. And the University teaching
job made me feel more adult. I wore a suit and tie. I had students. I
went to committee meetings. I argued crazily about the syllabus. I
even taught Logic. *That* made me feel indomitable.

I had a little apartment across from Stagg Field. I worked until
11:30 every morning teaching three sections, back to back, of
freshman composition. Then I'd hole up in the little apartment and
write until I was written out, and then I'd mark papers with, I must
say, the same ferocious energy I had for my writing. I was a very
intense fellow. I saw my friends in the evenings. I was intense with
them. Great fun, intensity, before it starts wearing you down.

I met Richard Stern that year I came back to Chicago, and Tom
Rogers and Ted Solotaroff. All of them were writers or wanted to be.
Tom was teaching freshman composition. Dick was teaching upper-
level courses. Ted was a graduate student teaching freshman English
in Gary, I think. They were all gifted and serious, and we became
friends.

I was writing the stories then that wound up in *Goodbye, Columbus*. (I had already written one or two of the *Goodbye, Columbus*
stories in the army.) One day, some six months into that first year, I
had lunch with Dick. I told him a story about a family I knew in New
Jersey who had plenty of dough and a terrific daughter. He was
amused by the picture I painted. He said, "Why don't you write
that?" I said, "But it's nothing. It's *stuff*. It's just where I come from."
It hadn't dawned on me yet that it was *my* stuff. I remember Dick
saying, "That's *something*. That's *it*."

I went home, started to write, and almost overnight this stuff
developed into the novella *Goodbye, Columbus*. Dick read an early
draft. He was appreciative but a tough critic. We were working
different sides of the street. Dick's approach seemed to me more
literary than mine back then—I was tempted more by what was raw
and vernacular. And yet *he* was the one who told me to *use* the
vernacular material. I didn't trust it; I didn't *see* it. I suppose I thought
I ought to be *more* literary.

Ted Solotaroff and I read each other's stories, too—rather edgily.
We had a tense relationship but also a warm one. Ted, Dick, Tom,
and I all gave each other pages and pages to read.

George Starbuck also read what I was writing. As I said, he later
became my editor at Houghton Mifflin. When I was in Europe during
the summer of 1958, I got a telegram from George saying that
Houghton Mifflin had accepted my stories, which he'd solicited from
me some months earlier. George selected the stories, giving the book
a Jewish focus which the random group of stories I'd submitted
didn't quite have. George, in a way, determined my future, because *I*
didn't think that was my subject. I didn't know what my subject was.

I had nothing to do with any but literary or bookish people. I
should say bookish men. With women I was more ecumenical.

Neurotic classmates? I suppose *I* would qualify. High-strung. Volatile. Opinionated. Argumentative. Playful. Animated. Quarrelsome. I'm sure I was as neurotic as any classmate I had.

I was instinctively fanatical about seriousness. Chicago didn't make me like that, but it sure didn't stand in my way. I wasn't a fanatical student—I was a fanatic about writing and books. I couldn't understand ordinary life. I didn't know what satisfactions it could possibly yield. Nor did I think that my fanaticism was extraordinary. I was in a community where it *wasn't* extraordinary. Hyde Park's the last place I lived where books seemed at the heart of *everything.*

I wouldn't describe myself at Chicago as "ascetic," and certainly not as a "bohemian." I was just a lively boy. (I think of myself as an ascetic *now,* unfortunately.)

One had to be careful about the temptation to become a gentleman. So many bright Jewish boys of my generation—and background—gravitated to literature because it was a prestigious form of assimilation that didn't *look* like assimilation. Not that I have any argument with what's called assimilation. I'm all for Jews reading Milton. But it was possible for even a Newark Jew to become a kind of caricature Noel Coward by virtue of "literary studies."

I wanted to be who I was from where I was. At the same time, I wanted mightily to escape those confines and breathe new air. Four or five of my friends—a small group of graduate students, of which Ted Solotaroff was one, and a terrifically entertaining and brilliant storyteller named Arthur Geffen was another—were able to make a lot of headway with the blunt neighborhood style that we'd brought with us. We took a lot of pleasure in having humble origins and high-minded pursuits. Either without the other was boring and looked to us like an affectation. Putting the two together was probably another affectation, but if so, it was a *deep* affectation, and that's the most you can ask of raw youth.

I was an audience for their high-spirited exhibitionism and they were for mine. A lot of it was being boys together. We provided each other with an audience and with terrific fellow feeling. What feeling there was flowing back and forth! That's because we were still close to those streetcorners where we'd first exhibited ourselves. Chicago didn't put a damper on this kind of raucousness. It allowed for a nice amalgamation of the raucous and the serious. Superego Fights Id to Fifteen Round Draw; Blood Drawn.

I met Saul Bellow in 1957, when Dick Stern gave a course in which he invited writers to come and talk to his undergraduates. I wasn't Dick's student; I was a colleague, teaching freshman composition. But when Bellow was coming, Dick asked me if, for the class, he could use my story, "The Conversion of the Jews," which I had written in the army and couldn't get published. It had been turned down by all the classy reviews.

I said, sure. I was delighted that Bellow would read it. Dick gave each student a copy, and I went to the class and sat in the back. (I don't remember whether, during the class, Saul knew I was the author or not.) Saul talked about the story. He laughed a lot and obviously had got a kick out of it. Then Dick and Saul and I had a cup of coffee. That's how I met Bellow.

I was so in awe of him, of course, that that meeting could hardly have developed into a friendship. He'd written *The Adventures of Augie March,* he'd written *Seize the Day*—how could such a person be your *friend?* Besides, he was eighteen years older than I, and when you're twenty-six and someone's eighteen years older . . . well, in the quaint old Fifties, even a lively boy felt somewhat constrained in the company of his distinguished elders.

Was my life then simple? I guess it was. I wanted to be a writer. It's simple before you're published, you know? It's simple—you write the things. That's the whole story then.

I prefer the writer I was in Chicago at twenty-three, even if I can't read his writing. But who doesn't? Who wouldn't? Unguarded! I was actually unguarded. Hard for me to believe. I didn't know who might be inspired by my writing to want to smash me one right in the face, and so I walked around with my kisser in the air as though I'd never heard of custard pies.

You know what it was? I was *stupid!* It was wonderful.

# Index

3 5282 00598 3856

Printed in the United States
38426LVS00003B/42